P9-CAA-292

AMERICAN GIVEN NAMES

AMERICAN GIVEN NAMES

Their Origin and History
in the Context of the English Language

GEORGE R. STEWART

New York
OXFORD UNIVERSITY PRESS
1979

Library of Congress Cataloging in Publication Data
Stewart, George Rippey, 1895–
American given names.
Includes bibliographical references and index.
1. Names, Personal—United States—Dictionaries.
2. Names, Personal—American—Dictionaries.
3. English language in the United States.   I. Title.
CS2375.U6S74   929.4'03   78-17603   ISBN 0-19-502465-6

Printed in the United States of America

CONTENTS

TO THEODOSIA

INTRODUCTION

The people of the United States—like other peoples generally—"give" names to their children. These "given" names, stand in contrast to the "family names," which are inherited, and so, ordinarily, involve no necessity of choice on the part of the parents or others who may participate in the naming.

Through the period of many centuries during which names have been thus "given," some conventions or customs have developed. All of these are subject to exception, but they are practical guides to usage. A few such principles may be listed.

1. In America, the name is bestowed soon after birth—usually almost as soon as the sex of the baby is known. It is not withheld, as among some peoples, until some incident gives occasion for it. In fact, the naming has frequently been discussed in advance and alternate names have been selected, final adoption awaiting the "Boy!" or "Girl!" pronouncement.

2. The name thus bestowed is considered permanent. Again, in contrast to the practice of other peoples, this name is not officially replaced by another one at some later period of life, though nicknames often develop.

3. The name is of specific reference to sex. It is "a boy's name" or "a girl's name." A few exceptions spring up as if by accident—generally, soon to vanish with the passage of time.

Examples are Francis and Marion, but both of these have used spelling to signal their difference.

4. With rare exceptions the namers select (at least at the conscious level) a name that is "good," according to their own standards. They may thus, without much imagination, choose a solid William or Sarah, but they may also choose something unusual or bizarre, or even coin a name.

5. The names available from which a name may be selected constitute a kind of "name-pool." As many as a thousand names are in continuing use ("viable"), and the number is vastly increased for men by the modern custom of using family names as personal names, as with Craig or Glenn. On the other hand, by mere disuse, a name may vanish from the name-pool, by simply being forgotten.

6. Just as names may be lost from the pool by lack of use, so also they may be added by borrowing from a foreign language, by adoption from literary sources, and by coinage.

7. The names thus chosen may have been originally from Hebrew, Greek, Italian, or some other language, but in their American usage they have been assimilated to the ways of the English language as spoken and written in the United States. There are differences even from British usage—not only with reference to general pronunciation, but also because of individual variations, as examples, Irene and Evelyn.

From the nature of this subject this work can put forward no claims to completeness, but must remain open-ended. Especially in recent times (including most of the twentieth century) many hundreds of personal names have originated by the use of family names or by coinage. The attempt to list all of these names would be fruitless. In any case, such a compilation would be of little interest or utility in view of the reference works already existing upon family names. Similar frustration would result from an attempt to list all the rare biblical names which were occasionally used in the seventeenth and eighteenth centuries.

San Francisco, California   G.R.S.
August 1978

AMERICAN GIVEN NAMES

HISTORICAL SKETCH

The Anglo-Saxons

"Anglo-Saxon" can serve as a general term, describing the Germanic tribes which invaded Britain about A.D. 500, and gradually conquered most of the island, establishing in it their customs, including their language. That language is known as Anglo-Saxon, sometimes as Old English. Modern English has developed from it. Since names are a part of language, the Anglo-Saxons in their new country continued to use their already established personal names, and some traces of them have even come down into modern times.

Documents of Anglo-Saxon times are numerous enough to give us a good idea of their naming-customs.

First, there were the names which are technically known as "dithemic," that is, consisting of two elements. In Alfred, for instance, the elements are *aelf*, "elf," and *raed*, "counsel." Women's names were similarly formed, as with Edith, from *aed*, "rich," and *guth*, "war."

This naming system is one which can be traced all the way back to the primitive Indo-European, possibly about 3000 B.C. Being so old, it is to be considered formal, conservative, and aristocratic. Naturally, the Anglo-Saxon kings used such names.

But also many Anglo-Saxon names were short, and showed only one element. Thus we have Budda, Bada, Wulfa. These names may have been commoner than the dithemic names. Some of them have "meaning." Thus Wulfa might be from the word "wolf." Some of them may have been shortenings of dithemic names, so that Wulfa may be considered to be from some such dithemic name as Wulfstan. There was no clear way of distinguishing between men's and women's names.

Politically, the Anglo-Saxon period came to an end in 1066, with the Norman Conquest. With respect to names, however, the effect was delayed for a century or so, though in the end it also was profound.

The Normans

As the result of the Conquest and of Norman rule, the Anglo-Saxon nobility disappeared, often adopting Norman customs and names. The peasants went on being Dene or Kragg or Cada, just as they had been before the Conquest. As for the Normans themselves, they were suffering what we might call a drought of names.

The Normans were of Scandinavian descent, and thus were eventually of Indo-European origin. They had used the dithemic name-system. But, having conquered a part of France and settled there, they had begun to speak French. There was, however, no dithemic name-system in the language of the French, who were descendants of speakers of Latin, a language which had lost the dithemic system. The Normans thus were without their name-elements and the possibility of forming large numbers of names. They took over into French, however, a certain number of men's names which they were already using. These names, naturally, went to England when the Normans established themselves there. We can thus account for the heavy—and even excessive—use of a few men's names. William was by all odds the favorite, and almost every family had a son thus named. But also numerous were Henry (Harry), Richard, and Robert. All of these names were destined to maintain themselves in the great tradition of naming throughout the English-speaking countries. Others of the Norman names failed to attain such great popularity, but have also been long-enduring—Walter, Roger, Ralph, Hugh.

The Normans were even worse off for women's names, but they made much use of Emma, Matilda (Maud), and Helewis (Héloise).

The Later Middle Ages

Given a century for the turmoil of the actual Conquest to settle down, and a new situation was well on the way to developing. The upper classes were beginning to use French less and English more.

The Norman names were no longer being used only by and for Normans. More and more often, instead of Budda or Wurth, the townsfolk, and even the peasants, were having children baptized as Robert or Roger. Actually it made less difference than might be imagined, because of shortenings that amounted almost to nicknames. Robert might be universally known as Hob and Roger as Hodge. The identity of this last pair comes out neatly in Chaucer's *Canterbury Tales*, where the cook is noted as being called Hodge, but on one occasion is actually addressed as Roger.

This dispersal of the Norman names did not, however, solve the problem of the scarcity of names in Norman-dominated England. In the end the Church took over, by sponsoring, so to speak, a large number of the names of saints, both for men and for women.

Some of these saints were biblical—such as, for men, John, James, Thomas, and Stephen, and, for women, Mary and Elizabeth (Isabel). The majority of the saints, however, were nonbiblical, and they originated (or the stories about them did) in every region to which Christianity had penetrated. Although male saints considerably outnumbered female saints, there were sufficient members of each to solve the naming problem. So, for men, we have, as nonbiblical saints, George, Nicholas, Benedict, and Dennis; and, for women, we have Katherine, Margaret, Helen, Agnes, and Cecily.

Since the Anglo-Saxons had themselves been good Christians, some of the saints' names were Anglo-Saxon and they were thus revived—notably Edward, but also Edmund, Edgar, and Audrey.

By way of illustration we may take a family that flourished around the year 1200, right in the middle of the shifting of names. In doing so we have to ignore the possible linguistic problem. Probably, however, the members of this family were bilingual, speaking French and English about equally well.

In the summer of the 1189, which was the first year of the reign of King Richard I, a famous knight named William, known as "the Marshall," married Isabel of Clare, a great heiress of feudal holdings in England, Wales, and Ireland. The marriage was highly fruitful, in nineteen years producing five boys and five girls. We know the names of all of them, and can even see why they were so named. The boys were William, Richard, Gilbert, Walter, and Anselm; the girls, Matilda, Isabel, Sybil, Eve, and Jeanne.

One need not justify the giving of William as a name to the eldest son of an aristocratic Norman family. It was the great Norman name. In addition, it was here the father's name.

As for Richard, that was another great Norman name, and also had been the name of the mother's father. He was none other than the famous Strongbow, the Norman conqueror of much of Ireland. Besides, the parents owed a great indebtedness to the ruling king, who was another famous Richard.

Gilbert and Walter, too, were notable Norman names. In fact, Anselm is the only saint's name in the boys' list, and it is a strange one, nonbiblical, and not at all common. The naming may have been the mother's doing, for Anselm was born in Ireland, at one of the family's castles, when the father was in England on the king's business. There is a churchly suggestion about Anselm, for its chief bearer was St. Anselm of Canterbury, who had been archbishop there about a century earlier. The mother may have been dedicating her son to the church, a career which a younger son sometimes followed.

To shift to the girls. Matilda was almost as much the outstanding woman's name among the Normans as William was

6

among the men. The elder William's father (himself named John) had fought in the service of Queen Matilda during the troubled times some years before.

Isabel is derived from Elizabeth, and is therefore the name of a biblical saint. It had been so much used by the Normans, however, that it might as well be considered one of their names. In this case, it was the mother's name.

Sybil is to be considered a kind of quasi-saint's name. The immediate reason for naming, however, was undoubtedly that it had been the name of the paternal grandmother.

Eve is certainly biblical, but it was not a commonly used name, and at first approach it is difficult to explain here. The situation becomes clear when we learn that this was the name of the maternal grandmother. She was the Irish princess who had married Strongbow, and there was no reason why she should have borne a Norman name. In the Irish household where she grew up, however, they undoubtedly knew her as Aoiffe, the Irish name which usually went into English as Eve.

Jeanne counts as a saint's name, the feminization of Jean, that is, of John.

To sum up, we can note that these parents did about as modern ones might do.

The naming in a great feudal family such as the Marshalls would probably be conservative, so it is significant to note the saints' names already working in.

They became more numerous by 1300, and then for more than two centuries there was little change, a small number of much-used Norman traditionals balancing off a larger number of saints' names.

This quiet period lasted into the sixteenth century. As the Normans themselves ceased to be a separate people, their names remained no longer distinct, and can better be termed "English traditionals." John, Thomas, James, and Edward came to join William, Richard, Henry, and Robert, each of these great names following its own historical course. Somewhat comparable to these, for women's names, are Mary, Katherine, and Joan.

There was thus only a small name-pool from which parents

picked names for their children. A score of English traditionals and a score of popular saints accounted for a large proportion of the names. Additions to the name-pool came only by what we may call historical accident—as happened with George, Francis, and Anne.

As we can scarcely fail to grant, the name-pool was too small for practical purposes. Even though people largely lived in villages, the repetition of names became troublesome. If you stood in the marketplace and called out in an authoritative voice, "John!" or "Nicholas!" or "William!" they would have come running from all directions. The result, since any society must be practical, was to give nicknames for clarity of distinction. In fact, the later Middle Ages became a great era of variations. A man might be baptized as Richard and never hear that name again, perhaps, until he came to be married. Ordinarily he would be addressed as Dick or Rich or Hitch or Hick or Dickon or Ricket, or something else.

The next great period of change arose with a religious change.

The Reformation

When a German monk nailed his propositions to the door of a church in Germany, he unwittingly initiated a revolution in the naming of English babies. This Protestant influence, one may say, ran its course and ended. But it was a course that extended over three centuries. Moreover, it left its permanent marks on history.

In England the decade of the 1540's shows the beginnings of this new movement. Moreover, we have available some statistics, and are not dependent upon impressionistic sampling. The count represents the complete baptismal record of five London parishes throughout the decade—427 boys and 392 girls.

In that decade the much-married old King Henry VIII died (in 1547). His weakly son succeeded him as Edward VI. The two princesses, Mary and Elizabeth, waited to see what fate might be in store for them. England could have been called

Protestant. By older tradition, however, the nation was still Catholic, and the name-pattern shows it.

To consider the women's names first—almost nine out of ten (84%) bore clearly religious names. Of these, 40 per cent were those of the nonbiblical saints, the favorites being Agnes, Katherine, and Margaret. The existence—we might say the persistence—of these names provides strong evidence of the strength of the Catholic tradition. But the future would not be with them.

Just equaling in numbers the names of the nonbiblical saints stood the names of the New Testament, most of them recognized as saints. The favorites were Elizabeth, Mary, Joan, and Anne.

Significant, though few (4%), were the names of women of the Old Testament. As the leaders marched Sarah, Judith, and Susannah. The last two show Catholic influence to be still strong, since they are from the Apocrypha.

Only 16 per cent is left for the total of all the nonbiblical names. Most of these seem to be what might be called survivals of the Norman period. One would guess that such names as Emma and Mabel then seemed old-fashioned to most people's ears. Alice was by far the most popular, though some of that popularity must be credited to an obscure saint of that name.

With men's names the situation was considerably different, but probably because it had traditionally been so, and not because it was reacting to the new Protestantism. The nonbiblical saints were an insignificant 7 per cent, chiefly existing because of George and Nicholas. On the other hand, the New Testament names totaled just about half, with John alone accounting for one name in four, and Thomas for one in eight. William was about equal to Thomas.

The Old Testament names totaled only about 5 per cent, with David, Adam, and Samuel as the leaders. Samuel is of great significance here, pointing toward the future when it was to be the typical Protestant name.

The chief difference between the men's list and the women's

lies in the number of male nonbiblical names (50.5%). William, Richard, and Robert are the leaders, all of them typical Norman names.

On the whole, both lists cry out in witness to a strong tradition and an essential conservatism. In the religion and the politics of the time, the winds of change were blowing, but (to continue a figure of speech) they had not yet disturbed the quiet waters of the baptismal font.

But change would come—as the Reformation took stronger hold, and, particularly, as the beliefs and ways of life known as Puritanism grew stronger.

The actual topic of this book, however, is the history of American names, and we can now, with the sixteenth century, begin to survey those names directly, rather than as a projection of still earlier names.

The First Immigrants

The earliest English-speaking community in the territory of the present United States was the Raleigh colony, which settled on the mid-Atlantic coast in 1587. It disappeared, mysteriously, thus to become known as the Lost Colony. By its lists of names, however, it left us some trace, and even has exerted some small influence on later naming.

Of 99 men and boys in this colony, 23 were named John; 15, Thomas; 10, William. Here we have nothing unusual. That triad was commonly heading any list of English men's names. Henry and Richard, with seven each, stood in the next places. Then came George and Robert, with three apiece. Hugh, Michael, James, and Roger were two to each. The list of singles totaled twenty-two.

To consider the various classes, we may note that the Norman traditionals were strong—William, Henry, Richard, Robert, Hugh, Roger. The New Testament supplied John and Thomas as the leaders, but elsewhere it was weak, with one or two for James, Mark, Peter, Simon, and Ananias. The Old Testament is almost absent, supplying only Michael. Most striking is the strength of the nonbiblical saints—including

George, Ambrose, Anthony, Clement, Cuthbert, Christopher, Nicholas, Martin, and several others. Lacking, however, is Francis, which would soon become popular.

Charles and Ananias call for special comment.

Charles was scarcely, at that time, to be considered English at all. There is even the possibility that this Charles was a Frenchman—some Huguenot taking refuge with the Protestant English.

Ananias is doubly unusual in that it is both untraditional and also of unpleasant or even sinister suggestion—having come to be the byword for "liar." To be sure, the name means "God-is-gracious" and there is another man of the same name in the Book of Acts who seems to have been a worthy person. It occurs also as a name of a high priest. On the whole, however, we may probably just as well classify the name as one of those oddities which occur now and then in almost any list. After all, not all parents have good taste, and some of them are downright eccentric. Aside from Ananias, we cannot see any possible Puritan influence in the names of the Raleigh colony.

Curiously, of all those people Ananias Dare is best remembered, for he was the father of the first English child born in America, herself named Virginia. That name, too, was very unusual.

Of women, only seventeen names are recorded. That is too small a number to be of much use, and actually no Mary or Anne happens to be included. For what it is worth there were three Janes, two Elizabeths, and one each for Agnes, Alice, Audrey, Eleanor (spelled Elyoner), Emma, Joan, Joyce, Margaret, Marjorie, Rose, and Winifred.

In 1607, in the next attempt at planting a colony, the boats went ashore at Jamestown. We have the lists of those names too, men only. Since most of them were young, we may assume that they show us how boys were being named in England around the year 1580.

Three lists, of the original settlers and of reinforcements, are available, and they total the respectable number of 238. As with the Raleigh colony, the names were clearly in the English tradition. William led, then followed John, Thomas, and Richard. Those are the ones that you would expect to find as the leaders ever since the year 1200. Then the names trailed off into doubles and singles.

Only when one looks at these doubles and singles does a suggestion of something new begin to appear. David (twice appearing, and actually listed as Davi) may be put down as Welsh rather than as religious. But a number of names are biblical and thus show what we have come to consider a Puritan suggestion. Two were named Daniel; one, Abraham; one, Jonas. Even more striking, there was a Nathaniel and a Samuel. These last two were becoming characteristically Puritan names.

We may see another forward-looking practice in the few surnames which have become baptismal names, such as Kellam and Harmon.

The names of the nonbiblical saints had fallen off, though George, Nicholas, and a few others survived.

There is also that great marvel, Edward Maria Wingfield. Not only did he possess one of the first middle names (Camden, our earliest scholar of names, makes special mention of it); but also Wingfield's middle name was that of the Virgin, which was commonly so used on the Continent for a man, but not in England. One guesses that his parents were bold eccentrics, under Catholic influence. This Wingfield himself was a leader of the colony, and should also be remembered as one of the first Englishmen in the New World to keep chickens.

In the Jamestown lists there was no Charles. There were, however, two Francises.

Unfortunately, the Jamestown lists fail to help us with women's names, though one Anne is mentioned.

Chiefly to be noted in this group is the flavor of Puritan naming, almost absent in the names of the Lost Colony.

What Happened in New England

Since the arrival of the *Mayflower* provides one of the dramatic moments of American history, we are fortunate in having the listed names of 68 of her men and boys who landed.

These names are not much different from those of James-town. John led, followed by William, Edward, Richard, Thomas. The apparent Puritan influence is a little stronger than in Virginia. Samuel occurs three times and Joseph twice. We have singles for Elias, Isaac, Moses, and Solomon. One Resolved, along with the Brewster boys, Love and Wrestling, are the only abstracts.

As a further exemplification of those who were landing in Massachusetts, we have the record of 452 freeholders, who must have been English-born, listed at Boston in the first four years of the colony, 1630–34. Again the name-pattern can only be described as "English."

These immigrants brought with them a commonplace cross section of English names, with only a slight Puritan flavor. The leading six were John, William, Thomas, Richard, Robert, and Edward. Only then, in seventh place, do we have what might be considered to be the test name, Samuel.

Since most of these immigrants were young men, we are dealing with people who were christened around the year 1600. By that time the Puritan influence was surfacing, particularly a fascination with the Old Testament. Showing up in some numbers among the freeholders are Daniel, Joseph, Abraham, Isaac, and Nathaniel. Even some of the more unusual names make an appearance, such as Ezekiah and Jehu.

The point to be emphasized, however, is that these immigrants show no heavy emphasis upon what might be termed Puritan names. In their religious opinions and possibly in their social ideals they may have been a special group, but scarcely in their names.

As a basis of comparison, we have a listing of 463 male children baptized in four London parishes in the decade 1640–49. The birthdates, therefore, are forty years later than those of the first Massachusetts immigrants. In that period Puritanism had been developing, and the current English name-pattern was just about the same as that of the Massachusetts freeholders. But what happened to naming-customs in the first years of the Massachusetts colony, among the children of those freeholders—that is a different story!

A commonplace of American history runs: "The Puritans attempted to establish the kingdom of God in the New World." Nowhere can we find a better exemplification of this idea than in given names. We can scarcely apply any word weaker than revolution. The traditional Norman names almost disappeared. Moreover, the movement cannot be credited to anything that was happening in the mother country. This was the period of the great Puritan push, followed by some reaction after the Restoration. We find a number of English children christened with Old Testament names, such prominent figures, for instance, as Joseph Addison, Daniel Defoe, Nahum Tate, Abraham Cowley, and Jonathan Swift.

But there was no mass movement in the home country. One reason undoubtedly was that the dedicated Puritans remained always a minority in England, whereas in New England they were a heavy majority, an Establishment.

Some actual percentages are illuminating. Among the freeholders, biblical names for men stand at 52 per cent, of which those from the New Testament comprise 41 per cent and from the Old Testament only 11 per cent.

The list of Boston births, however, shows a startling contrast, the corresponding figures being 90 per cent for the total of biblical names, with 50 per cent for the New Testament and 40 per cent for the Old.

The first ten in the freeholders' list were John, William, Thomas, Richard, Robert, Edward, Samuel, George, James, and Francis—chiefly the staunch Norman traditionals, and only Samuel being of the Old Testament.

The Boston list, in sharp contrast, had for its first ten John, Thomas, Samuel, Joseph, James, Nathaniel, William, Ebenezer, Isaac, and Jonathan. Nine of the ten are biblical. Of these Samuel, Isaac, and Jonathan are clearly of the Old Testament, with Joseph also drawing most of its strength from the patriarch. Nathaniel also is Hebrew, though the actual name appears only in the New Testament. Ebenezer provides a special case, but it is certainly of the Old Testament.

A similar shift occurred with women's names, but not so strikingly, since a movement toward biblical names for women had already been under way in England for a century or more.

Nevertheless, a tabulation of 707 names in the birth records for the first forty years of the Massachusetts Bay Colony (1630–70) shows some striking changes. Mary, with 21 per cent, is the leader; Elizabeth, with 17 per cent, is in close pursuit. Sarah, with 15 per cent, provides a good third. To complete the top ten we have Hannah, Abigail, Rebecca, Ruth, Lydia, Anne, and Martha. All of these are biblical—half from the New Testament, half from the Old. Almost appalling is the disappearance of the great nonbiblical saints. Katherine, Agnes, Margaret—they (and their aura of virginity) had dominated the roll of English women's names for centuries. Katherine and Agnes were wholly absent from this Boston list. Margaret barely survived with seven examples.

May we, on this basis of names, draw some conclusions as to a changed ideal of womanhood? No longer—and the Wife of Bath would have approved—was the prize set up for virginity. Mary remained, but she was conceived of chiefly as mother. The others emphasized the duties of wife and mother. Martha was notable as a good housekeeper. About some of the Old Testament women there was even a touch of sexuality. Sarah and Rebecca—did not Pharaoh and King Abimelech find them seductive? Ruth—just what did happen during the premarital night that she spent with Boaz? Abigail—after a scandalously short widowhood she was in David's arms! We can scarcely write the Puritans down as sensualists, but at least their names show that they had no truck with the idea that virginity was preferable to wifehood.

As the record itself indicates, the Boston parent must thus have begun with the idea that the name would be from the Bible. But why did he choose one name rather than another from that plentiful source?

We have a little contemporary testimony from the notable diarist Sewall, himself named Samuel. Writing near the end of the seventeenth century, he told why he named his children Judith and Sarah. Coming thus a little late, he already felt the pressure of a tradition. He wrote, "I named my daughter Judith for the sake of her grandmother and great-grandmother

. . . and the signification of it very good." When he was struggling over whether to call a daughter Sarah or Mehetabel, he consulted the Bible, and was (almost snobbishly) swayed by "Sarah's standing in the scripture."

Naming "for someone" can only maintain a tradition; it cannot inaugurate one. The actual building up of the name-pool, however, was doubtless the result of the same influences that swayed Sewall. The Puritan parent was likely to bestow a name because its original bearer stood out in biblical history. We must, however, add some provisos. Mere notoriety could not be enough. The name must be that of a character who could be construed as having been on the Lord's side. Eve was not popular, perhaps being conceived as the original sinner. Most of all, Christians rejected Judas. Melville was within his rights as a novelist to use the name of that "wicked" King Ahab. But who can cite historical justification for it? So also it goes with those other kings "who did evil in the sight of the Lord." Canon C. W. Bardsley hunted eagerly through English parish records to find Puritan "unpleasant" names. His findings were insignificant, and they would have been no better if he had come to America. He cites Antipas, the surname of Herod. But Herod is not mentioned by that name in the Bible, where the only Antipas is a respectable Christian martyr.

In general, the Puritans chose the shorter and simpler names. Seth and Saul probably flourished for this reason. On the other hand, many of the biblical names were long, and (to the English eye) grotesque in spelling. Some parents may actually have felt the attraction of such names. Even Elizabeth might be so classed. The fantastic Shearjashub occurs occasionally in the lists of Harvard students. Mahershalal-hashbaz—said to be the longest name in the Bible—actually existed as the name of a Newport tobacconist of 1668.

Nevertheless, we encounter difficulty in trying to explain why so many children received the names of insignificant biblical characters, some of these merely being mentioned in genealogical lists. There have been suggestions that names were, on occasion, chosen by lot. The Bible may have been opened at random, and the first name to be encountered could have been taken for the new baby. I have found no actual evidence to this effect, and the Puritan, generally speaking, was not given to reliance upon luck. On the other hand, there is no proof that such a system may not have been now and then employed. "Chance" seems to be about the only possible explanation for the selection of some of the rarer names.

In many instances, however, the parents chose the name (as we have seen Sewall doing) because of its good signification as translated. Many Puritan divines knew some Greek and Hebrew, and they could have interpreted the names to their own satisfaction—if not always to the satisfaction of modern scholars. Mehetabel ("God-is-doing-good") and Nathaniel ("God-has-given") offered good possibilities.

Scriptural analogies were also of importance. Benoni—and its associated Benjamin—might be used in a case when the child survived but the mother died. Samuel was apt when an older woman bore a son, having almost given up hope.

In many instances the name must have sprung from some mere quirk or whim of a parent or officiating minister. Such quirks or whims would be soon forgotten, or in any case would not get into the historical record. But this possibility helped give to Puritan nomenclature its remarkable variety.

The proliferation of a particular family, moreover, must have exerted its influence. A patriarch with many children would pass his name on to one son and to several grandsons. From there on, the name would prosper with the family. Dudley is a good example.

Puritan name-giving also showed originality in its use of "meaningful" names, although such names never became very common. In the beginning these show up about equally with men and with women, but they gradually specialized upon women, as with Charity, Mercy, and Patience. As the creative impulse of the first years faded out, these names faded too, although a few, such as Grace and Hope, managed to survive, their significance blunted.

Local variations also had their influence. Although William (like the other nonbiblicals) was rare, it was common in the towns of Eastham and Marshfield, where the citizens apparently stuck with the old names. Shobal was a specialty of Barnstable.

We rarely have direct evidence as to the reason for the more unusual names, and many of them seem to be, phonetically, very harsh—as with Jabez, Hephzibah, and Hezekiah. Probably the Puritan was not much swayed by mere euphony. In such case we should look to the literal meaning or to the associations of that character in the biblical record.

If we may accept the idea that the Puritans labored to found the kingdom of God, we must concede that in their establishment of a name-pattern they were, to a remarkable degree, successful in that endeavor.

Elsewhere Before 1700

In New England, throughout the seventeenth century, the settlers developed their important experiment in biblical names. Elsewhere the naming practices merely continued to be basically those which had been brought from the homeland.

In Northumberland County, Virginia, we have the record of births from 1661 to 1700. The pattern is English, but non-Puritan. There is a contrast between the men's and the women's list, in that the men preserve the traditional names but the women have, to some extent, "gone biblical."

Any English boy, as far as his name was concerned, would have felt at home in the county, where he would have found himself surrounded with boys who had been baptized John, Thomas, William, and Richard. Usually about half the boys bore those names; the other half, equally familiar ones. Names from the Old Testament supplied scarcely more than a flavor. Just before the end of the century they become a little more numerous, and we even find a few unusual ones, such as Abner and Micah.

The women's names also followed the English pattern, in general. Mary commonly headed the list, as compiled by decades, but with a narrow margin over Elizabeth—the latter commonly recorded as Eliza. Sarah and Anne were good followers-up. Those four names, indeed, tended to reach a monopolistic total, sometimes summing off at two-thirds. Unlike the New Englanders, moreover, the Virginians did not so completely eschew the nonbiblical saints. Katherine (good old English Kate) maintained a conspicuous place. There was also an occasional Charity, Mercy, or Patience.

In all the colonies, the settlers came to know the Indians, of various tribes and speaking different and highly difficult languages. The settlers discovered that the Indians, like other people, had personal names, usually long and hard to pronounce. Sometimes the speakers of English shortened those names, and sometimes they substituted English ones, so that the records were peppered with Indians who were merely listed as Ned or Jack or Joe. Of course, most of those Indians among their own people kept their own names. Thus the colonists knew the greatest of the early Indian leaders as King Philip, but he was Metacomet among his own people.

The white settlers, however, had no temptation to adopt Indian names, and there is no indication that they did so.

The blacks, though in many respects their experience has been unique, offer little that is remarkable in the history of given names. After a generation or two English became their usual language, and the name-pool came to them as a part of language.

Out of mere convenience, the early slaves received names from their masters, or themselves adopted English names. A short list from Virginia, about 1623, shows that most of the individuals bore commonplace English names such as William, John, and Edward. Also listed, however, are the Spanish forms—Angelo and Isabella. These names may be taken as evidence that the slave trade had not always been directly with Africa, but had also passed by way of some of the Spanish-speaking colonies. The use of Anthony, which appears most frequently in this list, is confirmatory, for it has never been common in English. The only name tha suggests an African origin is Jiro, and even that might be a twisted form of some Spanish name.

Like other peoples, the blacks had their own ways of giving names, and they brought those customs with them to America.

As in other non-English-speaking groups, however, their systems rapidly fell into disuse as the people learned English.

The so-called "day-names" constitute an interesting part of the system of nomenclature among various African tribes. It consisted the two lists (one for males and one for females) of seven names each, and one of these names was bestowed upon a child born on that day of the week. As time passed and African customs began to break down, some of these names went out of use and others became commoner, as did Cudjo and Cuffee in the course of the eighteenth century.

Probably by confusion with these day-names arose the custom of using classical names, commonly Roman. The name for a girl born on Monday was Juba. But this was also, by accident, a name that would be known to any reader of the Roman historian Sallust. This Juba was king of Numidia, and therefore an African, even though presumably a Berber, not a black. So also Phibba was sometimes used as the equivalent of Phoebe. Sambo, another of the African names, gained strength from its identification with Samuel and Sam (see the Pompey entry).

The usage of classical names among the blacks was never widespread, and was chiefly limited to the house servants. Such names, in fact, may have been chiefly in the nature of nicknames, since some owners were amused at having a servant whom they could address by such a famous name. Out in the quarters he probably went by some other name—perhaps an African one like Quash, or, more likely, as Bob or Harry.

After the English takeover of New Netherland in 1664, the Dutch language lingered in the country places. But it exerted no clearly evidenced influence upon our names. One reason was that it resembled the English language in both linguistic origin and in cultural background. Pieter, for instance, was so much like Peter that it merely vanished into English. Possibly Derrick (or Derek) is from the Dutch, among whom it was a popular name. But Derrick has always been a rare name in English.

Toward the end of the seventeenth century came a heavy immigration of Germans into Pennsylvania. These people held to their own language tenaciously, and they had some effect upon the names. They were the first group to use two given names—that is, to have what we call a middle name. The first name was conventionally Johann—our John. The use of the middle name grew steadily throughout the eighteenth century and we can ascribe this, in considerable degree, to the German example.

These Germans added a few names to the pool. One of them was Frederick, which can hardly be considered as English before this time. With its shortening to Fred, it became a common American name, aided by its introduction into the British royal family with the coming of the Hanoverian kings.

Of all the special groups, the Scots were the most influential in shaping the name-pattern. Some of them were direct immigrants from Scotland, but the larger number came as the so-called Scotch-Irish, after a stopover of three or four generations in the north of Ireland. Their native language was English, though with a northern burr. Their cultural tradition, however, differed considerably from that of the English settlers. They had their own favorite names, and they kept them in America in sufficient numbers to effect the naming statistics notably. James, the name of seven of their kings, serves as a good indicator. In any colonial list, if James gets up into the first three, you may suspect Scotch-Irish influence. Andrew and Alexander serve as other such indicators. Archibald established itself as Archie.

Both in Scotland and in Ireland these people had lived in close association with the speakers of Gaelic. Thus had come into their name-pool such names as Duncan, Donald, and Kenneth. Already anglicized, these names, along with others, passed readily into a general colonial usage.

The Eighteenth Century

In the political area the eighteenth century brought revolution, but in the naming of babies it displayed only the slow, evolutionary change that may be expected in any society with the passing of the years.

It was a so-called classical period. But this Greek and Latin influence had really begun its work with the Renaissance, in the time of Elizabeth. In the eighteenth century, throughout the colonies, we have only a minor growth of classical influence. There is, at this time, a somewhat greater showing of names with distinguishing forms for men and women, after the Latin usage—such as Julius and Julia. On the whole, however, the speakers of English have never manifested much liking for such pairs, so that they have generally preferred Mark to Marcus.

A few names show classical influence without preserving classical form. Horace and Vergil (not Horatius and Vergilius) reflect admiration for two of the most widely read Latin poets. Horatio, which also became popular at this time, is the Italian form, probably owing something to its use in *Hamlet*.

By and large, however, the classical influence upon American naming has never been very strong. The appearance of some latinized form can usually be credited to a particular cause rather than to pervasive classical tendencies.

One of the most important developments of the eighteenth century was the growth in the use of middle names. Among Harvard undergraduates, during the first half of the century, a third name was almost as rare as a second head. Then something happened, and, decade by decade, in steady and even progression, the middle name became commoner. By 1800 one Harvard student in four was thus endowed.

Also within the time limits of the century came the continued heavy use of biblical names, and the beginning of their decline.

During the middle years of the century the Harvard students show a consistent pattern. About half of them bore Old Testament names, with Samuel, Joseph, Benjamin, and Jonathan being the most popular. About a quarter of the students bore New Testament names, concentrating heavily upon John. The nonbiblical names comprised about one quarter of the total, with William easily the leader—the others scattering widely, and including some family names.

During the last quarter of the eighteenth century the popularity of the Old Testament names finally began to recede at Harvard. In their place came some of the newly popular names, such as Charles. Also important was the revival of Robert, Henry, and some others which had once been Norman, but were now rather to be considered as traditionally English.

Some new names primarily gained popularity, we may say, from the widespread desire to have something just a little different. Some of the impulse may be called patriotic, since the new dynasty of Hanoverian kings supplied a number of the new names. George enjoyed a surge of popularity. Frederick and Augustus became common. From queens and princesses came Charlotte, Caroline, and Sophia. Charles also rose in popularity, though definite causes are hard to assign. Francis was a favorite, displaying the definite strangeness of being used for both men and women—sometimes, for the latter, being spelled Frances.

After the middle of the century, Princeton provides an interesting means of comparison with Harvard. Harvard drew its students almost entirely from the Congregationalists of New England. Princeton drew from the Middle Colonies, had a Presbyterian background, and, as the names indicate, also felt the influence of the German settlers.

In the decade of 1800–1809 (births of 1780–89) the first ten, with their percentages, stand:

Princeton (328 individuals)			Harvard (449 individuals)		
John	53	16.2%	John	47	10.3%
William	37	11.3	William	37	8.3
James	21	6.4	Samuel	29	6.5
Thomas	21	6.4	Benjamin	20	4.5
Robert	17	5.2	Joseph	20	4.5
George	14	4.3	Charles	19	4.2
Samuel	12	3.6	James	19	4.2
Charles	10	3.0	Thomas	16	3.6
Jacob	8	2.4	George	13	2.9
Richard	7	2.1	Henry*	11	2.5
		80.0%			51.5%

(* A triple tie with Nathaniel and Timothy.)

The two lists show many resemblances—the result of their common tradition, which arises from their use of the English language. John leads and William follows, an often-recurring situation. Seven names appear in both lists. The great names of New Testament origin—John, Thomas, and James—appear in both lists, but somewhat more strongly at Princeton. On the other hand, the names from the Old Testament at Harvard show the solid triumvirate of Samuel, Benjamin, and Joseph, but at Princeton only the unusual Jacob. Robert and Richard reinforce the traditional color of the Princeton list, as Henry does for Harvard. George (in both lists) shows that a trend in names is not easily broken off, even though revolution may make a particular king unpopular. Charles, a new name, shows in both lists.

The most surprising of all these names is certainly Jacob. It is probably to be taken as German in background. To reinforce this conclusion we may point to other German-favored names—which stand lower—Nicholas, Augustus, and Gustavus.

The Scotch-Irish influence displays itself with the high score of James, and the the occurrence, in small numbers, of Archibald and Alexander.

An excellent offering of lists arises from the preservation of many muster rolls of the Continental Army. We may examine, for instance, the names of the enlisted men and noncommissioned officers of the Third South Carolina Regiment in 1779. These names represent a sample of the naming usage for a Southern Colony in the middle of the century.

John leads, followed at a respectful distance by James and William in a tie for second place. The list is, on the whole, thoroughly English. It includes a few of the rare Old Testament names, but so, we must remember, did the English pattern itself at this time. New Testament names are rare except for the leaders, John, James, and Thomas. The English traditionals stand high—William, Henry, Robert, and Edward. The chiefly used Old Testament names, also, are those which had become by this time traditional—Samuel, Benjamin, Joseph, and Daniel.

24

The high position of James indicates Scottish or Scotch-Irish influence. So do the two occurrences of Alexander. We have possible German influence in Michael and Matthew. Probably Irish are Malachi and Patrick. On the whole, however, the list is probably not much different from those of the British regiments against which this one was marching.

Let us shift now to the roll of the enlisted men and noncommissioned officers of the Fourth Regiment of the Connecticut Line for 1781. John leads. William stands in second place, James in fifth. The other seven names of the first ten are all from the Old Testament—Jonathan, Samuel, Joseph, David, Benjamin, Daniel, and Isaac. Far down the list, except for William, are the famous English traditionals—and even Thomas. The differences from the Southern regiment are striking.

Far different, again, is the situation when we consider two regiments of a Middle Colony. One of these (its number not recorded at the time of the compilation of the list), was recruited in Cumberland County, Pennsylvania, about 1776. That area was a stronghold of the Scotch-Irish. John and William lead the list, and James trails William closely, to stand in third place. Totally unexpected is it to find Patrick in fourth place. The other leaders are Robert, Thomas, Charles, Samuel, Edward, and Joseph. Also showing are Alexander, Archibald, and Andrew—all indicators of Scottish influence. Except for Samuel and Joseph, names from the Old Testament are rare. Even Benjamin occurs only once.

Most surprising is the high position of Patrick. It indicates either a considerable adoption of that name among the Scotch-Irish during their sojourn in Ireland or else a mingling with them in their migration of a number of the native Irish.

Still another situation holds with the Pennsylvania Rifle Regiment. Basically its name-pattern appears to be German, the population of the colony being largely German. John dominates, accounting for one man in four. (And we must remember the German liking for Johann.) William manages to make only fourth place, and Thomas drops clear down to eighth. Frederick and Matthias are among the leaders and are

German. The regiment shows other elements as well—the Scotch-Irish display themselves with James, Andrew, Alexander, and Archibald. There is even a Welsh suggestion in Hugh and Owen, as well as in the more widely used David. What is most strikingly lacking is the traditional English element. Robert occurs only once; Edward and Richard not at all. Equally lacking are the namings from the Old Testament which so dominate the Connecticut regiment. Benjamin and Samuel retain a little popularity, but Joseph fails to appear.

Shown by these contrasts between the muster rolls of Connecticut, Pennsylvania, and South Carolina, the differences between the regions are only what would be expected. National origin is partly to be held responsible, but so also are the differences in cultural development, as with the Puritanism of New England and its people's concentration upon the Old Testament. Moreover, the regions are isolated from each other, by modern standards.

The muster rolls also provide an opportunity for testing the influence of social class upon naming. We have available, for instance, the list of officers in the first to eighth regiments of the Connecticut Line for the years 1777–81.

As compared with most societies, that of Connecticut of this period would have to be rated as highly egalitarian. Nonetheless, significant differences between the two lists are clear. For instance, a person named Hezekiah was about ten times more likely to be an officer than to be an enlisted man. Isaac and Amos, on the other hand, are more characteristic of the enlisted personnel.

Such differences are difficult (or impossible) to explain. They are not, however, the less real for that reason. The situation is probably involved with wealth, education, and social status, small as those differences would have been in colonial Connecticut. The son of the farmowner probably went as a lieutenant and the hired man enlisted in the company. By this time, we must remember, the biblical names were becoming slightly old-fashioned, and might therefore have been somewhat commoner in established families, in which the tendency would be to name the child for the father or grandfather.

The Continental Army having possessed no women's auxiliary (unless we count an occasional Molly Pitcher) we are put to some difficulty to provide adequate lists of women's names for the period. We may present an analysis of some five hundred names of women who were married in Orange County, Virginia, in the years 1772–1800. These names may be said to represent, roughly, the naming practice in Virginia during the third quarter of the century.

The first ten names, in their order, are Elizabeth, Mary, Sarah, Ann, Nancy, Sally, Lucy, Susanna, Frances, and Betsy. This first ten suggests a strong English tradition, and there is indeed, no reason to suspect any other influence upon it. The great New Testament names—Elizabeth, Mary, and Anne—had been standing high in lists of English women for two hundred years at least. Their counterparts from the Old Testament, established soon after the Reformation, were Sarah and Susanna (having already become Sally and Susan in common speech).

The other names are also of interest. Nancy, developed from Agnes, had by this time almost wholly replaced the name of that once popular saint. Betsy shows a diminutive coming to be a name in its own right. Lucy is of special interest as being the name of a nonbiblical saint, such as would not readily have been accepted among the Puritans. Finally, Frances shows a recent development which has already become established.

Further analysis of the list reveals much of interest. Such Old Testament names as Rebecca, Rachel, and Ruth scarcely make an appearance. Abigail, that favorite in New England, is missing entirely. On the contrary, the nonbiblical saints (almost to be called outlawed in New England) make a considerable total—Margaret, Katherine, Alice, Barbara, and Winifred.

The classics make their contribution with Lucretia, Cynthia, Lavina, and others. Here we must include Zantipey (for Xantippe). On the other hand, the Southern custom of giving family names to girls has not yet developed. We note a single Sidney.

Most striking, and of great importance in the next century, is the custom, already noted with Nancy, Sally, and Betsy, of developing independent and official names from what were originally affectionate diminutives. Thus, occasionally we already have Milly, Polly, Frankie, Molly, Sukey, and others.

As in the seventeenth century, the colonies of New England call for a special report also in the eighteenth century. Here, once more, we note a basic stability, as demonstrated by the Harvard list, with the number of biblical names as the most interesting indicator.

At the opening of the century these names were over the 40 per cent mark, and they remained there for many decades, but never exceeded 49 per cent. Near the end of the century, however, the figure fell sharply, to 35 per cent. At the time it could have been written off as a mere temporary adjustment, but it was actually an early indication of a revolution which was to appear fully in the nineteenth century.

Thus, both for men and for women, the name-pattern of the eighteenth century developed steadily, not spectacularly.

The Nineteenth Century

The nineteenth century in the history of the United States was an intense and colorful period—the Civil War, heavy immigration of non-English-speaking people, a turbulent frontier, the economic chaos of the burgeoning Industrial Revolution, a new attitude to life and art which is known as Romanticism. Nonetheless, in the giving of personal names it may be characterized as showing only a steadily developing tradition.

We may, indeed, accept this basic stability of naming as an evidence of self-confidence among the people, especially shown by their ability to absorb the names of the polyglot mass of immigrants. A man who had been Shamus in County Clare became James in Cook County. Heinrich and Johann shifted to Henry and John—and, in speech, even became Hank and Jack.

Once any name developed into a stereotype, parents tended to avoid it. When Pat and Mike had become comics, the upwardly mobile Irish grew doubtful about them. So also, Bridget and Norah seemed to suggest a cook and a housemaid, and sent prosperous Irish parents to scanning the *Mayflower* list.

Among the "old Americans" changing social customs had some influence. The large family was disappearing. When parents expected to have only one or two sons, they still had a tendency to name one of them after the father, and thus the proportion of such names increased as the use of "Junior" flourished.

Highly characteristic of the early nineteenth century was the increased use of a middle name. Common custom in America viewed the first name as dominant over the second. In speech the middle name was rarely used, and in writing it was commonly reduced to the initial.

This usage created a sharp distinction from the usage of Britain, where the use of a third name was developing at the same time. The British conceived the middle name to be dominant, and reduced the first name to an initial. Also, more commonly than in America, the British in their writing reduced both given names to initials, or else all three names were spelled out.

Explanations of such folk customs are difficult. The American practice, however, seems to spring from a belief that the middle name, being considered as less important, was given the less emphatic position. Actually to address a person by his middle name was so rare as even to lead to comic effects. On the other hand, the British usage emphasized the middle name, which usually was a family name and would be considered, in some degree, as honorific.

This growth in the use of middle names—as indicated specifically by the Harvard and Princeton lists—had begun before 1800. It continued into the nineteenth century, and at such a rapid rate, indeed, as to suggest that by mid-century the process would be complete. In fact, this is roughly what happened. At Princeton, in the decade 1840–49, 92 per cent of the students had middle names. At that point, however, there seemed to come a sudden resistance, and the percentage fell to 72 during the next decade. From that time on, the percentages

29

at Harvard and Princeton alike leveled off at about 80 per cent—that is, only one undergraduate out of five lacked a middle name.

Some practical utility helped to power the movement toward the third name. As towns grew larger, there was more chance of having two people with the same first and last name, and the middle name (even if reduced to an initial) was of immense value in distinguishing one of these people from the other. Moreover, the middle name was commonly the mother's maiden name, and its use thus ensured the enduring of that family name for one more generation. The middle name also bestowed a certain dignity upon its bearer. No longer was he merely, among a hundred others, another Thomas Jones or Benjamin Bailey. Now he could be, for all to know, Thomas K. Jones or Benjamin Henry Bailey. Sometimes, also, when the parents had seen fit to give only one name, the person himself assumed a middle name. Or he might merely assume an initial, as in the famous case of Harry S. Truman.

We may grant that in the mid-nineteenth century the middle name was commoner in the colleges than in the general population. Eventually, however, the custom ceased to be elitist. In the drafted army of World War I, a highly egalitarian assemblage, every American was presumed to have a middle name. If he lacked one, some name or initial could be inserted into his record.

A different but somewhat comparable situation arose with women's names. The parents of a girl baby were likely to avoid such a complication as Mary Ann Jones, and sent their daughter into the world as Maryann Jones. Throughout the century there was a flourishing of such combinations as Susiejane, Rosemay, and Annamarie.

Another effect of the middle name was to increase the use of family names. In practice, however, the distinction between given names and family names cannot be totally maintained. Henry, Charles, and a host of others may be either. Exact percentages, therefore, cannot well be compiled.

In general, we have enough evidence to indicate that the family name as a given name appeared in isolated instances from Elizabethan times onward, becoming gradually commoner. It was used regularly for men, but its use for women became prevalent in the Southern states during the nineteenth century.

Actually, the family name never became dominant. In the mid-nineteenth century it stood only at 10 per cent, approximately, most of the examples occurring as "singles." Only an occasional name, such as Franklin, had as yet made the passage and was fully used by people who were not members of a family so called.

The family name gained what success it did from a kind of need for new names. The decline of the biblical names, especially those of the Old Testament, had begun in the last quarter of the eighteenth century, and it continued through the first half of the nineteenth century until such names might have been designated an endangered species.

In 1770 the Harvard list showed biblical names at 72 per cent, with the Old Testament supplying 49 per cent and the New Testament 23 per cent. The nonbiblical names were obviously, then, 28 per cent. In the Harvard of 1870 the names of the Old Testament had dropped to 9 per cent and those of the New Testament to 13 per cent. The nonbiblical names had thus soared to 78 per cent.

With biblical names thus falling out of use, there would seem to be a kind of crisis. What names were going to be bestowed upon the millions of newborn babies who may be envisioned as crying out for names as well as for milk? The 10 per cent supplied by family names did not go far, in spite of their potentially great number.

As if to solve the crisis, parents turned for aid not to the family names, but to what we may term the English traditionals. They were chiefly the Norman names—William, Robert, Henry and Harry, Richard. Included with them were Edward and George. One might also join to this group the three chief New Testament names—John, Thomas, and James. Few people thought of these as having religious suggestion. Jack, Tom, and Jim seemed equally as traditional as Bill, Bob, and Hank.

A few names of the Old Testament were so well fitted into popular usage that they survived with some degree of popularity through the nineteenth century. Here were Benjamin, David, Samuel, Joseph, and Daniel. All of these commonly appeared in their well-worn short forms—Ben, Dave, Sam, Joe, and Dan. Certain newly popular names also helped to supply the deficiency—Charles, Frederick, Frank, and Arthur.

Aiding in the use of the family name was the practice of naming for heroes—and the new Republic boasted a large number of celebrities. The great Washington doubtless aided in the continuing popularity of George, and he was certainly responsible for the use of that family name as a given name—as with Washington Irving, the writer, and Washington Allston, the painter.

A special group of family names comprises those of the English and Scottish nobility—Percy, Sidney, Stanley, Chester, Douglas, Clare, and a few others. Howard was especially popular near the middle of the nineteenth century. In general, however, Americans of that period were not highly susceptible to this infection of Romantic snobbery, and these names met with strong opposition, often being classified as "namby-pamby" or "sissy." In the long run, however, Howard and a few of the others managed to establish themselves. In this book names of this sort have, for convenience, been called "feudal."

Certain family names became especially popular, even coming to be considered as being primarily given names, not requiring any actual family origin. Such a one was Elmer, of interesting though not altogether explained history. Franklin furnishes an example of a name that flourished, partly from hero worship, partly because it suggested Frank, a name already in use and therefore not clashing with tradition. Many of the Franklins, indeed, went commonly as Frank.

Some interesting situations arose with the Civil War. As heroes and their names went, the Confederates were the more happily situated. Either Robert or Lee, or (often) both, provided an easy and apt christening, and became traditional. Derived from the second great Southern hero, Stonewall sometimes appeared. The initials of the *beau sabreur* J. E. B. Stuart gave rise to his nickname, "Jeb," and even established Jeb as an occasional name in its own right.

The two great Northern heroes bore the unusual names Abraham and Ulysses, but neither of these became popular. On the other hand, Lincoln and Grant became common as given names. The rejection of Abraham and Ulysses, however, is worth remembering as an evidence that hero worship as such is probably not as potent in name-giving as many people suppose.

In the later part of the eighteenth century, throughout Europe and its American appendages, there arose that way of looking at things which we have come to call Romanticism. Along with so much else, it affected the giving of names, chiefly by its love of the past. Anglo-Saxon names sprang into a new popularity—Alfred, Egbert, Harold, Edmund. The same source produced Edith, Ethel, and Audrey.

The Arthurian story supplied names, especially after the popularity of Tennyson's *Idylls of the King.* Arthur itself showed a renewed life, and the names for women were also in common use—Guenevere, Enid, Elaine, Vivian.

Largely because of the writings of Sir Walter Scott a kind of Scottish cult arose, gaining strength from the large number of Americans who recognized their Scottish ancestry and were proud of it. We may note Bruce, Douglas, Donald, Roy, Ronald, and Kenneth. But Sir Walter was also responsible for some non-Scottish names, such as Quentin and Rowena.

Though a kind of basic conservatism kept a few traditional names at the head of the list, the total effect of Romanticism upon names was strong. The number of names in common use increased noticeably because of it.

With women's names, the nineteenth century brought various new developments. Some names were beginning to seem old-fashioned and out of date. At the same time the increase in the size of towns tended to produce a monotonous repetition. To meet this problem (if we may assume a conscious motivation for a procedure which was chiefly unconscious) several devices arose. By a kind of evolutionary process new names came out of old ones—Eliza from Elizabeth, Nancy from Agnes. To arrive at these new forms, the namers made much use of the diminutive, -ie or -y. Thus arose Sally from Sarah, Annie from Anna, Carrie from Caroline.

The needed additions to the name-pool came also from revivals of names which had been fashionable in some earlier period. Lucy, for instance, one of the notable virgin saints (but not biblical), had been popular in pre-Reformation times and then almost disappeared, only to be revived strongly after 1800.

The Romantic mind also took an interest in the foreign and exotic. Charlotte thus came from the French; Maria from Latin or Spanish; Henrietta from Italian.

The nineteenth century, moreover, was highly literate. In fact, it may well end by being considered the period of the greatest triumph of the book. In the English-speaking lands the great majority of people knew how to read, and at the same time cheap printing was available. There was at yet no competition from other forms of mass media.

Shakespeare (read more than acted) supplied or aided several names for women—Juliet, Rosalind, Viola. Tennyson helped to re-popularize Maud, as well as the Arthurian names.

Actual coinage of names also had its place. Such coinage, in its simplest form, was merely the use of a common noun for a name. Usually a few names were selected from some group. Thus, from the precious stones we have Pearl and Ruby. Others, such as Beryl, Emerald, and Diamond, also appeared. In the flower list, Rose made a good precedent, having been long recognized as a saint's name. In the nineteenth century we have such additions as Lily, Violet, Iris, Heather, and Hazel. More fully developed coinage often involved the invention of a new feminine form to stand beside the old masculine form. Harriet, an English equivalent of Henrietta, sometimes made the top ten.

Most people would accept the suggestion that this nineteenth-century coinage reached its zenith with Lulu—best explained as baby-talk for Louise.

By and large the namers of the nineteenth century, if we may put it in that way, met the challenge and overcame the dangers. The name-patterns displayed no excessive monotony. As Romantic ways of thought advanced into a new century, the name-pattern for women displayed some basic conservative traits. Never having, like the male pattern, exhibited an excessive urge for Old Testament names, this pattern for women had no need for much reconstruction. Mary remained in general the commonest name, with Sarah and Elizabeth in second and third places. These three leaders generally accounted for a third of all the namings. Susannah, usually transformed into Susan, remained popular.

With women's names, however, the most interesting developments of the period were those which arose from the half of women's namings which were nonbiblical. The chief trend might be described as "feminization." It drew its strength from the lack, in the English tradition, of any clear means of expressing whether a name was borne by a man or a woman.

The new development began in the eighteenth century and showed up strongly in the opening decades of the nineteenth. The method was merely to transform the masculine name by adding a suffix, usually borrowed from French or Latin, and indicating something small and at the same time, usually, something feminine. Thus George might shift to the Latinate form Georgia or Georgiana, or could become, with French help, Georgette or Georgine. Robert, with a mere addition of a letter, became a passable Latinate form as Roberta.

There was also much use as a formal name of the diminutives which had previously been colloquial, such as -ie and y. Again the ambiguity arose. "Is it," we might ask, "a diminutive (and so applicable to both male and female children), or is it a feminine?" A certain tendency developed to maintain -ie for the feminine and -y for the diminutive. But this was, at best, only a distinction for the eye, and it was never carefully maintained, Many Americans, however, have a basic feeling that Billie indicates a woman and Billy a man.

Less formalized than the eighteenth century, the Romantic period allowed many of these nicknames to become full-fledged names. A somewhat easier-going religion moved in the same direction. Thus even Mary became Molly. The stately old name Elizabeth frequently ended, in almost jocular tone, as Betty or Betsy, or—fixing upon another syllable—became Eliza, Lizzie, or Liz. In certain cases the once-informal name actually tended to supersede the original one. Thus the formidable and rather ugly Mehetabel became the popular and very feminine Hetty.

On occasion, we may turn to the artificial world of fiction to establish people's ideas about names. To this end Mark Twain's dichology of *Tom Sawyer* and *Huckleberry Finn* is highly illuminating.

Huckleberry itself is obviously fanciful, but its common abbreviation, Huck, may be explained as a diminutive of Hugh. The other hero, however, bears a name—Tom—already, for centuries, typically English. With this name, we can only expect him to be a "good guy."

On the other hand, his sneaky little brother is Sid—that is, Sidney—one of the recently introduced snobbish names of English aristocracy, which Twain disliked.

Twain seems to be considering his fictional St. Petersburg as an American village of his own time, that is, of the middle 1840's. Indeed, he was seeing the life of that time through the rosy-tinted glasses of nostalgia. The names which he gives to the schoolchildren project this idea. The boys are Ben and Bennie, Billie, Johnny, Jeff, Jim, Bob, Joe. The girls are Becky, Mary, Gracie, Sally, and Susie.

Though the bearers of such names may occasionally lapse from virtue, they in general maintain the old American tradition. In fact, in this mythical St. Petersburg an unusual name signals aberrant behavior. The hated model boy, for instance— being opposed to Bill or Billy—is Willie, a name that had come to suggest something of a namby-pamby. There is also an Alfred, from whose name we can obviously expect little that is good. Actually, he turns out to be the unsympathetic smartie from St. Louis.

Huckleberry Finn—leaving the village behind and entering somewhat into the larger world—shows a comparable enrichment of its names. With Harney Shephardson we have an example of the new custom of using a family name. The six Graingerford children display an interesting split. The boys are named in the long-established tradition—Tom, Bob, and Buck (this last, probably, a nickname). The girls, however, echo the Romantic names—Emmaline, Charlotte, and Sophia.

The names of slaves, as Twain presents them, offer no distinction from those of the general population—Jim, Betsy, Elizabeth, Johnny, and Nat. Only Balum (for Balaam) is unusual, but there is no reason why one of the masters should not also have borne that Old Testament name.

As far as American personal names are involved, we may say that Romanticism extended well into the twentieth century.

The Twentieth Century

Of all the misty regions of the past, the most recent is, in general, the most difficult to present. The natural readjustments have not yet become clear, so that we have trouble is distinguishing trenchant movements from ephemeral shiftings.

The name-pattern of the mid-twentieth century differs strikingly from the earlier ones—both that of the earlier twentieth century and those of more distant times. The differences, however, may represent only a kind of temporary revolution.

Two practices—originating in the nineteenth century or even earlier—came into much importance in the twentieth. One of these exercised its influence chiefly upon men's names; the other, upon women's names.

The use of the family name as a personal one for men has flourished particularly in the twentieth century. These family names are exceedingly numerous. Elsdon C. Smith has attempted to ascertain their number in the United States, and comes up with the almost incredible total of 350,000. We must, however, note that many thousands of these names are non-English, and are probably destined in large number to be absorbed into the general pool, and to become conventionally English in spelling and pronunciation. Other names represent partial assimilation. Thus Schmidt is normally so spelled in

German, but in the United States—on its way in many instances to becoming Smith—it may appear as Shmit, Schmitt, Schmit, and in other spellings.

The vast number of American family names is important in that it provides an enormous pool of names. We have no reason to fear that the name-pool will ever run dry.

Although less characteristic of women than of men, the family name has also contributed notably to the women's pool, especially in the South. We need only think of Beverly, Lee, and Shirley.

The second new influence upon names in the twentieth century may be described under the general heading of coinage. It essentially is the expression of a desire to furnish the child with an original name, and not merely to draw from the name-pool.

Coinage begins with very slight changes, such as those of mere spelling, as in Debra from Deborah and and Kathryn from Katherine. Slightly more radical is Deeann, with which no one is certain whether to make the starting-point Diane or to think of the name as Ann with a prefix from Diane or Diana.

A further advance into coinage comes with the breakdown of names by syllables and their reconstruction. So we may have Kathella or Kathann or Kathmar. The syllables are normally conceived as having no meaning. An enormous number of names becomes possible, once this procedure is recognized as workable. The system resembles the dithemic one of the Anglo-Saxons.

In other instances the namers attempt to break with the past entirely, and to construct a new name from syllables which were not previously known to them. One trouble here is that no means exist by which anyone can be sure that the constructed name really is new.

These manufactured names have been the subject of much interest among those attracted by oddities. For instance, H. L. Mencken, in his *American Language,* devoted considerable space to such coinages, as also Puckett/Heller have done with special reference to names for blacks. Actually there is no reason to assign such names as characteristic of blacks, since they seem to flourish also among whites.

On the whole, the manufactured names should be enjoyed, but need not be taken too seriously. They are never numerous, probably not more than 15 per cent of the total. At the same time they show that originality is still not lacking among the givers of names.

Of the material at hand no assemblage of data is more enlightening than the Princeton list, largely because it is available, either in whole or by sampling, all the way from 1748 to 1975. The top ten for the men of the class of 1975 runs:

David	6.2%	Richard	2.9%
Robert	4.6	Thomas	2.7
John	4.5	Paul	2.5
William	3.2	Jeffrey	2.4
James	3.1	Michael	2.3

The list has both its conservative and its radical suggestions. David and Michael represent what is left of the once formidable Old Testament names. Neither of these, actually, has any appreciable biblical suggestion still remaining. The New Testament names (John, James, Thomas, and Paul) still stand strongly, though also with little suggestion of anything biblical. The Norman names show Robert, William, Richard, and Jeffrey. We must note also the lack of many of the once-popular names. No Charles, no Samuel or Benjamin, no Henry or Harry, no George, no Frank, no Frederick! Not one of these makes the first ten. Thus even this Princeton list suggests change rather than permanence.

The recent admission of women to Princeton enables us to present their top ten (here, eleven) also for the class of 1975:

Elizabeth	6.3%	Anne	4.3%
Susan	6.3	Barbara	4.3
Deborah	5.5	Cynthia	3.0
Linda	5.0	Ellen	3.0
Mary	5.0	Margaret	3.0
Nancy	5.0		

As with the men's names, these of women show old favorites jostling with upstarts. Elizabeth—historically, first or second—still maintains its high position, but Mary—commonest favorite of all—has dropped into a tie for fourth. The staunch Old Testament Deborah has risen to third place. Susan—biblical in some connotations—actually ties for first place. At long last, the nonbiblical saints have largely regained the status which they lost in the Reformation, though—as with Anne and Ellen—the spellings suggest Romantic influence. Barbara and Margaret preserve older spellings, but Nancy has been so fully worked over that few realize its connection with Agnes and thus with the nonbiblical saints. Finally, to complete the list, we have two newcomers—Linda and Cynthia.

Most strikingly absent from this list is Sarah, which was regularly in the first three over a period of centuries.

Thus the class of 1975, men and women, at Princeton (individuals born about 1955) shows a basic maintenance of tradition, but some striking shifts in the popularity of traditional names.

Since the Princeton lists may be thought elitist and conservative, we can shift, for less conservative lists, to those of Berkeley (Calif.) High School—the men and women of the graduating class of June 1974, births around 1955.

In the men's list the changes from a nineteenth-century list are extreme. The top ten run:

David	4.8%	Steven	2.7%
Michael	4.8	Kevin	2.0
John	3.4	Paul	2.0
Mark	2.7	Donald	2.0
Robert	2.7	Bruce	1.4

(This last being a tie for tenth place with Eric, George, Glenn, Gregory, Jonathan, James, Kenneth, and Thomas.)

Since David has been showing up regularly in the top ten during the twentieth century, its appearance in first place is not surprising. The rise of Michael is more remarkable. Even more striking is the breakup of the Norman names and the New Testament names. Of the Norman names only Robert is clearly in evidence. Of the great New Testament names, John has slipped to third place. Mark, Paul, and Steven have risen sharply. No fewer than three Scottish names appear—Donald, Bruce, and Kenneth. The most remarkable newcomer, however, is Kevin.

A top ten for women is also available for the same school and year:

K[C]atherine	3.5%	Cynthia	1.8%
Susan	2.8	Kim	1.8
Deborah	2.5	Linda	1.8
Karen	2.5	Sarah	1.8
Mary	2.1	Sharon	1.8

In this list Anne and Elizabeth fail to appear. Mary and Sarah are well down. But the top three names (and Sarah also) are firmly grounded in tradition, three of them being biblical. Cynthia, Kim, Linda, and Sharon, however, are essentially new favorites, even though Cynthia and Sharon are based on older traditions.

Also, we should note, the total of these top ten is only 22 per cent, but in many older lists it is as high as 50 per cent. Centainly the list shows greater variety than in earlier periods.

To bring the analysis down as closely as possible to the date of the actual writing of this book (1977) we present some data on infants born and named within five years of that time.

In 1972–73 Patricia Anne Davis collected material in Charlottesville, Virginia. Her method of presentation was somewhat different from that used in my own countings, but can be easily compared. Her eight most common men's names are Christopher (4.3%) James, John (3.7%), and Brian (Bryan), Charles, David, Michael, and Robert (2% to 3%).

Her list for the most popular girls' names for the same period and town gives eight names "in alphabetical order because there is no significant difference between the first and the last." The list is Amy, Angela, Jennifer, Katherine (Catherine, Kathryn), Katrina, Lisa, Melissa, Stephanie.

We pass on to the work of Cleveland Kent Evans at Ann Arbor, Michigan, for 1973–74:

Michael	4.8%	Brian	2.9%
Matthew	3.9	David	2.8
Jason	3.4	Jeffrey	2.8
Christopher	3.2	Daniel	2.4
John	3.1	Stephen	2.4

In the corresponding women's list he presents only the first five:

Jennifer	4.5%	Kimberly	2.3%
Amy	3.5	Michelle	2.1
Sarah	2.8		

To subject these lists to detailed analysis would involve too much for what is, after all, a mere introduction. Possibly the reader has already absorbed enough to draw some inferences.

The immediate general conclusion must be that some kind of revolution has struck the name-pattern. In all the lists the continuity of tradition seems to have been destroyed. New names suddenly have risen far upward, and centuries-old leaders have fallen back into obscurity.

As to why this has happened, we can present possible causes—at least by analogy.

The middle part of the twentieth century has been, everyone must admit, a time for rejection of ancient standards and of flight from old social customs. The name-pattern has reacted to this social ferment. If we ask whether such a change is "good" or "bad," we come to uncertainty and personal preference. Considered from one angle, the shift may be taken as something new and creative. Differently viewed, it may be considered a sign of the disintegration of a culture. There is as yet, indeed, no indication that the change is a permanent one. In another few decades there may well be a conservative drift. It is just as likely, however, that a still different list of names will appear.

THE DICTIONARY

Headnote

This portion of the book may be described as a dictionary, for it is an alphabetically arranged list of names, with the commentary presented under the individual heading. The information which is supplied may be analyzed in the order in which it stands in the entry:

The spelling or spellings of the name, usually being the entry heading itself.

Whether the name is (or was) applied to a man or a woman—or, occasionally, to either. Used for symbols are the conventional biological ones: ♂ for male, ♀ for female.

The language from which the name is derived, or from which it was taken into the English language.

The meaning of the name, which is commonly supposed to be the meaning it bore when it was taken into English, or first appeared in that language.

Information which may be described as a history of the name among the people of the United States. With many rare names this last category may not appear at all, and for many others it is brief. Some names, however, demand space (as do Charles and Nancy).

Cross-references to other entries are indicated by small capital letters, as: **Ian** ♂ The Scottish form of JOHN.

Information upon pronunciation is supplied when necessary or especially useful, but not when the pronunciation seems "regular."

A

Aaron ♂ Attempts to interpret it as Hebrew are unconvincing, and it is probably (like its counterparts Moses and Miriam) of Egyptian origin. In the United States, throughout the period of the popularity of Old Testament names, Aaron is found, but remains rare. After the mid-nineteenth century it virtually disappeared, except for occasional Jewish usage.

Abel ♂ If Hebrew, the name could mean "God-is-the-father." It occurs, however, only in the Creation story and therefore we can suspect that it is a borrowed name. A well-known and "good" character, Abel would have been, we should have thought, a popular name in the colonies. But (like Adam, Eve, and Cain) it is rare. It exists chiefly in New England, and its principal period of use is 1800–1850. Its possibility of confusion with the common adjective "able" may have contributed to its lack of popularity. Nab existed as a diminutive. (*See* ABIGAIL.)

Abiel ♂ Hebrew, probably "God-is-the-father." It may have been considered a mere variant of Abel. It is fairly common in early New England, but becomes rare after 1800 with the decline of Old Testament names.

Abigail ♀ The Hebrew may be translated as "father-joy," probably with the idea of the child's being "a joy to her father." According to I Samuel 25, Abigail was a woman of practical sense and efficient action. She was, however, far from being a model of constancy. Her husband having died, she hastened to David's bed—in (it would seem) a matter of days, or even hours. This action, indeed, may be construed as a necessary one (rather than one of mere concupicence) to preserve life and property in a world which was overrun by predatory gangsters, such as David was at that period.

Still, it sets no high ideal of human conduct, and by early Puritan standards Abigail did not create a heroine after whom parents would wish to name their daughters.

Abigail appeared rarely in the earliest records of Massachusetts, but became more popular after 1675. It also became a common name in the non-Puritan colonies. This situation maintained itself throughout the eighteenth century, when Abigail was regularly in the first ten. This popularity suffered, however, in the general decline of biblical names in the nineteenth century, and by 1900 the name was again rare. It has still further declined in the twentieth century, until—indeed—it scarcely exists at all.

Abigail developed the diminutive Abby, which functioned as an independent name (even commoner that Abigail) from about 1800 onward. The *n*-forms Nab and Nabby were also common. (*See* ABEL.) GAIL, still in use, represents yet another name derived from Abigail. Gale is probably a variant.

Abijah ♂ Hebrew, probably "Jehovah-is-the-father," fairly common in early New England, dying out after 1800 with the decline of Old Testament names.

Abner ♂ Hebrew, "father-light," or more likely (since his father was named Ner), "his-father-is-Ner." Captain of the Host to King Ishbosheth, Abner displayed many good qualities, and the name itself was both simple and short. Abner is current but never common in the period of Old Testament names.

Abraham, Abram ♂ The original name was Abram, which may or may not be Hebrew (or may be partly Hebrew). The translation is "father-of-height," or "high-father," neither making much sense. The suspicion thus arises that Abram, like other names in Genesis and Exodus, may be a borrowed name, not one constructed from Hebrew (*see* e.g. MOSES, MIRIAM). In Genesis 17 ("Almighty God" Himself being the speaker) the name is changed: "thy name shall be Abraham; for a father of many nations have I made thee." As usually translated it reads "father-of-a-multitude," Abraham thus at one shift becoming wholly Hebrew and wholly apt for a patriarch.

During the popularity of Old Testament names Abraham was current but never common; Abram also occurred occasionally. A slight increase in popularity shows up near the opening of the nineteenth century, including "Old Abe" himself (born 1809).

By the Civil War, however, Abraham was becoming wholly old-fashioned, and it has remained rare in spite of hero worship of the Great Emancipator. Actually a slight increase of Abram occurs in the post Civil-War period, and is probably to be taken as a tribute, though the advantages of the briefer name were to be rated more determining. In the twentieth century neither form of the name seems to remain current.

Absalom ♂ In the biblical story Absalom is both a wrongdoer and an unfortunate person. In favor of the name, however, is its literal meaning ("father-of-peace"), along with the personal beauty and charm of the character. It occurs occasionally in the period of Old Testament names.

Ada ♀ A short form of some such name as Adela, Adelaide, or Adeline. Ada was introduced into England directly from Germany near the end of the eighteenth century. It spread across the United States with the Romantic wave, but remained uncommon.

Adam ♂ In its opening passage, the Book of Genesis (with what may be taken for conscious literary art) employs the Hebrew word *adam* in at least three senses: first, as the personal name of a particular man; second, for man in the general sense; and third, for the color red. Some scholars even take the meaning to be "earth" or "likeness."

In the later Middle Ages (1100–1400) the name was much used in England, and was even commoner in Scotland, this popularity arising partially from the cult of two Celtic saints named Adamnan ("Little Adam"). This usage failed to survive the Reformation. Possibly the Puritan divines recognized some impropriety in using a generic word for a personal name. (And "red" did not help, one way or another.) While not becoming wholly obsolete, Adam came to be little used. In America it held a precarious but tenacious foothold. At Harvard, for instance, there is rarely a period without at least one Adam and probably there was never a time when there were more than two of them. The later eighteenth century was possibly the period of Adam's greatest use. One Pennsylvania regiment in the Revolution had four of them.

Possibly because of its old-fashioned suggestions the later centuries have not picked up the name, and it commonly fails to occur at all in recent lists. Another reason for its lack of popularity was Adam's association with the idea of Original Sin, a doctrine which was given high respect among the Puritans.

Adela, Adele ♀ Germanic, from *athal*, "noble." Introduced in England after the Norman Conquest, it never became common. Some amalgamation in the twentieth century with the French form, Adele, has helped to keep it from becoming extinct.

Adelaide ♀ Germanic, from *athal*, "noble," and *haidu*, "kind, sort." It was well used by the Normans, though it may be considered chiefly important as having given rise to ALICE. It became extinct in England, but was reintroduced in the early nineteenth century, largely because of the popular Queen Adelaide. From England it reached the United States, but it has never been much used.

Adeline ♀ Germanic, from *athal*, "noble," with diminutive-feminine *-ine*. A Norman name. It was revived in England in the early nineteenth century, and was used a little in the United States during that same period, when women's names ending in *-ine* enjoyed some popularity, partly because of the song "Sweet Adeline." The form Adelina also exists.

Adlai ♂ Hebrew [?], "lax, weary." Occurring only once in the Bible (I Chronicles 27:29), as the name of the father of Shaphat, who (under King David) had charge over "the herds that were in the valleys." The use of this utterly faceless name

48

suggests a choice by chance or by lot. What the name may lack in distinction of numbers it overbalances by distinction of achievement. It has supplied three generations of notable public servants, and has become a fixture in the Stevenson family.

Admire ♀ It occurs once in the Plymouth list, and doubtless occurs elsewhere. The word appears in the King James Version only once, as "admired" (II Th. 1:10). The meaning should probably be taken as "admire-virtue," or something similar.

Adolph, Adolf ♂ Germanic, "noble-wolf." It is generally to be found in German context, and is scarcely established as a name in English. Its association with Hitler probably worked against the name.

Adonijah ♂ Hebrew, "God-is-my-lord." It appears as the name of three persons in the Old Testament, the most prominent being David's fourth son. It was rarely used during the period of biblical names.

Adrian ♂ Latin, a name indicating originally that the bearer was from the Adriatic coast. It occurred chiefly in the late nineteenth century, but was always rare. The form Hadrian also appears.

Aeneas, *see* ANGUS.

Agatha ♀ Greek, "good." As the name of a widely venerated saint, Agatha was used in Anglo-Saxon times, but like the other nonbiblical saints it was largely rejected at the Reformation. It has never been favored in the United States. Its shortening, Aggy (or Aggie), is indistinguishable from that for Agnes, and this lack of individuality probably worked against Agatha.

Agnes ♀ From the Greek adjective *agnos,* "pure, chaste." The name was a popular one in the pre-Reformation period when it was supported by the cult of St. Agnes, one of the virgin-martyrs (cf. KATHERINE, BARBARA, MARGARET). The Reformation almost annihilated the name. In America it has been in continuing use, but has to be classified as almost rare, unless we consider it as represented by NANCY.

The modern pronunciation is based directly upon the classical form. In pre-Reformation times, however, the spelling was commonly "Annes," probably indicating a pronunciation which we would roughly represent by the spelling "Annyess." The diminutive is commonly Aggy or Aggie.

Agur ♂ Probably Hebrew, "gatherer," mentioned in Proverbs 30 as the author of that "prophecy." It has been very rare name in America.

Aileen, *see* EILEEN.

Alan, Allen, Allan ♂ Probably Celtic, literal meaning uncertain. It was the name of a fifth-century bishop of Quimper in Brittany, which was an area of Celtic speech. Contacts between Brittany and Normandy were close, and two of the Conqueror's lords bore the name (spelled Alain or Alein). It later became current, especially in Scotland, so that it may even be held to be a Scottish name.

In America it has been primarily a family name, but in the later twentieth century it became somewhat popular as a given name.

Albert ♂ Germanic, "noble-bright." The history of the name presents interesting differences between British and American development.

According to Withycombe, Albert was current in England during the Middle Ages, but fell out of use in the early modern period, to be revived after the marriage (1840) of Queen Victoria to the German Prince Albert. As Prince Consort he became highly popular among the English, and his name, curiously, became much more popular than Victoria's ever did.

In America, Albrecht, the German form, occurred among German immigrants of the seventeenth century. This German influence may be responsible for keeping the name alive, and it recurred in the rolls of the Continental Army.

The name shows in the Princeton lists for men born at the end of the eighteenth century, and slightly later it appeared at Harvard. The earlier appearance at Princeton may be attributed to the heavy German immigration to the Middle Colonies, but Romanticism may have had its influence. (Albert is a chief character in Scott's *Anne of Geierstein*.) In the earlier decades of the nineteenth century the name remained more common at Princeton than at Harvard, but the situation was suddenly reversed for men born in the decade 1840–49. This wave of Alberts struck Harvard in the decade 1860–69, and can be attributed to the popularity of the name in England rather than to any direct influence of the Prince Consort. Princeton did not show the new popularity until a decade later.

The popularity of Albert remained high throughout several decades, reaching its summit in 1880–89, thus putting the name into the top ten at Harvard (ninth place, in the decade 1900–1909.) Princeton showed a similar trend. Since that time the popularity has waned, but Albert remains a viable name.

Some confirmation of the dual development of Albert shows in the familiar form—Bert in Britain, as opposed to Al in the United States. The diminutive Bertie is regular in Britain, but very rare in the United States. There is, moreover, no corresponding term, possibly because such a one as Allie strongly suggests a feminine, as if from Alice.

Alberta, though never popular, has served as a feminine, along with various modernisms, such as Albertine.

Aldo ♂ Germanic, from *hild,* "war, battle," an Italian adaptation. It is very rare.

Alethea, *See* ALTHEA.

Alexander ♂ Greek, *alex-,* "defend," and *ander,* "man." It is an additional name or title borne by Paris in the *Iliad.* It was a common name in later classical Greece, partly because of Alexander the Great, who, in the Middle Ages, became the hero of a cycle of romances. There are also some twenty saints bearing the name. Nevertheless, Alexander never really flourished in England. In Scotland, however, it was a name borne by three successive kings (1214–85), and became generally used.

In the American colonies, Alexander may even be employed as a kind of test for Scottish influence. The name, for instance, is much more common at Princeton than at Harvard. In the nineteenth century, however, it declined.

Sandy, historically, is a variant of Alexander, not (as common belief now runs) a nickname for someone with so-called "sandy" hair. In the Celtic speech of the Scottish Highlands the name became Alistair.

Alexander has been strictly masculine. Its counterpart Alexandra failed to establish itself even with a queen as sponsor. On the other hand, the Italian form Sandra is in current use as a woman's name.

The colloquial American form Aleck or Alec has occasionally been used as an actual name.

Alexis ♂ Greek, "helper, defender" (cf. ALEXANDER). Alexis is a borrowing from the French, which in turn took it from Russian or some other language of eastern Europe. In the United States it is very rare, and normally is used in a Russian context.

Alfarata ♀ A coined name, originally appearing in a popular song of the nineteenth century. It is the name of an Indian girl, wholly fictional. The latter part of the name is used as a rhyme with "Juniata" (the river). Various spellings developed when the name was used after it had lost connection with the song, e.g. Alphareta, Alpharetta. The ALPHA may have been taken from the Greek, coiners of names being notoriously careless in their literary borrowings. The name has been very rare, and may not have survived the nineteenth century.

Alfred ♂ Old English, "elf-counsel." In spite of the Christianization of the Anglo-Saxons, pagan customs lingered, such as the belief in elves as friendly supernatural creatures, and "elf" was a recognized name-component. In addition, this royal family regularly used names beginning with A.

After the Norman Conquest, the name Alfred went out of use. It reappeared in the late eighteenth century when interest revived in the Anglo-Saxon heritage. In the United States the name dates from about 1780. It rose through the next century, sometimes getting into the second ten, and reaching its height about 1850–70. Its decline may be linked with that of the feudal names, with which it may be said to have a kinship. After 1870 its popularity fell off rapidly over the course of a few decades, and by 1950 it was little used. (*See* HOWARD.)

One difficulty has been the lack of a comfortable short form. Albert tends to monopolize Al, and Frederick dominates Fred. The British solution of using Alf (considered a vulgarism by many, even in England) remains a Briticism to most Americans in spite of "Alf" Landon, candidate for President in 1936.

Algernon ♂ Old French, "with whiskers [moustaches]," originally a descriptive nickname of William de Percy, founder of the Percy family. Revived in that family in the later fifteenth century, it remained in English usage, chiefly in aristocratic families, and then enjoyed a modest popularity in the nineteenth century. It barely reached the United States, being too closely associated with the British aristocracy and thus with decadence and effeminacy.

Alice, Alison ♀ A development into independent status of a form derived from the same original as ADELAIDE. It was highly popular in the Middle Ages. Though it survived the first effects of the Reformation, it gradually declined, and it is rare in the colonial period. In the nineteenth century it revived, probably because of the Romantic trend of thought and a general interest in the past, especially the Middle Ages. The popular *Alice in Wonderland* (1865) also affected the situation. Around 1900 Alice was second only to Mary in numbers. Throughout the twentieth century it has remained in use.

Alison, a diminutive, or "pet-name," came from France in the Middle Ages, and became popular, especially in Scotland. It has come into popularity again in the twentieth century.

Allan, *see* ALAN.

Allen, *see* ALAN.

Alma ♀ As a woman's name, it came into British usage as a by-product of the publicity following the Crimean battle (1854). The Latin adjective itself (familiar to most Americans because of the phrase "Alma Mater") means "loving, nourishing," and this connection must have aided the development of Alma in the United States. It has always, however, remained rare.

Almon ♂ Germanic, meaning "German." In the United States it occurs rarely, being probably a family name used as a given name.

Alpha ♀ Greek, for the first letter of the alphabet, used occasionally in the nineteenth and twentieth centuries with the suggestion of being the first daughter.

Althea, Alethea ♀ Greek[?]. The name occurs in Greek mytho-

logy as that of Althaea, the mother of Meleagar. It may not be
a Greek word. If it is, it can be associated with a root which
means "heal, make wholesome."

Addressing a lady in poetry, Richard Lovelace used Althea
in the seventeenth century. The name has thus been transmitted by its literary status, but it has remained very rare in English. Lovelace accented the word on the second syllable, but
modern usage has tended to shift the accent to the first syllable.

Alethea, though it may not actually exist in the American
name-pool, is from Greek, "truth," and should not be confused with Althea. It is accented on the second syllable.

Yonge associates Alethea with Ireland, and with the diminutive Letty, but this latter can equally well arise from Letitia.

Alva, Alvah ♂ ♀ This is a curious name, and may, indeed, be
two distinct names. Alvah is a minor biblical name, for one of
the dukes of Edom, and Alva might be only a variant spelling.
But Alva may be connected with Alvin, itself of uncertain origin. Any relationship to the Spanish Duke of Alva seems unlikely. The names, always rare, are chiefly of the eighteenth
and nineteenth centuries. Another curious feature is that they
have been applied both to men and to women.

Alvin ♂ Of uncertain origin, though perhaps from an Anglo-
Saxon name. Three possibilities are Ealdwine, Aethelwine, and
Aelfine. The name, however, was apparently not in use during
a long period. Its "revival" in the late nineteenth century may
not be an actual revival, but may be a coinage. It does not
occur in Yonge, and seems to be essentially an American form.
It has had some currency from the later nineteenth century on.
See ALVA.

Amanda ♀ In the seventeenth century, and even later, names
were coined from the Latin by poets addressing themselves to
ladies whom they wished to keep unidentified. We have
Amanda, "worthy to be loved;" Amata, "beloved."

Also connected with *amo* are Amabel, Amable, and Amiable
(all from the adjective *amabilis*). (*See* MABEL.)

These names are very rare, but may occur in a Latin context.

Amariah ♂ Hebrew, "God-has-spoken." It was the name of nine characters in the Old Testament, though not one of them was a person of importance. The name occasionally appeared in New England during the period of biblical names, but there seems to be little reason why it should have been used.

Amasa ♂ Hebrew[?]. The meaning usually given is "burden-bearer," but this is an unlikely term to be given for a name. Amasa was David's nephew, but his career was not very distinguished and at his death he "wallowed in blood in the midst of the highway" (II Samuel 20:12). It is difficult to account for even the occasional use of his name in early New England.

Ambrose ♂ this pagan name (meaning "ambrosial, divine") came into Christian usage with the canonization of St. Ambrose, the heroic bishop of Milan, in the fourth century. It occurs in the United States as a rare name, chiefly in the mid-nineteenth century.

Amelia ♀ A latinized form from *amal*, which is a common element in early Germanic names, of uncertain meaning. The name came to England with the Hanoverian kings and became popular there in the mid- and late-eighteenth century—and more so in the colonies. In America the classicism of its Latin form was becoming old-fashioned by 1800, and it was more or less replaced by the similar sounding EMILY.

Ammi ♂ Hebrew, "my-people." As a personal name Ammi occurs in the Bible as part of some longer name, e.g. Ammishaddai, "my-people-are-mighty." Ammi was the usual form in America, and the name had some currency in New England during the period of biblical names.

Amos ♂ Hebrew, "burden-bearer," one of the minor prophets and a book of the Bible. It was a fairly popular name in early New England throughout the period of biblical names.

Amy ♀ From Old French *amée*, "beloved." Common in the Middle Ages, it later passed out of ordinary usage, but was revived as a Romantic name in the nineteenth century, only to become old-fashioned again in the twentieth.

The early use of Amy is probably not to be attributed to the two French (male) saints of that name; it is, more likely, based directly upon the meaning. If it were from a saint's name we should today expect a masculine equivalent. By the later twentieth century, however, this volatile name had again become an ordinary resident member of the top ten.

The existence of a certain Amy in the White House is another testimony to the ability of her parents—named CARTER—to identify themselves with a popular movement.

Amzi ♂ Probably Hebrew. In the Bible it occurs only once, in a genealogy, and may mean "my-strength."

It appears regularly at Princeton in the period 1810–60, but not at Harvard. Apparently Amzi represents a development in the Middle Colonies, one which did not reach New England. The contrary is more usual.

The reasons for the choice of this obscure name are unfathomable. Possibly we may have to fall back upon an origin by some casting of lots.

Andrea ♂ ♀ The Italian form of ANDREW. The feminine-looking form, however, has caused it to be taken for a woman's name, and it is sometimes thus used.

Andrew ♂ The name is from the Greek adjective *andreios,* "manly," and entered the Christian tradition as the name of the Apostle and saint who became the patron of both Scotland and Russia.

Although the association with Scotland began at an early date, it was possibly more formal than popular. In America the Scottish immigrants brought the name with them, but it was not much used, possibly because of its "papist" suggestions. In the mid-nineteenth century it was fairly common, doubtless because of the extreme popularity of Andrew Jackson.

Andrew has failed to develop a one-syllable form, but the use of Andy is almost universal.

Angela, Angeline, Angelina, Angelia ♀ All are the result of attempts to derive (or adopt) a feminine name from the Latin or French word for "angel." These forms enjoyed a mild popularity in the late nineteenth century, and some of this has carried over into the twentieth. Angela, in particular, has appeared in the top ten.

Angus ♂ Scottish, common as a name in Scotland, but of uncertain meaning. It has failed to attain popularity in the United States, where it must be classified as a rare name.

In Scotland it has sometimes been shifted to Aeneas, as if from the name of the Trojan hero, but no such practice has been noted in the United States.

Anita ♀ Spanish, a diminutive of Anna in its Spanish form, Ana. It has shown some popularity in the twentieth century.

Ann[a], Anne ♀ Hebrew, "grace." (For further discussion of the meaning, *see* GRACE.) The name, spelled Anna, represents the Greek form of Hannah, as it appears in the New Testament (Luke 2:36). This Anna has become St. Anna, whose feast day is September 1. Much more widely known is St. Anne, whose feast day is July 26, and to whom we may attribute the ubiquity of the name. Though this Anne is not mentioned in the Bible, early Christian tradition identified her as the mother of the Virgin Mary.

She was especially honored in the Byzantine Empire, whence her cult spread to Russia, and then to France in the eleventh century, when King Henry I married a Russian princess named Anna. The name, however, failed to become popular in England until the fourteenth century. It survived the Reformation better than did most of the nonbiblical saints. In their new colonies, however, the Puritans rejected it, replacing it by its alternate form. (*See* HANNAH.)

In the non-Puritan colonies Ann remained about as popular as it was in England. Gradually, in the nineteenth century, it replaced Hannah, even in New England. It continued to be popular (usually in the first ten) until the counterculture of the mid-twentieth century. Even so, Anne still remains current.

One reason for its continuing use is undoubtedly that it is both short and euphonic. It has also developed new forms. The diminutive Annie was popular in the nineteenth century as an independent name. Nan and Nanny also flourished in that period. The case of NANCY is different, but many people associate it with Ann rather than with Agnes. Ann is popular in compounds, such as Maryann and Annamarie.

Of the variant spellings, Anna represents the biblical (Greek and Latin) tradition. Anne, with its diminutive Annette, shows French influence. Other forms appear in Anita, Anabell, etc.

Annabel ♀ The name is of medieval Scottish origin. It may be, as Withycombe suggests, a derivative of the Latin *amabilis* (*see* MABEL). Though Poe's poem *Annabel Lee* gave wide circulation to the name in the United States, it never was much used. Perhaps the funeral atmosphere of the poem was too marked.

Anne, *see* ANN(A).

Ansel ♂ The etymology is uncertain, but the name is most likely a shortening of Anselm, which is Germanic ("god-helmet"), chiefly used among the Lombards, and brought to England by Anselm (himself a Lombard) when he became Archbishop of Canterbury in the late eleventh century. It has been of rare use in the United States.

Antipas ♂ Greek, apparently a shortened form of Antipater, "like-his-father." It appears rarely in America, being probably derived from a Christian martyr mentioned in Revelation 3:12. *See* SALOME.

Antoinette ♀ The French feminine form of Antony, in occasional use from the eighteenth century onward. *See* ANTONY.

Ant[h]ony ♂ A Roman family name, meaning uncertain. The modern usage, however, is chiefly due to St. Antony of Padua. In the United States the intrusive *h* has influenced the pronunciation, and the *th* pronunciation is now the more common one. The name has never been popular, and Antonia and Antoinette, its feminine counterparts, have been rare. *See* TONI.

The common masculine shortening is Tony.

April ♀ In the twentieth century a slight use of April has occurred, probably on the analogy of May and June.

Along with the masculine August this seems the total extension of personal names taken from months, and for May and August the source is not primarily the month.

Aquila ♂ In the Greek text of the New Testament the name stood as Akulas, which may mean "acorn." In Latin and in the King James Version this name became Aquila, "eagle." It occurred rarely during the period of biblical names.

Arabella ♀ Like Annabel, which it resembles, the name appears to be of medieval Scottish origin, but it involves some uncertainty. Withycombe favors an actual development from Annabel by a *n-r* sound shift.

It has been a little-used name in the United States, but enjoyed a slight vogue in the early nineteenth century.

Archelaus ♂ Greek, "chief-[of]-[the]-people." He was a son of Herod and succeeded his father, but was a tyrannical and unsuccessful ruler. He is mentioned only once in the Bible, and is in no way characterized.

The name may be classical rather than biblical, since its biblical association is actually against it. It occurs very rarely in early New England.

Archibald ♂ Germanic, a typical two-element name, with *ercan,* "true," and *bald,* "bold." It was an established name among the Normans, but failed to survive in England, except in the North, and especially among the wide-ranging Normans of southern Scotland, where it became a common name.

In America it appears in some colonial listings, where it is to be considered as evidence of Scottish influence. It has scarcely survived on its own, coming to be associated with Algernon and other such names of aristocratic (and decadent) suggestions. Archie, however, has been well americanized, though still remaining uncommon.

Ariadne ♀ Borrowed from the Cretan heroine in Greek mythology. It is probably from a pre-Greek language. It has scarcely been used in the United States.

Ariel ♂ ♀ Hebrew, "Lion-of-God" or "God-is-a-lion." A man in Ezra bears this name, and it is also used in Isaiah as a symbolic name for Jerusalem. Shakespeare used it in *The Tempest,* and in the list of characters Ariel is noted as "an airy spirit," suggesting that the playwright was attracted rather by the punning suggestion than by the linguistic meaning.

In the Bible as well as in *The Tempest* the association of the name is thoroughly masculine, but in the modern American tradition the adjective "airy" has a strong feminine suggestion, and Ariel, a very rare name, has been used for women and probably not for men.

Arlene ♀ Its origin is doubtful, but it is probably best divided as Ar-lene, with the first syllable derived from Arthur. The second syllable may come from Caroline or some other form in *-lene.* If divided as *Arl-ene,* it may be derived from the well-established Charlene. It is a moderately common name in the mid-twentieth century.

Arnold ♂ Germanic, from *arin,* "eagle," and *vald,* "power." It may be found as an occasional usage from the later eighteenth century onward, sometimes from the family name.

Artemas ♂ Greek[?]. From its single use in Greek context (Titus 3:12), we presume a Greek origin, but no specific Greek word seems to fit. The derivation from *artamos,* "butcher," is not satisfactory either for form or for meaning. There may be a connection with Artemis, the goddess, or with the adjective *artios,* which has various commendatory meanings, e.g. "complete, proper."

It is chiefly remembered from General Artemas Ward, of the Revolution (born 1727). But there are other examples. In the mid-nineteenth century the humorist C. F. Browne took Artemus (thus spelled) as his pseudonym.

Artemisia ♀ Greek, from the name of the goddess Artemis. It was the name of two much-admired ancient queens. In America it appears under classical influence in the nineteenth century, but it never attained much currency, and has apparently disappeared in the twentieth.

Arthur ♂ The origin of the name has been the occasion of much controversy—as, we may say, so has everything else about King Arthur. The name may be from that of a Roman family, recorded as Artorius, but various Celtic origins have also been plausibly proposed. Its origin from the legendary King Arthur is, however, certain.

The name was nearly extinct in the seventeenth century, but increased interest in the Middle Ages, and the general Romantic approach to life, brought the name gradually back into use in Britain, and its association with the Duke of Wellington assured its popularity. In the United States it began to appear about 1780, and grew steadily. In the decade 1870–79 at Harvard it made the top ten, and in the class of 1905 it stood in sixth place. No exact explanation of this advance is to be

given, but the popularity in Great Britain was of some importance.

As the twentieth century advanced, the name, as is only to
be expected, came to seem old-fashioned, and its popularity
declined steadily until by the middle of the century Arthur was
to be considered uncommon—possibly ready, indeed, for another run of popularity.

Arthurine, a feminine form, has made little progress.

Asa ♂ Hebrew, "physician[?]," an Old Testament name used in
the biblical period. It was borne by one of the outstanding
kings of Judah, and may also have had some appeal because of
its brevity. It occurs infrequently in early New England.

Asahel ♂ Hebrew, "God-acts." It is the name of four people in
the Bible, of whom David's nephew, the younger brother of
Joab and Abishai, was best known. Although Asahel was
killed before he had distinguished himself, something in his
character apparently caught people's fancy, and the name was
viable during the period of biblical names.

Asaph ♂ Hebrew, "collector, gatherer," the name of five people
in the Bible, most notable among them one who was given
charge by David of the service of song and was appointed by
Solomon to administer the temple service. Possibly this name
was used in families who were musically minded. It went out
of use when biblical names lost popularity.

Asarelah ♂ Hebrew, "joined-[is]-God." It appears once in the
Bible as the name of a man "appointed by David for the service of song." The name might thus have appealed to a family
devoted to singing.

Asenath ♀ In Genesis this is the name of Joseph's wife. (It is not,
as sometimes stated, a modern coined name.) Its meaning is
unknown, but its language is probably Egyptian. It occurs
rarely in the Old Testament period.

Ashbel ♂ Hebrew, "man-[of]-Baal[?]," a son of Benjamin, mentioned only in passing. Baal was generally a foreign deity to
the Hebrews, but its use in a name is not impossible. Ashbel
was very rare in America, even during the period of biblical
names.

Asher ♂ Hebrew[?], the name of a son of Jacob and of the tribe taking its name from him. As with most of these tribal names the origin is doubtful, and it may be from some pre-Israelite source. The name was rarely used in America. Some of its later occurrences are probably from the family name, which indicated a man working with wood-ashes for making potash.

The spelling Ashur is probably a mere variant.

Aubrey ♂ A French form of the Germanic Alberich, "elf-rule." It came into England with the Normans. The later history of this rare name is not clear. It may be Romantic revival.

Audrey ♀ Anglo-Saxon, from Etheldreda, "noble-strength." Etheldreda, a queen of Northumbria in the seventh century, became a highly venerated saint, and her name was thus passed on after the Norman Conquest. It suffered severe changes in pronunciation, and by the sixteenth century the spelling was shifted to agree with the new pronunciation. The name came to have a rural and countrified association, and Shakespeare used it, with that suggestion, for the shepherdess in *As You Like It*.

The name, by the seventeenth century, had become rare in England, and at that period it scarcely appeared at all in the colonies. In the early twentieth century it was revived in England, and became somewhat popular. This English interest stirred up some usage in the United States. It has not, however, become as much used in America as in England.

Augustus, August[e], Augusta ♂ ♀ Latin, a title, "venerable, consecrated." In the United States it regularly appears as Gus. It is commonly taken from the German form August, and has never been wholly naturalized in general usage in the United States.

The feminine Augusta (with its diminutive Gussie) was viable in the eighteenth and nineteenth centuries.

Aurelia ♀ It was a Roman tribal name, but is generally considered as the adjective, "golden." It has been occasionally used in the United States.

Averil ♂ The Anglo-Saxon form is Everild, and is probably "boar-favor." The name was in use in the medieval period, particularly in northern England, where a local saint was so named. The history of the name is uncertain, but it survives (though very rarely) in the United States.

Aylmer, *see* ELMER.

Azalea, *see* LILY.

Azariah ♂ Hebrew, "God-[is-his]-helper." It was the name of one undistinguished king of Judah, but is more remarkable for its great general popularity in ancient Israel, being borne by no fewer than 28 persons in the Bible. It occurs very rarely in early New England.

Azel ♂ Hebrew, "noble." It was the name of a Benjamite, mentioned only in genealogies—a very rare name in America.

B

Babette ♀ Commonly a diminutive of Bab, itself a short form of Barbara. In some instances it may have arisen from a French version of Elizabeth. It has been a rare form.

Barachiah, Barachias ♂ Hebrew (Barachias is the Greek form), "blessed-of-God." It occurs rarely in the Bible, always in a genealogy. In America it is very rare, and is one of those names which may have been selected by mere chance.

Barbara ♀ Greek, feminine of *barbaros,* a term (noun or adjective) applied to anything or any person to indicate "not Greek," or, in general, "foreign, outlandish." In the Christian countries the naming tradition begins with St. Barbara (Syrian, 3rd century) one of the great virgin saints.

   The name was not popular in England before the Reformation. In the following period, with its widespread rejection of the idea of sainthood, Barbara almost disappeared—especially in America, where it was vestigial in the eighteenth and nineteenth centuries. In the twentieth century Barbara came into use again to some extent because of its Spanish suggestions (cf. DOLORES, LINDA, etc.). By 1950 it had become highly popular, a regular among the top ten.

   The common short form has not been well explained. Bar and Barb may have been rejected because of unpleasant suggestions of meaning. Babs, however, is not easily explicable; there is no ready source or analogy for the added *s*.

The older English familiar form was Barbary, but it has made little impression on American usage, a further indication that the recent popularity of the name is not a development from British practice, but is an independent growth, probably from a literary or dramatic (Hollywood) source.

Barnabas, Barnaby ♂ Hebrew, Aramaic, "son-of-exhortation[?]." The name of St. Paul's companion was in regular use among the first immigrants to New England, but it declined in popularity as time passed. It has enjoyed a mild revival in the twentieth century. The form Barney has also commonly been used.

Barry ♂ Irish, derived from a word meaning "spear." The name came into use in English in the nineteenth century. Its introduction must have been aided by Thackeray's novel, *Barry Lyndon* (1844). In the mid-twentieth century it has enjoyed some popularity in the United States.

Bartholomew ♂ Hebrew (Aramaic), "son-of-Tolmai." As one of the Apostles, St. Bartholomew was venerated in England during the later Middle Ages, and his name was popular. Like others of the New Testament names (partly, perhaps, because of its length), it failed to maintain that popularity in America, although the recurring short forms Bart and Bat indicate its use in the nineteenth century. It is scarcely to be considered current in the later twentieth century.

Barzillai ♂ Probably Hebrew; some connection with *barzel,* "iron, strong," is possible. It is a rare name—possibly selected by chance, though Barzillai appears as a friend of David in an episode narrated in II Samuel 19.

Basil ♂ Greek, "kingly." St. Basil the Great has been one of the widely known saints in the Eastern Church. The name is rare, except in groups having a connection with that Church.

Bathsheba ♀ Hebrew, "daughter-of-the-oath," one apex of the triangle in the scandalous story of David-Bathsheba-Uriah. The name had some currency in medieval England. Perhaps this tradition led to the name's continuance in America, chiefly in the Puritan colonies, even though Bathsheba's habits and motivations, as the biblical story presents them, are not Puritanical. The name, however, scarcely established itself in the colonies, and it probably ceased to be current about 1800. *See* BATHSHUA.

Bathshua ♀ Hebrew, "daughter-of-prosperity." In the biblical text this name is sometimes only another form for "Bath-sheba," though at least once it is the name of another person. It occurs rarely among names in early New England. It may represent an attempt to provide a substitute for Bathsheba, without that name's evil suggestions. Bathshua, however, failed to become established. *See* BATHSHEBA.

Beatrice ♀ Latin, a feminine form of *beatrix,* "one-who-blesses" or "one-who-makes-happy." St. Beatrice (4th century) was well known in medieval England, and the name was popular, but in the post-Reformation reaction against the names of nonbiblical saints Beatrice nearly disappeared. It regained some popularity in the eighteenth century from the general revival, under Romantic influence, of interest in the Middle Ages, and also because of increased interest in Dante and his Beatrice. The name has remained in moderate use in the United States.

The alternate form Beatrix has had some usage in Britain but scarcely exists in the United States, unless the diminutive Trixie (itself rare) is to be counted.

Belinda ♀ Germanic, with *lind-*, "snake," and the other element not known. Preserved as a literary name, it occurs in current usage, but is rare.

Bell, Bella, Belle ♀ All are to be considered short forms of Isabel, though the direct influence of the Latin *bella,* "beautiful," is possible, as well as that of "belle," Southern usage for an attractive girl. The names are chiefly of the nineteenth century.

Benjamin ♂ Probably Hebrew, "son-of-the-right-hand." The original name, however, may have been applied to a tribe.

The usage as a baptismal name arose among English Puritans of the early seventeenth century. Brought to America by immigrants to the Puritan colonies, the name flourished, its popularity there surpassing that in England itself. Countings for New England in the seventeenth century show Benjamin regularly in the top ten, characteristically about in seventh

66

place. After 1700 its popularity fell off, and it made the top ten for the last time in 1720–29.

In regions other than New England the name was less used, but can still be considered popular. At Princeton it never attained the top ten, but reached twelfth place in 1850–59.

The decline, even in New England, sharpened after the mid-nineteenth century. Though still current in New England, Benjamin is to be reckoned, after 1890, a rare name over the country in general. It still remains viable, though old-fashioned, and shows no sign of a revival, nor of the adoption of the forms Ben, Benny, and Benjy.

Benjamin must thus be accepted as one of the most characteristic American names—the whole history of the country being considered.

The reasons for this popularity are (as usual) difficult to assign. The biblical story, however (though but lightly sketched), is an appealing one—the child orphaned of his mother in childbirth, the solace of an elderly father. Benjamin was probably a name given after the death of the mother in childbirth, an all too frequent reality in those years. The name, also, was a suitable one for a son born to elderly parents, and thus likely to be the youngest of the family and to receive special cherishing. (*See* BENONI).

Certainly, from the latter part of the eighteenth century and on through the nineteenth, the influence of Benjamin Franklin was of importance. As a folk-hero Franklin's only rival was Washington, and in some respects Franklin even exceeded Washington.

Benjamin is thus of importance as a thoroughly biblical name which shifted to become a traditional and popular name, and so survived the collapse of the vogue for biblical names. (*See* FRANKLIN.)

Bennet[t] ♂ From the Latin *benedictus,* "blessed." The popularity of the name in the Middle Ages sprang chiefly from St. Benedict himself (490-*c.* 542), founder of the Benedictine order. The name (as that of a nonbiblical saint) went largely out of use at the Reformation. It had, however, given rise to a family name, and Bennet once more became a given name.

Benoni ♂ Hebrew, "son-of-my-sorrow." The name occurs only once in the Bible (Genesis 35:18), in the pathetic story of Rachel's death in childbirth: "as her soul was in departing . . . she called his name Benoni." Apparently considering this too much a name of ill omen, the father, Jacob, changed the name to BENJAMIN.

Bernhard, Bernard ♂ Germanic, "bear-[animal]-hard." This typical Germanic name was propagated largely by the Normans. In the United States it is probably to be considered a family name which is occasionally used as a given name.

Bernice ♀ Greek, "bearer-of-victory," A person of this name is merely mentioned in the Bible (Acts 25). The name never became popular, and probably is used as much in the twentieth century as at any period.

Bert, *see* ALBERT, HERBERT.

Bertha ♀ Germanic, a short form of one of the numerous names with the element meaning "bright." Popular with the Normans, it lost favor, but was revived in the nineteenth century and enjoyed some moderate prosperity around 1900. Since that time it has again gone almost out of use.

"Big Bertha," a name for a heavy German gun in World War I, did nothing to glamorize the name.

Bertram, Bertrand ♂ Germanic, "bright-raven," brought into English usage by the Normans. It has been less current in America than in Britain. The American use of the name may be from Romantic tastes of the nineteenth century rather than from a continuing tradition from the Anglo-Saxon.

Beryl, *see* PEARL.

Bethia[h], Bethya ♀ Hebrew, "daughter-of-Iah" (i.e. "of-God"). The name was fairly common in New England during the seventeenth century, but went out of use. Berthier may be a variant spelling, and it may have been confused with Bertha.

Bettina ♀ Although it looks like a derivative of Elizabeth, the name is from the Italian feminine-diminutive of Benedict. It is of rare occurrence.

Beverly, Beverley ♀ ♂ Anglo-Saxon, "beaver-stream," a place-name in England. It occurs rarely as a family name. From the family name Beverly is to be found occasionally as a man's name in the later nineteenth century, e.g. at Harvard.

In the early twentieth century the name was much used for women, largely because of the enormously popular novel by G. B. McCutcheon, *Beverly of Graustark* (1904). The particular reasons for the author's choice of the name are unknown. The heroine was from the South, where the giving of family names to girls has been more practiced than in other regions.

In the mid-twentieth century the name has been moderately popular for women. It has shown an occasional variant, such as Beverlee.

Bezaleel ♂ Hebrew, "God-is-[my]-protection[?]." In Exodus 31:2 God called "by name" Bezaleel to work as a master craftsman in the construction of the tabernacle and the ark with their furniture—"to devise cunning works, to work in gold, and in silver, and in brass." The cause of the flourishing in colonial America of this rather strange name may be that certain families with a tradition of craftsmanship viewed Bezaleel as a kind of patron. In the same passage and elsewhere, in more general but highly commendatory terms, he is recorded to have been filled with the spirit of God "in wisdom, in understanding, and in knowledge." Bezaleel thus bore a name to be highly regarded.

Bezer ♂ Probably Hebrew; meaning uncertain. It occurs only once in the Harvard lists, and may have been selected by chance.

Blanche ♀ French, "white [feminine]." In some instances the name may have been given because the baby gave evidence of blondness. It has been rare in the United States.

Boaz ♂ Hebrew[?]; of uncertain meaning. The biblical person was the husband of Ruth, and, as the great-grandfather of David, stands in the genealogy of Christ. It is also the "name" of a brazen column in Solomon's temple. During the period of biblical names it appeared occasionally.

Bonnie ♀ A Scottish form, from the common adjective for "pretty." It is an interesting case of a name being based upon an ordinary word in modern usage.

It has been a moderately popular name in the mid-twentieth century.

Boris ♂ Probably Russian, meaning uncertain. It is of rare occurrence, usually with a Russian background.

Brenda ♀ Probably to be connected with Norse *brand,* "sword," but uncertain. It is a literary name, used by Sir Walter Scott. It came into fashion in the mid-twentieth century and has continued to be moderately popular.

Brendan ♂ Celtic, the name of two Irish saints, literal meaning uncertain, but *see* BRENDA. In the United States the name has appeared chiefly in Irish context.

Brian, Bryan ♂ Celtic, particularly Irish, of uncertain meaning. It is also a family name. It flourished in England during the Middle Ages, but fell into disuse. Revived in the twentieth century, it is fairly popular.

Bridget ♀ The English adaptation of the Irish form Brighid, a pagan fire-goddess; eventually from *brigh,* "strength." It has traditionally been, after Mary, the commonest woman's name in Ireland. Because of the tremendous transatlantic imigration of the Irish in the mid-nineteenth century the name became common, but it failed to establish itself in general usage in the United States. It thus became a mark of the Irish (especially of domestic servants), and the Irish themselves tended to abandon it as a handicap to their integration into American life. Though a revival seems possible, the name in the later twentieth century is only to be classified as rare.

Brigham ♂ Anglo-Saxon, from the family name, meaning "settle-at-the-bridge." It has derived some special usage because of the Mormon hero, Brigham Young.

Bruce ♂ The village Braöse in Normandy gave its name to the Norman family which became established in Scotland and from which sprang King Robert the Bruce, victor over the English. Its use as a given name has chiefly developed in the twentieth century. Since Bruce is a well-established family name, its use as a given name has been aided by that source. In most Americans' minds Bruce would be considered primarily as being a given name.

About 1975, for no established reason, Bruce (especially

Brucie) came to be used as a generic term for a "gay." We may therefore expect it to lapse from general usage.

Brutus, Cassius ♂ Popularized by Shakespeare's play rather than by historical sources, these two names were in occasional use during the nineteenth century and have not become altogether obsolete. As revolutionaries, the two Romans were, in a small way, conceived of as American heroes, and Cass became an established short form.

Bryan, *see* BRIAN.

Bud, Buddy ♂ Baby-talk, from "brother." It has been a very common short form, occasionally attaching itself to a particular person, and even doing duty as an official name. It has been widely used in the armed services.

C

Cadmus ♂ From the Greek mythological (or partially historical) character, possibly a Phoenician name taken over by the Greeks and originally meaning "easterner." Its occasional appearance as a personal name is chiefly of the nineteenth century.

Caesar ♂ In early slave lists it occurs, often the commonest of the classical names—presumably given by masters rather than by slaves. The great fame of Julius Caesar certainly accounts for this popularity, but there seems to be no specific reason why the name was thought an apt one for slaves. In later usage it has been used for non-blacks, sometimes being applied to a boy born by Caesarean section. The spelling Cesar also can be found. At the present time Caesar is scarcely to be considered viable.

Caleb ♂ Probably Hebrew, "dog," possibly a tribal totem. It was a viable name in the American colonies, especially in New England, down until the general decay of biblical names about 1800. Its moderate popularity sprang, perhaps, from its shortness and simplicity as compared with biblical names such as Jehoshaphat and Nehemiah.

Calvin ♂ The name begins at Harvard in the early eighteenth century. As a Protestant reformer, John Calvin was a highly respected and even heroic figure among both Congregationalists and Presbyterians, but more so among the latter. That situation is emphasized by the greater popularity of Calvin at Princeton as compared with Harvard.

Cameron ♂ A family name, itself derived from the clan-name, meaning "wry-nose." Like so many Scottish names it attained some popularity along with the Romantic movement.

Camilla ♀ Etymology uncertain. The name comes from the warrior-queen of Vergil's *Aeneid,* and may have been the poet's creation. It probably does not occur in the United States before the nineteenth century, and it has always been rare.

Candace, Candice ♀ Usually pronounced as two syllables, language and meaning uncertain. Candace was in ancient times the hereditary name or title of the queens of Ethiopia or Nubia. One of these queens figured in a story which represented her as involved in incest with her brother. Chaucer, though attributing the story to Canace, contributes the line "Who loved her owne brother synfully." The name was also attributed to the queen of Sheba who visited Solomon. In addition, "Candace queen of the Ethiopians" has a passing mention in Acts 8:27

Putting all this together, we have little reason to expect to find the name in American usage. It has, however, so occurred—in spite of the suggestion of incest which clung to it. In fact, that taboo topic might even have an attraction—as, in fictional setting, it has in Faulkner's *The Sound and the Fury.* Occurring rarely in the nineteenth century, it has become more used by the counterculture, perhaps because it is one of the few traditional names which can bear a suggestion of unusual sex relations.

Carl ♂ Its etymology is the same as that of CHARLES, but its later history is quite distinct. The earlier (German) form is Karl, and that spelling is often retained, especially among immigrant groups and in situations where Germanic influences have acted strongly.

Carl was, generally speaking, confined to German immigrant groups until about 1850. It showed a sharp rise about 1880, doubtless due to being connected with the rise in German prestige following the victorious war of 1871–72 and due to the general expansion of German influence upon western civilization. By the time of World War I the name had established itself. Especially in its C spelling, it was well entrenched and had lost its closer Germanic origins. It thus escaped most of the reaction against things German which necessarily tended to appear under wartime conditions, and it still survives in moderate usage. It is highly unusual for a name thus to survive and to offer alternate spellings.

Carl is also unusual in having no common short form or diminutive—a situation which many people think advantageous. The actual connection with Charles is no longer considered, and Carl does not share the nickname Chuck. Carla serves for a feminine, but is not common.

Carlos ♂ The Spanish form of Latin Carolus (Charles), it occurs rarely as a Romantic or literary form, never having become fully naturalized.

Carmella ♀ Eventually the name must be from the biblical Mt. Carmel. Through the Carmelite order the name came to western Europe. As a given name it was not used until the twentieth century.

Though it suggests a Spanish origin, it is more likely a development within the United States. It stood at 98 in the Smith list (1942) but has fallen off sharply since that time.

Carol, Carole, Carroll ♂ ♀ The origin is the same as that of CHARLES. The development in several European languages (e.g. Polish, Romanian) arrived at the simplest possible form, such as would be spelled merely Carol in English. In Continental usage, the name was the equivalent of Charles, and was used for men.

In Great Britain the name Carol, beginning to appear near the end of the eighteenth century, naturally applied to men. In America, however, it soon was used for women—perhaps being so influenced by its attraction to the obvious Caroline instead of to the less obvious Charles. As a result, Carol (applied to a man) is so rare in the United States as scarcely to exist. Instead, the spelling Carroll has been used, as if it were a family name.

Carol continued in use for women, and two later-coined

forms (also for women) were Carole and Carola. All these forms, however, remained rare. Other coined spellings may be found, e.g. Caryl.

Caroline, Carolina, Carolyn ♀ Its origin is Italian, and the *-ine* form is probably French (or possibly Italian). *See* CHARLES for further etymology. The popularity of the name, however, came to England from Germany in the mid-eighteenth century with the marriage of George II to Princess Caroline of Ansbach.

As Caroline the name was moderately popular in the United States through the nineteenth century. In the mid-twentieth century it was again popular, but in the spelling Carolyn. (*See* LYNN.)

Carolina (probably an adjectival form based on Latin) did not establish itself as a viable name, though used for two states. Probably its four syllables seemed too many.

Carrie, the diminutive, was popular through the nineteenth century and into the twentieth. It is often to be considered an independent name.

Carter ♂ From the family name, which springs from a man who drives a cart. The name has developed some glamour because of the social status of certain branches of the family, and may well continue to so develop because of the prominence of the Georgia branch.

Cassandra ♀ In the *Iliad*, Cassandra is one of Priam's daughters, notable as being the prophetess who was never believed. The element *-andra* is "man" in Greek, but the name may not be Greek or may only seem Greek because of having been transmitted through that language. Like Hector (her brother), she became well known to the English. Her name was common in the Middle Ages, and a faint tradition of it hung on, usually in the diminutive Cassie.

The local-color writers of the nineteenth century (e.g. Bret Harte) used the name as a characteristic one for a primitive American of that period. If it has survived into the twentieth century, it must be exceedingly rare.

Cassius, *see* BRUTUS.

Catherine, *see* KATHERINE.

Cato ♂ The name is limited to black males of the period of slavery, but in that group it is a common name. It is derived from the Roman name—in particular from M. Porcius Cato (95–46 B.C.), known as Uticensis, from his death by suicide at that African city. One of the heroes of the Roman Republic, he became by association a hero of the young American Republic, to which places called Utica give testimony. His association with Africa was established by his military services there, and his place of death. Though not a black, his connections with Africa were sufficient to lend a certain rational background to the use of his name for blacks.

Curiously, his great-grandfather of the same name, known as "the Censor," in his treatise on Roman agriculture supported the idea of slavery, even in its harsher forms.

The name also may owe something to Cata, a name of West African origin, and enough like Cato to suggest that name. It is no longer viable.

Cecil ♂ Latin, a tribal name, Caecilius, literally meaning "blind." It is the masculine of Cecilia, but much rarer. In the United States it occurs chiefly in the later nineteenth century, and is to be classed with the feudal names such as Sidney and Percy. *See* CECILIA.

Cecilia, Cecily ♀ The femine of Caecilius (see CECIL), its use is more particularly based upon the cult of St. Cecilia, the patroness of music. As a nonbiblical saint, Cecilia was not much regarded in the Protestant tradition, and the name has been rare in the United States. In the twentieth century its use has increased somewhat.

Cedric ♂ It was not in use before it appeared in Scott's *Ivanhoe* (1820) as the name of a character who was known as "Cedric the Saxon," and who would presumably have an Anglo-Saxon name. The name most like it in Anglo-Saxon records is Cerdic. Possibly by mistake but more likely by conscious coinage Scott apparently shifted this name to Cedric (cf. ROWENA). In America, however, the name was as rare as scarcely even to be termed viable.

It was, however, the name of the chief character in Burnett's *Little Lord Fauntleroy* (1886), a highly popular novel, which gave great circulation to the name but at the same time gave among American boys a strong "sissy" suggestion. Cedric enjoyed a slight boom at the time, but soon disappeared.

Celeste ♀ French, "heavenly," but originally Latin and chiefly inspired by St. Celestine. It is a rare name.

Celia ♀ Latin, from a family (tribal) name, probably independent of Caecilius (*see* CECIL), and remembered largely from its occurrence in Shakespeare's *As You Like It*. It has never been a much used name. (*See* SHEILA.)

Cephas ♂ For its origin, *see* PETER. Loughead gives Cephas as an American name, but I have not seen it in my listings. There is no reason why it should not occur, but it must be exceedingly rare. (*See* John 1:42.)

Chad ♂ Anglo-Saxon, from Ceadda, the name of a bishop in the seventh century; later he attained sainthood. The name is probably a nineteenth-century revival in England and has remained very rare in the United States.

Charity ♀ In the New Testament it has the meaning "love" (in the spiritual sense), and the early namers in New England probably so realized. Later namers have echoed the earlier ones, with little thought of meaning. The name is one of the commoner of early Puritan abstracts, and has managed to maintain a slight usage down to the present.

Charleen, Charlene ♀ In recent years, with sex distinctions breaking down in much usage, there has been a constant tendency to adopt masculine forms to serve for women. To supply a feminine for Charles, several adaptations have been improvised, and Charleen and Charlene have attained some popularity in the later twentieth century.

Charles ♂ Germanic, from a word meaning "man" in the complimentary sense, seen in the modern German and Scandinavian as Karl. It seems to have been especially a Frankish name, and was borne by their famous leader Charles Martel (d. 741) and by Charlemagne, that is, Charles the Great (d. 814).

The Frankish form was put into Latin as Carolus. From this form, with retention of the final *s*, and some phonetic shifting, the Old French developed Charles. Retaining the tradition of Charlemagne, Charles continued to be a common name among the French, whose early seat of power was in the Île-de-France, the region around Paris.

But the French and the Normans were again and again at war, and from the Norman point of view Charles became a hostile name. At least this is the obvious reason by which to account for the failure of the Normans to use the name and thus for its almost total absence from England of the Norman period. Also, since there was no St. Charles before the sixteenth century, the Church exerted no influence in favor of the name. In a list of 427 male children who were baptized in London in the 1540's, there is no Charles at all.

For that name the road to England (and a wholly new road) began in France and detoured by way of Scotland. The young Scottish princess named Mary was betrothed in 1548, when she was only six years old, to the heir apparent of France, and went to live in that country, where she became more French than Scottish. The princess—later known as Mary Queen of Scots—married her Frenchman, but provided no heir to the French throne. After a few years her husband was accidentally killed, and she returned to Scotland, where she continued to speak French and otherwise to follow Gallic customs.

As a second husband she took a Scottish nobleman, and by him had a son, whom she had christened as Charles James. The second of these names was obviously appropriate since five Jameses in succession had held the Scottish throne. At the same time the name Charles was a natural result of Mary's own French background.

This baby, on maturity, did not use the name Charles, and is known to history as James the First of England and Sixth of Scotland. Before attaining the crown of England he had married and had called his first son Henry. This naming was a natural political move, since James was already working to become the English monarch, and Henry was the closest thing to a conventional name for English kings.

King James gave his second son, born 1600, the name Charles; no one knows why. It had been one of his own names, but his discarding of it would indicate, if anything, that he did not particularly care for it.

By this time Charles was being occasionally used in England, but was still, definitely, a French name. An Englishman named Charles in Shakespeare's time (such as Charles Chauncey, born 1592) was in much the situation of an Englishman now bearing such a name as Gaston or Hippolyte.

In the same decade of the 1590's Shakespeare gave the name to a character in *As You Like It,* but this merely goes further to indicate that the name was not English, for this Charles appears in a group of characters bearing such thoroughly non-English names as Le Beau and Jaques.

In any case, the little prince named Charles seemed destined to be one of those historical zeroes. His elder brother, the heir to the throne, was strong and vigorous; he himself, the second son, was weakly and not expected to live long—certainly not the kind of person for whom people name their sons.

Then, when Prince Henry died in 1612, everything changed. Charles was now destined to be king of both England and Scotland. Even his health seemed to improve—though in the end he died in the prime of life by the stroke of an ax.

In any society the name of the monarch gains tremendous publicity, and so did Charles from 1612 onward, especially after that king's accession in 1625. Some London lists of baptisms (1640–49) show Charles even with George, in what is a very respectable standing.

The name, however, became involved in a civil war, and the large body of Puritans rejected it. In the lists of immigrants to Massachusetts the name is only a vestigial one. Among 1288 Plymouth births (1640–99) there is only one Charles. In a list of 675 Massachusetts births (1630–69) there is not a single Charles. From the beginning until 1680 no Charles attended Harvard, and only one did so in the decade 1680–89. After this adventurer three more decades passed before a second specimen arrived.

Charles remained a rare name at Harvard until about 1780, in which decade the count jumped from two to eight, thus enabling Charles to make (barely) the top ten in a tie with Daniel for tenth place.

But, from then on, it was ever upward. Advancing with

scarcely a falter, Charles-at-Harvard took seventh place in 1780–90, and went to a tie for sixth in the decade of 1800. Then, successively it moved to fifth, fourth, and third. Finally, in the decade of 1840, Charles was the most used name in the Harvard roster.

Naturally, it could then only fall off, but it has always remained high. Typically, in Harvard lists, Charles has stood in second or third place, or at least in the first five.

Whether New England—Harvard, in particular—is to be held typical of the whole nation, is a question to be asked. Such far-from-complete evidence as we possess cannot return a secure answer.

As evidence pointing the other way, however, the Princeton records (the only available ones comparable with the Harvard ones) show that those lists of undergraduates from the Middle and Southern Colonies were slower to register evidences of the new name. Three Charleses at Princeton showed up in 1770–79; the same number in 1780–89; four in the next decade. Then with ten in 1800–1809 the name skyrocketed to eighth place. From that point Charles-at-Princeton rose slowly; but with a stubborn solidity. In 1820–29 it was ninth on the top ten list. Thence, by decades down to the end of the century, its record ran 5, 4, 4, 4, 3, 3, 3. In the class of 1935 a special count finds Charles in fourth place.

This steady rise of a name points to the influence of a prevailing social "climate" rather than to the influence of special events, and some evidence seems to be confirmatory. In that whole period, for instance, we find no great American hero named Charles. The popularity of the name seems to build up by a kind of self-generated momentum.

Moreover, in the counterculture of the 1960's, though losing a place in the top ten, Charles still maintained itself as a current and much-used name, in a position to rise again to high popularity.

Charles, its origins being wholly male, has developed no standard feminine. Charlotte, Caroline, and Carol (all are etymologically derived from Charles) have usually been taken as names in their own right. The manufactured Charleen has shown some recent popularity.

In its diminutive—as in everything else, indeed!—Charles follows few rules. Charlie developed regularly enough, and the Jacobites in 1745 were singing a song, "Charlie is my darling." But there was no short form until the Americans began to use Chuck, and that form scarcely became popular until the end of the nineteenth century. Possibilities such as Charr, or Charl, never developed.

Just where Chuck came from is uncertain. There was an Elizabethan pet-name which had no special connection with a particular name. When Lady Macbeth thus addresses her husband as "chuck," we cannot conclude that his given name was Charles.

Even the transition from the French is irregular, and suggests a period when the spelling exercised great influence, so that English pronounces the final *s* and anglicizes the initial *ch*.

All in all, Charles provides the most remarkable history of any of our names.

Charlotte ♀ From the same Germanic word that has yielded CHARLES, Charlotte has evolved through the use of the French diminutive-feminizing suffix *-otte*. In British-American usage, however, the connection of Charlotte with Charles has been forgotten, or, probably, one would better put it, the idea of the association with Charles failed to make the transition from French to English.

Charlotte, before the later eighteenth century, was essentially a French name, rare in England and scarcely existing in America. The shift came with the marriage of George II to the German princess who bore the half-French name Charlotte-Sophia. As queen she was a popular figure, and the name even crossed the Atlantic.

The establishment of Charlotte drew support from its uses for fictional characters, since it seems to have had an appeal to writers. In Goethe's widely read *Sorrows of Young Werther* it is the name of the heroine, and it serves both as heroine and title for Rowson's immensely popular *Charlotte Temple* (1791).

Charlotte, however, failed to equal the success of Charles, and enjoyed only a moderate popularity throughout the nineteenth century. This popularity, as if in compensation, has been long-enduring, and Charlotte is still a current name. (*See* LOTTIE.)

Charmian ♀ Greek, a diminutive of "joy." The name is known from its use in Shakespeare's *Antony and Cleopatra*. It occurs rarely, probably used because of its association with the idea of charm.

Chaunc[e]y ♂ It is probably from a French place-name, which became an English family name and was brought to New England in the early years. It began to be used as an "elegant" given name in the nineteenth century and was continued into the twentieth, but the usage has largely lapsed.

Chere ♀ The French adjective (in feminine form) is translatable as "dear, darling." It was popular enough in the mid-twentieth century to develop such forms as Cheri, Cherie, Cheryl, and Cherylyn. Of these, Cheryl has been the most common. With different spelling, Sherry has appeared (cf. SHARON, CHERRY).

Probably the common words "cheer" and "cheery" have been an influence in popularizing this group of names.

Cherry ♀ This name appeared in the mid-twentieth century. It may be another plant name on the analogy of LILY, but it is more likely to be a derivation from CHERE.

Cheryl ♀ Possibly a development of Cherry, more likely of Chere. It appears also as Sheryl. It is essentially of the twentieth century, about the middle of the century making the top ten in some lists.

Chester ♂ In Scott's Romantic poem *Marmion* the dying hero exclaims:

Charge, Chester, charge! On, Stanley, on!

This appearance of Chester at the climax of a very widely read poem is probably the cause of its being used in the nineteenth century as a given name.

Although it failed to become as popular as Clarence and some others of the feudal names, it managed to survive somewhat better. It has been the name of President Arthur and of Admiral Nimitz. The diminutive, for reasons not clear, is not Ches, but Chet.

Chloe ♀ Greek, "a burgeoning shoot," a name used once in the New Testament. Its adoption as the name of a prototypical black household servant, Aunt Chloe, has not been explained. It is rare in the twentieth century.

Christian[a], Christina, Christine ♂ ♀ Greek, "Christian." The name has always been rare for men, and is generally to be associated with German immigrants or some other non-English-speaking group. Christina, however, is somewhat commoner, and has tended to lose its religious connotations and become "just a name."

Christopher ♂ Greek, "Christ-bearer." Originally meaning merely a Christian, its literal sense inspired the story of the stalwart saint who carried the Christ-child across a stream.

In the United States the name has been remarkable for its stability, being present in nearly every list from Raleigh's colony onward. It is seemingly immune to fading. It fails to show the great popularity of the name in England since 1950, but it nevertheless has continued to be used. It stands high, and has reached the top ten in many twentieth-century lists. In one list (Charlottesville, Va.) it is the leader.

Clair[e] ♂ ♀ French. The ordinary dropping of the e should give the masculine form, and in the nineteenth century the name was commonly used for men. Gradually, however, the name with either spelling came to have feminine suggestions, and in the twentieth century it has come to be used ordinarily for women. The history is approximately that of the Latin form. (*See* CLARA.)

Clara ♀ Latin, feminine of *clarus,* "bright," but more directly from one of the several saints so named. The anglicized form is Clare, but it has been less popular, and in the United States has occasionally been borne by men.

Used in the Middle Ages, Clara was revived in the Romantic period, and was popular in the United States throughout the nineteenth century. The counterculture has not favored it, and in the mid-twentieth century it is to be considered rare.

Clarence ♂ In 1362 King Edward III arranged a marriage for his third son, Lionel. The bride was of the Clare family, one of the leading English feudal houses. Apparently because no geographical area was available, a title was coined from the bride's name, and in the official Latin of the time Lionel became Duke of Clarensis or Clarencia, which second form, in English, became Clarence. Duke Lionel failed to establish a succession, but the title remained available, and it was used, now and then, in later centuries, for one of the royal princes.

That it should, occasionally, have been given as a man's name is natural enough. More surprising is its sudden rise into popularity in the United States during the 1860's. We may assume some special incident of the time—probably English, but spreading, as news, across the Atlantic.

In the decade of the 1870's Princeton had one Clarence. In the next decade there were nine, and in the following decades there were seven and ten. Harvard, we may note, felt the influence less strongly, and two decades later—at a time, indeed, when the creation of a new Duke of Clarence (1890) could account for some interest in the name.

But it was only a flash in the pan. The new duke died after two years, interest in Clarence slumped, and it soon became a rare name again.

Like others of the feudal names (as PERCY, SIDNEY), Clarence suffered in the long run from its suggestions of an effete aristocracy, from which it had originally benefited. Its use fell off in the twentieth century, until it became rare.

Mark Twain, always careful with his names, used Clarence for a character in *A Connecticut Yankee in King Arthur's Court* (1889). The name apparently had for Twain some namby-pamby and unheroic suggestions. Incidentally, we may note that that book was written during the time of the greatest popularity of Clarence.

Clarissa ♀ *See* CLARA. Various forms evolved in France from Clara, such as Clarice and Clarisse. The novelist Richardson apparently latinized (or hellenized) the name to produce the heroine of his novel *Clarissa Harlowe* (1747–48). It has appeared occasionally in American usage. We have here the rare case of a name which has evolved from Latin form to French and then back to Latin.

Clark ♂ From the family name, arising from a man who was a clerk—that is, one able to write, keep records, etc. Being common as a family name and at the same time being simple to pronounce, it has become a fairly common given name.

Claud ♂ *See* CLAUDIA. The form Claude also occurs.

Claudia ♀ Latin, feminine of Claudius, a tribal name which was derived from *claudus,* "lame." It was a common name under the Roman Empire, and there are some half-dozen saints named Claudius. In the United States it was a rare name until its moderate usage (for unknown reasons) by the counterculture in the mid-twentieth century.

Clay ♂ From the family name, to denote one who lived near a clay-pit or was otherwise thus associated. The longtime popularity of Henry Clay helped to establish Clay as a given name in the nineteenth century, but it is probably not now current.

Clement ♂ Better known in America as Clem, it is from the Latin, "mild, merciful," and is the name of several saints. It had something of a revival in England during the nineteenth century, and may thus have spread to America.

Clifford ♂ From the family name, i.e. "cliff-ford." The Cliffords were a notable English aristocratic family, and the name became known through its use in Shakespeare's historical plays and in other poetry, especially through Rosamund Clifford, the "fair Rosamund" of song and story.

   The name made its American appearance in the later nineteenth century, but remained rare.

Clyde ♂ From the family name, which indicates a person living near the River Clyde (Scotland), or in some other way thus associated. As a given name it appears in the later nineteenth century, and exclusively in the United States. It seems to have no reason for being thus taken, except for its brevity and euphony. Being limited to American usage, it has sometimes been taken as a typically American name. Cf. ELMER. It remains viable.

Cof, *see* CUFF.

Colin ♂ The name has two origins, now completely fused. First, it can be a French borrowing, the equivalent of "Little Nicholas." Second, it can be from a Scottish (Gaelic) name, such as Colum or Malcolm. Whatever its beginnings, the name has remained rare in the United States.

Comfort ♂ ♀ The word occurs frequently in both the Old Testament and the New, and in several famous passages, so that no particular passage can well be selected as the source of the name. More likely its use rests upon the general human feeling that a child (especially a daughter) may be a comfort to the parents.

It had a scattered usage down through the eighteenth century, and was occasionally borne by a man.

Connie, *see* CONSTANCE.

Conrad ♂ Germanic, "bold-counsel." In America it has occurred chiefly in German context, and is scarcely to be considered fully naturalized.

Constance ♀ The name-element *constant-* (with the general meaning of "firm, constant") was common in the period of the later Roman Empire, as may be illustrated by the name of such a figure as the Emperor Constantine. From the Latin *constantia,* "constancy," came the French-English form Constance. The use of this name in Chaucer's *Canterbury Tales* gave it an enduring literary reference. Probably, however, the use of the name in America sprang chiefly from the meaning itself.

Although never attaining high popularity, the name has demonstrated itself by remaining stable in its use over the period of American history.

The diminutive Connie has not infrequently functioned as an independent name. Constance appears in early New England lists, being probably considered as one of the "meaningful" names, and as standing for constancy, which was not used.

Constant ♂ Functioning as a masculine, Constant has been occasionally used as the equivalent of CONSTANCE.

Consuelo ♀ Spanish, "consolation," from a title of the Virgin Mary, *Nuestra Señora del Consuelo,* "Our Lady of Consolation." Although not more than minutely in use in the United States, the name is of interest for its form, being a Spanish word used as a woman's name but ending in the masculine o, because of the need to cut it down to reasonable length by canceling out all but the one word of the title. (Cf. DOLORES.)

Content ♀ Presumably to be taken as an adjective, i.e. "contented." The King James Version supplies several texts that might be applicable here, e.g. "be content with such things as ye have" (Hebrews 13:5).

Cora ♀ Withycombe, usually reliable upon name-origins, states "apparently of American origin," and ventures no etymology. With some confidence, however, a Greek origin may be assigned, viz. from *cora,* "maiden, daughter." As suggested by Withycombe, the usage may be American. This simple borrowing would require only minimal knowledge of ancient Greek, scarcely more than the ability to use the dictionary. In the late nineteenth century many hundreds of Americans would have been thus capable. Moreover the shift of a common noun to a personal name, by transliteration, is common, and so is the use of an element meaning "son" or "daughter." CORINNA may also have provided a suggestion.

Cora is rare. It appears in the United States about the end of the nineteenth century.

Cordelia ♀ Its etymology is uncertain, but for practical purposes its slight usage in the United States is based upon its appearance in *King Lear.* Shakespeare even modified the spelling from the original, "Cordeilla," probably to make the name more like a Latin one, since the atmosphere of the play, being pre-English, is to some extent conceived of as Roman. There is, however, no suggestion in the play of any Cordelius.

Corinna, Corinne ♀ From an ancient Greek woman's name, probably including *cor-, "maiden, daughter." See* CORA. In England, Herrick used it for his famous poem "Corinna's Going A-Maying" (1648), and it may thence have been taken over as an actual name, though its appearances in America are scanty and late (probably 19th century).

Corinne is the French form, which was somewhat popularized by Madame de Staël's novel *Corinne* (1807). It has been used occasionally in America.

Cornelius, Cornelia ♂ ♀ Latin, the masculine and feminine of the members of a Roman tribe or family. Cornelius once occurs in the New Testament, and is the name of several saints, principally those with cults in the Low Countries, thus giving usage to the name in Dutch contexts.

In the United States the name is primarily to be associated with the Dutch of New Netherland, who maintained their language long after they had lost political independence. Such a combination as Cornelius Vanderbilt shows the Dutch coupling. Thus gaining a small but persistent usage, Cornelius appears regularly, but scarcely enters what we may call the mainstream of American naming.

Among the Irish the name met with some favor, having been at an early date used as a substitute for the native Conchobhar.

Cotton ♂ From the family name, itself from Anglo-Saxon, "at-the-cottages." It is scarcely remembered in the United States except from Cotton Mather, the eminent colonial figure.

Craig ♂ Scottish, from the place-name ("Crag," in English). It is derived from the family name, and has become fairly common in America as a given name in the twentieth century.

Cudjo ♂ A name of African origin, given to a male child born on Monday. It was common during the slave period, but declined in the nineteenth century.

Cuff, Cuffe, Cof, ♂ This is a name brought from Africa, perhaps with the intermediate step of the Spanish-speaking West Indies. It was a name-day, one of the names given because of the day of the week, here the equivalent of Friday. It was a common name for a black during the slave period, but died out in the late nineteenth century.

Curtis ♂ English, "courteous," but in the older sense of the word, i.e. "fit for court-life." From being a nickname it became a family name, and then, for unknown reasons, it became popular as a personal name, especially at the end of the nineteenth century.

Cyndy, Cindy ♀ A shortened form of Cynthia might be Cynthy, but the commoner forms are Cyndy and Cindy. In the mid-nineteenth century they occasionally appeared as independent names.

Cynthia ♀ An epithet of the ancient Greek goddess Artemis, presumably because of associations with Mt. Cynthus. The Romans identified Artemis with their own moon-goddess, Diana.

Artemis was a virgin goddess, and in the later sixteenth century the poets often celebrated Elizabeth, "the Virgin Queen," by comparing her with Artemis, often using the name Cynthia. Doubtless thus inspired, a few uses of the name are cited in England from the seventeenth century. Yonge, however, writing in 1863, merely stated, " a title of the moon, and a name of girls in America."

Actually, Cynthia was not more than very rare in America, since it fails to occur in what tabulations are available for the nineteenth century. For some unknown reason, however, it became popular in England at the end of that century, and also began to be used freely in America. In a recent list (1974) it has risen to a five-way tie for fifth place! No special reason for this recent popularity can be assigned—certainly not a special devotion to the ideal of virginity.

The shortened forms are Cyndy and Cindy.

Cyril ♂ Probably connected with the Greek *curios,* "master," perhaps a diminutive from it. The name is borne by several saints, chiefly associated with the Eastern Church. It has been rarely used in the United States.

Cyrus ♂ Persian, "throne," probably with the idea of "royal, kingly." In the Bible this name refers to the great founder of the Persian Empire, whose policies favored the Israelites. Though a number of references to him in the Bible are friendly, his name is not recorded as having been adopted by the Israelites. It was, however, used in America.

Cyrus is not to be considered merely another biblical name, since information about him was abundant in the writings of Herodotus and Xenophon. In fact, Cyrus can almost be held to be counterbiblical, since it is outside the main current of the Bible and since it was much better known from lay works than from the Bible.

Cyrus did not appear until around 1750, when the full sweep of the biblical names was over—another indication of its being counterbiblical. After 1750 it remained viable for a century, and can, in fact, still be found—for instance, with Cyrus Vance, Secretary of State in the Carter administration, born 1917.

D

Daisy ♀ The name is one of the few which spring from two origins. It may be taken as one of the earliest of the flower names, or it can equally well be taken as the translation of the French name Marguerite. It enjoyed some popularity in the second half of the nineteenth century.

Henry James, in his *Daisy Miller* (1879), used it for a girl whom he considered to be, in many ways, typically American. Apparently Daisy remained American rather than British. The name had lyrical possibilities, and one Daisy was the heroine of the popular song "A Bicycle Built for Two."

Dale ♂ From the family name, designating a man living in a dale or in some way associated with one. Favored by its short and euphonic form, it has attained popularity as a given name in the mid-twentieth century.

Damaris ♀ Origin and meaning uncertain, the name of an Athenian woman converted by Paul (Acts 17:34). During the period when biblical names flourished it appeared occasionally, and it continues to appear.

Damon ♂ It may be from the family name (origin uncertain), but it may also be an echoing of the ancient Greek story of Damon and Pythias, the ideal friendship.

Dana ♀ ♂ The family name is not very common. It was used occasionally as a given name for men in the nineteenth century, occurring in the Harvard lists. In the twentieth century the name has been used for women, and it may be considered viable in that usage. The derivation of the family name is uncertain.

The shift to a woman's name probably results from the fact that Dana looks like what an average American considers to be a name for a woman—particularly its ending in an *a*. Also, however, it is much like several other such names—e.g. Diana, Anna, Donna.

The pronunciation varies, the first vowel being either long or short.

Daniel, Dan ♂ The question may be raised as to whether there are two names here. Dan may be merely the short form of Daniel, or it may be from the name of the Israelite tribe. In any case, names derived from the tribe would have been few, and Dan is usually to be considered as being from Daniel.

This name is Hebrew, "God- [is]-judge." It is the name of a book of the Bible, which takes its name from one of the prophets. This prophet is the leading character in the spectacular and widely spread story commonly known as "Daniel in the lions' den." From such a background Daniel naturally passed over to being a name used by early Christians. It was also, as luck would have it, a name which much resembled certain Celtic names such as the Irish Donnall and the Welsh Deiniol. One such Welshman became, in the sixth century, the first bishop of Bangor. From all these influences Daniel established itself as a regularly used English name, standing in the first ten at Harvard throughout most of the eighteenth century.

Though falling off with the general decline of Old Testament names in the nineteenth century, Daniel did not (as many names did) vanish altogether, apparently now being established as a regular American name, having lost its biblical connection.

The form Danny has also survived.

Daphne ♀ Greek, "laurel." By the twentieth century the daphne had become known as a garden bush, and it was then occasionally used as a girl's name. (Cf. LILY, etc.)

Darius ♂ Probably Persian, but meaning uncertain. The name appears in the Bible, but its associations are rather with the great Darius of Persia, known more from Herodotus than from the Bible (cf. CYRUS). Darius was an extremely rare name, but it did appear occasionally in the nineteenth century.

Darlene, Darleen ♀ An adaptation of "darling," occasionally appearing in the twentieth century. Other adaptations are Darla, Darylyne, Daryl.

Datus ♂ Latin, "given." It is apparently a latinized (masculine) translation of the Hebrew (*Nathan*) and of various Greek words formed around the element *dor,* as in Dorothy. It has been very rare.

David ♂ The linguistic origin is uncertain. If Hebrew, it may have the meaning "darling, beloved," and thus be a kind of honorific nickname. (Cf. such names in the Book of Judges, e.g. Barak, "lightning;" Gideon, "hewer.") As an outstanding biblical lay-hero David would have been likely, under any circumstances, to be a much used name. It had the particular fortune to be the name of the archbishop (7th century) who became the patron saint of Wales. It was also borne by two kings of Scotland in the Middle Ages. The name thus came to have solid patriotic support in Wales and Scotland, in addition to its biblical aid. A mild popularity of the name spread also to England, and it was in regular use at the time of the Reformation, *c.* 1540.

It suffered in popularity among the Puritans, with whom David's notorious sins would have had a strong negative influence. Among 452 names of early immigrants to Massachusetts there is only one David, together with one Davy whom we should be able to set down confidently as a Welshman.

Once settled in their new home, the Puritans seemed to view David's sins more lightly. Among 675 Boston births of 1630–75 David failed to rank in the top ten by slipping into eleventh place—just below Richard and just above Jacob.

In the Harvard lists David is actually missing for several decades at the beginning, and then leaps into tenth place. From that time on, in the colonial period, David appears regularly but not in numbers sufficient to make the first ten.

In the other colonies we find David a little more favored than at Harvard. One would suspect Scottish and Welsh influence, but its actuality has not yet been clearly demonstrated.

The highest popularity of David yet established for the eighteenth century (1781) is in the officers of eight regiments of the Connecticut Line where the name stands in a second place tie with Samuel and William.

Along with the other Old Testament names, David faded out in the later nineteenth century, and in the early twentieth century it was rare. It revived sharply after 1930. In one college list for births c. 1948 it stands in fifth place. In a high school graduating class with births c. 1955 it stands with Michael in a tie for first place. The reasons for this popularity are obscure.

Dawn ♀ A recent usage, described by Withycombe as "a 20th-Century invention of novelette writers." It has failed to escape from the "rare" category, though offering some advantages for a name, such as brevity and euphony.

Dean ♂ From the family name, which originates from someone associated with a dean, that is, a church official. In the United States the word is more widely known in its academic usage, but we may question whether this connection has influenced naming. (*See* EARL.) The brevity of the name has been a factor in its popularity, together with its resemblance to the popular names Don and Dan.

Deborah ♀ The name is simply the Hebrew word for "bee," and must have been taken with that meaning by speakers of Hebrew. This is, however, an unusual meaning for a personal name, and Deborah possibly (like other early biblical names) represents a name borrowed from one of the many languages with which early Hebrews were in contact.

As prophetess, poet, and ruler of the people, the great Deborah (Judges 5) was encroaching upon fields of endeavor which the Puritans reserved for males. Perhaps for this reason they were slow to use her name. Like Abigail, Deborah scarcely appears until after 1675. It then enjoyed some popularity, only to decline sharply in the early nineteenth century.

Writing in 1863, Yonge stated that the name was no longer

used in England "except by the peasantry." Revived once more in the twentieth century, it has prospered greatly, and for children born near the middle of this century it stands close to the top. The reasons for the recent popularity are not well established, but we cannot ignore the widespread publicity for the name which was engendered by actresses, such as Deborah Kerr.

As with all highly popular names, the by-forms have tended to become independent, thus giving us Deb and Debby functioning by themselves.

Deirdre ♀ The etymology is uncertain, but its Irish connections make a Celtic origin likely. The writers of the Irish Renaissance in the early years of the twentieth century did much to popularize this heroine of early Irish tradition, but the name itself has never been more than occasional in the United States.

Delia ♀ Greek, an epithet of the goddess Artemis, from her association with the island of Delos. It has occasionally appeared in the United States, but has failed to establish any strong tradition. Yonge suggests that it sometimes originated as a clipping of Cordelia, but since Cordelia itself is not a common name, such origin seems unlikely.

Deliverance ♀ Probably to indicate such an idea as "deliverance-from-sin." It was among the more common abstracts in early New England, but died out in the eighteenth century.

Della ♀ Appearing occasionally in the late nineteenth and the twentieth centuries, it is probably a coinage in the search for euphony, apparently developed from such established names as Delia, Ella, and Adeline.

Denise ♀ For the background, *see* DENNIS. The form Denise is modern French, and its American usage is that of a name borrowed from the French. Like its masculine counterpart, but to a lesser degree, it has had an increase in use in the later twentieth century.

Dennis ♂ It is derived ultimately from the name of the Greek god Dionysius, of uncertain etymology. By the beginning of the Christian era personal names which were derived from that of the god were already in use, and a man of that name was among the early converts (Acts 17:34). This Dionysius the

Areopagite, according to tradition, attained sainthood and was martyred in Paris. As a result he was much venerated in France, whence his cult spread to England, his name appearing in English most commonly as Dennis. As the name of a non-biblical saint, Dennis ceased to be a popular name in the Reformation period.

During nearly all the course of American history, the name may be said to have lain quiescent, but it has enjoyed a certain renaissance in the later twentieth century—possibly from the long-continued popularity of the cartoon Dennis The Menace. It also must owe something to the family name being used as a first name.

Derrick, Derek ♂ Dutch, the equivalent of the German name Diederich, which is from Theodoric, "people-rule." The name probably survived from the early Dutch settlers, but has always been rare.

Desire ♀ Though rare, Desire was a viable name in early New England. About all that can safely be said about it is that it was not used with sexual suggestions. The word, in fact, was a favorite one with the translators of the King James Version, and appears many times with many shades of meaning. Doubtless, in naming it was taken to suggest some such phrase as "desire-salvation." It remains, however, a highly vague name. It occurs chiefly in the seventeenth century.

De Witt ♂ Dutch or Flemish, a family name originating from a person who came from a place named Witt. It has had some usage in the United States in the twentieth century. Coupled with De Wight, it has even supplied names for twins.

Diana, Diane ♀ Latin, the name of the virgin goddess whose Greek counterpart was Artemis. As the goddess of the chase, her name was well known among the European aristocracy of the Renaissance, a period in which the authority of the Church was slack. One of the first modern uses of the name was that by Diane de Poitiers, mistress of King Henry II of France, though we have difficulty in seeing how (or why) she should thus move in on the virgin business.

Diana made little impression on the United States until the

mid-twentieth century, when the French form Diane became popular enough to make the top ten on occasion. In that period the name was plagued by the development of many spelling variants, such as Deanna, Deanne, Dyanne.

Dinah ♀ The name of a daughter of Jacob; probably Hebrew. The etymology is uncertain. If (as some think) it is from a Hebrew word meaning "avenged," the name may have been given secondarily, i.e. Dinah, having been dishonored, was avenged by her brothers (see Genesis 34).

Dinah occurs rarely except as borne by blacks. The cause of this association is uncertain. Most likely some African name was enough like it to stimulate its use.

Dixie ♀ The origin is uncertain, but "Dixie" commonly indicates the South or the Southern state of mind. The slight use of the name is too late (20th-century) to be taken as another manifestation of loyalty to the Confederacy, but has probably been picked up for a name from its suggestion of lightheartedness in connection with the tune. It may occasionally have been taken as being derived from Dick.

Doll, Dolly ♀ Since r shifts commonly to l in English names, Doll may be considered a normal development from Dorothy, but it can generally be treated as an independent name. In fact, to many people it may not suggest Dorothy at all.

Only with the twentieth century has Dolly fallen off, the modern short form being Dot, with the diminutive either Dotty or, occasionally, Dotsy." The modern use of "doll" as a generic for "girl" may have resulted in a counter-movement against Doll as an actual name, even though the use may be a complimentary one.

The immensely popular song "Good-bye Dolly Gray" (c.1900) roughly coincides with the decline of the name. People may just have gotten tired of it, so that song and name died together of acute iteration.

The spelling Dolley was used by President Madison's wife, but has not been popular.

Dolores ♀ Spanish, a shortening of *María de Dolores,* "Mary of Sorrows." It is a rare name, except as used in a strong Spanish context. More nearly naturalized are the short form LOLA and the diminutive LOLITA. Dolores itself has enjoyed a certain popularity in the mid-twentieth century.

Donald ♂ Celtic, "world-strong." It is probably the commonest of Scottish names of Highland origin. Although an occasional Donald appears in the eighteenth century, its generally late entrance into the names in the United States (about 1850) suggests that it was the result of Scottish immigration. The writers of the Romantic revival, such as Sir Walter Scott, were fond of using such exotic names.

In the mid-twentieth century Donald became highly popular, reaching the top ten in some lists. The reasons for this strength of Scottish names are probably that they offered a relief from the conventional John, William, etc., and at the same time were names that had a certain stability. Scottish names tending to follow the same course as Donald are Douglas, Malcolm, Kenneth, Ronald, and Alan.

There has been no comparable movement with feminine names, but some Scottish forms have circulated and even become popular, especially ELSIE and MAISIE. A little-used feminine is Donaldina.

Donna ♀ Italian, "lady." It is chiefly of the twentieth century, and by mid-century was clearly viable.

Dora ♀ Although the ending in *a* is unusual, Dora probably should be considered merely a short form of Dorothy. It is rare, but is to be found occasionally in the nineteenth century.

Dorcas ♀ Greek, a kind of deer or antelope, often rendered as "gazelle." Acts 9:36 tells of "a certain disciple named Tabitha, which by interpretation is called Dorcas." In her life she was known for the "good works and almsdeeds which she did."

The name Dorcas—thus well recommended—was in regular use in colonial America, particularly in New England. With the decline of biblical names in the nineteenth century, it became rare, lapsing wholly in many areas.

Her being known by both Aramaic and Greek names is an interesting commentary upon the complexity of the linguistic situation—especially its bilingualism in names—in ancient Palestine during the period when the New Testament was written.

Doreen ♀ Withycombe suggests origin from an Irish Doireann or from a popular novel entitled *Doreen* (1894). In the United States, however, it seems more likely to have been a twentieth-century coinage from DOROTHY and the suffix *-een*. It has had a certain currency in the twentieth century.

Doris ♀ The name occurs in ancient Greek mythology as that of a minor divinity or nymph, and also as a place-name. The name apparently consists of *dor*, "gift" (as in Dorothy), and a feminine ending, "*-is*." Doreis is probably nothing more than a modern variant.

Although Withycombe cites a (questionable) New England example of 1819, Doris fails to make much impression until about 1900, when it seems to move in to fill the vacancy left by the decline of DOROTHY. Since that time Doris has remained in use, sometimes showing a modest popularity. Its persistence may well have prevented another boom of Dorothy.

Dorothy ♀ Greek, "gift-[of]-God." The rather little used alternate, Dorothea, is merely the original Greek or Latin form.

The history of Dorothy is complicated and has by no means been definitively studied as yet. It became established, apparently, before the Reformation, since the name of a non-biblical saint would not have become popular in post-Reformation times. Moreover, by 1550 the forms Doll and Dolly were fully established, and such a situation demands a long-term familiarity with the name. In Shakespeare's time Doll (e.g. Doll Tearsheet) had come to be used as a generic for a loose woman. Partially for this reason, we may assume, the name fell from popularity (at least in Puritan circles), and among the immigrants there were few named Dorothy. (But then many names had gone that road.)

Nevertheless, a name which has once been highly popular may be trusted to maintain at least a vestigial usage, and Dorothy thus lingered throughout the seventeenth and eighteenth centuries and most of the nineteenth. Doll and Dolly also lingered, apparently outliving their derogatory suggestion. We may note, for instance, Dolley Madison, the President's wife.

On both sides of the ocean a marked revival occurred about

1880, and Dorothy became a highly popular name, its boom peaking about 1900. The name was notable for its euphony, and a general catchiness, and we find it in two famous juvenile books published close to 1900—*Dorothy Vernon of Haddon Hall* and Dorothy of *The Wizard of Oz*. Like most sudden booms in name-usage this one was short-lived, so that the typical Dorothy of the mid-nineteenth century was, like the century, middle-aged.

A complicating factor in the development of Dorothy is the use of the highly popular DOLL, DOLLY.

Dougal, *see* DUGALD.

Douglas ♂ Originating as a place-name, Douglas became widely associated with the "Black Douglas," one of the heroes of the Scottish War of Independence against England in the fourteenth century. The Douglases remained a leading Lowland family thereafter. In the United States the name has generally been less popular than DONALD, but has followed a similar course.

Drusilla ♀ A Latin diminutive-feminine from Drusus, the name assumed by the Roman warrior who had killed a Gaul of that name. It occurs once, as a passing reference, in Acts 24:24. It remained rare, even in the flourishing of the biblical names. It cannot even be well termed "biblical" except in a superficial way.

Duane ♂ A family name of uncertain origin. It appears, rarely, in the twentieth century as a given name.

Dudley ♂ In Anglo-Saxon times it was a place-name, "Dudda's clearing." It became a family name, and its early use as a given name is to be traced to the New England family—that is, the descendants of Thomas Dudley, who emigrated to Massachusetts in 1630 and was a prominent person there until his death in 1653—three times married, the father of seven children. In the lines descending from his daughters the use of Dudley as a given name sprang up naturally. Eventually it came to be a given name among people having no family connection with any Dudley, and it turns up in this fashion in the various periods.

In England, also, the Dudleys were a prominent family, and English influence is probably responsible for the increase in the use of Dudley in the later nineteenth century in the United States. Like so many of the feudal names, it came to have a suggestion of snobbishness or excessive elegance.

The short form Dud may possibly, about 1880, have given rise to the popular term "dude," the etymology of which has not been satisfactorily explained. Also uncertain is the use of "dud" for something which fails to function properly, and some connection with the name (through "dude") is, again, possible.

From Dudley, about 1900, developed the slang phrase "Your Uncle Dudley," meaning the speaker himself. Though the actual source is not known, a stage origin seems likely.

Dugald, Dougal ♂ Gaelic, literally, "dark stranger," a curious name applied by the Irish to the invading Danes, later becoming a common personal name, especially in the Scottish Highlands. It is rare in the United States.

Duke ♂ From the family name, which originated from someone associated with a duke or else as a shortening of MARMADUKE. Bardsley assumes that these names from titles were given for a kind of snobbish suggestion (cf. DEAN, EARL, PRINCE). Although such feelings may have influenced the choice, the origin from the family name seems to be the basic one.

Dulcie ♀ In this and other spellings the name seems to be derived from Latin *dulcis,* "sweet," but its etymology is not certain. It is possibly a seventeenth-century borrowing from the Spanish (Latin-derived) Dulcia, and thus it could be a name brought in with the slave trade. Or, as a literary name, it could be from Dulcinea in *Don Quixote.*

It has not been a common name, but was conventionally used for a housemaid during the slave period.

Duncan ♂ Celtic, "brown-head." This well-established Scottish name is found occasionally in American usage, but has failed to attain the popularity of Donald, Douglas, and others with which it is naturally associated.

Dwayne ♂ The origin of the name is uncertain, and it is possibly a coinage of the twentieth century, being formed from Wayne on the analogy of Dwight. It may, however, be a variant of Duane. It is of rare use.

Dwight ♂ From the family name, which is of uncertain origin. Most likely it is a French form contracted from *de Wight* and meaning "from-[the-Isle-of]-Wight." The family was a numerous and prominent one in early New England, and the name itself is attractively direct and short. It had a period of some popularity about 1870. President Eisenhower, commonly known as Ike, was actually named Dwight.

E

Earl ♂ It is an English family name, apparently to indicate a person associated with an earl. It occurred as a family name in the colonies (often as Earle), and was occasionally used as a given name. Its buildup in the early twentieth century is not wholly explicable, but may be because of its association with the feudal names. (*See* HOWARD.) Its best period is the mid-twentieth century, and it stands at 53 in Smith's list of 100 (*c.* 1941). Since that time it has fallen off. Chief Justice Warren is probably its most famous bearer.

Ebenezer ♂ Hebrew, "stone-of-help." In the Bible it is a place-name, its significance made clear in I Samuel 7:12:

> Then Samuel took a stone, and set it between Mizpeh and Shen, and called the name of it Ebenezer, saying Hitherto hath the Lord helped us.

The aptness of the name for the colonists is striking, and equally remarkable is the transfer from a place-name to a personal name.

Since Ebenezer has always been rare in Britain and since the earliest English example (and that a doubtful one) is of 1668, the likelihood is that the practice originated in New England, where it can be cited as early as the decade 1640–49.

The name grew rapidly in popularity. The Boston birthlist of

675 individuals (1630–69) includes eight Ebenezers; in the Plymouth list of 1288 (1640–99) there are 49 of them (3.8%), and the name stands in eighth place. Even more strikingly, in the Plymouth list of 473 for the decade 1690–99 Ebenezers number 28, and the name stands in second place, exceeded only by John.

Although the use of the name spread to all the colonies, its chief flourishing was in New England in the years of births between 1670 and 1790. With the decline of Old Testament names in the nineteenth century, Ebenzer also declined strikingly—partly, we may suppose, because of Dickens's Ebenezer Scrooge. By the time of the Civil War it was almost out of use, definitely old-fashioned. It became a rustic name, still keeping its background of New England. Novelists and dramatists (such as Eugene O'Neill) made much use of it for their characters of the backwoods New England farms and villages. In the twentieth century it is to be considered only a vestigial name.

The short form Eben was regularly used and occasionally appears as a name in its own right.

Edgar ♂ Old English, *ead,* "rich," and *gar,* "spear." Important in the Anglo-Saxon period, Edgar declined, and was probably not in use during the period of the settlement of the American colonies. The name revived in the later eighteenth century under Romantic influence, and it also appears in the title of Charles Brockden Brown's *Edgar Huntly* (1800), one of the earliest American novels. Though never common, Edgar continued in use through the nineteenth century and into the twentieth.

Edith ♀ Anglo-Saxon (Eadgyth), "rich-war." As a saint's name Edith survived the Norman Conquest and was common in England down through the Middle Ages. It faded into disuse in the sixteenth century, partly (we may believe) because of the generally unfavorable reaction to the names of nonbiblical saints. In the United States it apparently came into use as a Romantic name, but had its chief flourishing at the end of the nineteenth century, when many medieval names were revived. It has remained in modest use through the twentieth century.

Edmund, Edmond ♂ Old English, *ead,* "rich," and *mund,* "protection"; the name of two Anglo-Saxon kings and of two saints. Many of the early settlers of New England were from the English county of Suffolk, of which the chief town was Bury St. Edmunds. Doubtless Edmund was firmly established among these people. At least it did not lapse from usage, but has remained viable clear into the later twentieth century. It is an excellent example of an ancient and "conservative" name showing some fluctuations with time, but on the whole remaining steady.

Edna ♀ Its resemblance to an Anglo-Saxon name is coincidental. Edna occurs in the Apocrypha, but its etymology (even its language) is unknown. Its use in England began in the mid-nineteenth century, the earliest certain example (1860) being a fictional character in a novel by C. M. Yonge, who was herself the author of a much-respected two-volume *History of Christian Names* (1863). In the extensive list of names in that work Edna is not included—strong evidence that it was not then in actual use in England despite its having been used for a fictional character.

Curiously, still another stage of development in English appears in the use of the name in the pseudonym Edna Lyell, which the much-read novelist Ada Ellen Bailey employed in a series of popular works from 1879 onward. The source from which she took the name is not known. One can note, however, that all the letters of Edna are included in Ada Ellen, so that the influence of some linguistic game is to be suspected.

Possibly because of this use of the name by a best-selling writer, Edna appeared in the United States. It enjoyed a mild popularity in the decade or two following 1890. Since then it has faded, but it still makes an occasional appearance.

Edward ♂ Old English, formed from the conventional name-elements *ead*, "fortunate, happy," and *weard*, "guardian." It was the name of two Anglo-Saxon kings, of whom the second was canonized as St. Edward the Confessor.

The name survived the Norman Conquest, and acquired new vitality in the later part of the twelfth century because of the devotion of King Henry III to this particular saint. He gave the name to one of his sons, who succeeded him as Edward I. Other Edwards reigned in the fourteenth and fifteenth centuries, so that the name became firmly entrenched throughout England.

The first stirrings of the Reformation had no apparent influence on the case of this particular nonbiblical saint. In fact, the accession of a Protestant prince as King Edward VI must have done something to strengthen the name. One actual count of 1540–49 shows Edward in seventh place.

The early colonists included many of the name. One Edward was with Raleigh's colony, and several appeared at Jamestown. In the list of those landing from the *Mayflower* in 1620 were fifteen Johns, eight Williams, and six Edwards.

Among the colonists themselves, however, Edward was not a popular name for their children. Its thoroughly English quality had no special appeal to the many Dutch, German, and Scotch-Irish settlers of the Middle and Southern Colonies.

Even in New England the name made little showing on the baptismal records. During the first forty years of Harvard's existence there was only one student named Edward. The most likely supposition is that Edward was spotted as a nonbiblical saint, and the Puritans viewed such names with suspicion.

This prejudice was slow to fade, but a more liberal attitude is discernible in Harvard names from 1700 on down, that is, for actual namings from about 1690. Throughout the whole eighteenth century, however, Edward is scarcely to be called popular at Harvard. In one decade it ranks in sixth place, but in another decade it almost disappears.

In the eighteenth century, however, Edward became fully established, not only at Harvard but at Princeton as well, and in fact throughout the country. Its typical place is the lower half of the top ten.

At Princeton a significant number of Edwards began to appear in 1780–89, and the name continued in use without great variation of popularity until the mid-twentieth century. Its lowest position (13th place) occurred in 1700–1709, and its highest position (7th place) in the 1780–89 and 1860–69. Although not a favorite among the modernists, Edward still continues to be a viable name.

In the United States the regular variants are Ed and Eddie. The use of Ned is not unknown, but has a slightly British suggestion. Ted and Teddy seem to have little current use. (*See* THEODORE). Their development out of Edward is not easily explained.

Edwin ♂ Old English, *ead,* "rich," and *wine,* "friend," commonly in use before the Norman Conquest and immediately after, but fading out. It was probably not in use at the time of the settling of the American colonies. About 1800 it began to make an impression upon American naming, being revived, like many obsolete names, under Romantic influence. It grew in popularity through the nineteenth and twentieth centuries, and in 1920 surpassed all the other Anglo-Saxon names. Since that time, however, it has fallen off sharply. The feminine Edwina has been rare.

Effie, *see* EUPHEMIA.

Egbert ♂ Old English, *ecg,* "sword," and *beorht,* "bright." A well-known name of the Anglo-Saxon period, it went out of use after the Conquest. Revived in the late eighteenth century under Romantic influence, like so many other Anglo-Saxon names it remained in use through the nineteenth century and into the twentieth. It has not, however, been popular.

Eileen, Aileen ♀ Though actually from a Celtic name, Eibhilin, it has been generally conceived to be the Irish equivalent of Helen. It has shared in the general revival of Irish names in the twentieth century, though it was scarcely used earlier.

Elaine ♀ A medieval French form of Helen, occurring in Malory's *Morte D'Arthur.* From that work Tennyson took it for his *Idylls of the King* in the mid-nineteenth century, and it has remained in occasional use.

Elbert ♂ The name may have been manufactured from Albert by substituting *El-* for *Al-.* We may note that *El-* is a common first element, e.g. Elmer, Elijah. Elbert seems to have originated in the mid-nineteenth century, but has remained rare. It is also, though rare, a family name.

Eleanor[a] ♀ The name (or at least the form) apparently originated in the south of France, where in the Middle Ages it existed as Alienor. It came to England in the later twelfth century with Eleanor of Aquitaine, queen of Henry II. The etymology is doubtful, though some connection with Helen is probably to be assumed. The -*or* ending, however, is not to be derived from Helen, and suggests Honora, also a popular name of the period. The possibility exists that Eleanor[a] may be in some degree a manufactured name, a blend of Helen and Honora.

Eleanor became a standard name in medieval England. Not being a saint's name, it did not suffer in the Reformation. In the earliest list of American settlers (the Raleigh colony of 1587) there was one Eleanor (spelled Elyoner). The name remained in use, though it was never highly popular.

Like so many of the medieval names, Eleanor came into favor during the Romantic period of the nineteenth century and reached a modest height of prosperity in the later part of that century.

Eleazar, Eliezar, Eleasar. ♂ In all of the spellings, the name clearly shows the Hebrew word-elements *el*-, "God" and -*ezar*, "help." It has various slightly differing English renderings, such as "God-is-help" or "God-is-helper." In the Bible it is borne by no fewer than 18 persons. Although never a popular name, it was in regular use in New England down until 1800.

Eli ♂ Hebrew, meaning uncertain, but with *el* probably "God." During the period of the popularity of biblical names it appeared occasionally, doubtless to some degree because of its brevity. Moreover, Eli was the father of Samuel, who bore one of the names most widely used as a personal one.

Eliab ♂ Hebrew, "God-[is]-father." It is the name of six persons in the Old Testament, but none of these is of importance. Probably because of its literal meaning, the name appears in some lists during the period of biblical names. It was, however, rare.

Eliakim ♂ Hebrew, probably "God-establishes." It is a very rare name, chiefly of the early eighteenth century.

Elias, *see* ELIJAH.

Eliezar, *see* ELEAZAR.

Elihu ♂ Hebrew, meaning uncertain, except that *el* is presumably to be taken as "God." It was used rarely in the period of the popularity of biblical names. A vestige of the use of the name shows in the well-known political figure Elihu Root (1845–1937).

Elijah, Elias ♂ Hebrew, "Jah-is-God." Elias is the form of the name in the New Testament, under Greek influence. The name is also related to ELIHU. As a notable major prophet, Elijah occurs with some degree of popularity in the lists of colonial New England, and the name was also viable in the other regions. It died out in the general nineteenth-century decline of biblical names, but not before it had established its shortening to be Lige.

Eliphalet ♂ Hebrew, translatable as "God-helps-to-escape"; the name may be taken in general to mean "God-saves." It exists in the Old Testament in several different spellings, but these do not seem to have been transferred to English. The alternate spelling, Eliphabet, is very rare.

Elisabeth, *see* ELIZABETH.

Elisha ♂ Hebrew, "God-is-[our]-savior." As the name of a prophet and an outstanding biblical character, Elisha was moderately popular in early New England, and its use spread also to the other colonies.

Elizabeth, Elisabeth ♀ Hebrew, "God-has-sworn-[a-covenant]," with reference to the oath or covenant which God swore to Abraham (Genesis 17). The spelling with *z* has been the regular English usage, *s* being indicative of French influence.

The name was borne by the mother of John the Baptist (Luke 1). In the Middle Ages Elizabeth was little used in England, and mainly was in honor of St. Elizabeth of Hungary (1207–31). The name, however, entered the royal family in the fifteenth century, from Elizabeth Woodville, the queen of King Edward IV. The still rare name eventually passed on to the younger daughter of King Henry VIII. In her early years that Elizabeth was little known, but circumstances put her into the position of being the symbol of Protestantism as opposed to her Catholic sister Mary. One curious result of this rivalry was the sudden popularizing of the name Elizabeth (*see* Introduction).

Elizabeth Tudor eventually became queen and ruled

gloriously for almost half a century, usually with great personal popularity. The glamour of the queen, who was a symbol of the nation itself, shed glamour also on her name. Elizabeth was the leading woman's name in that reign, and so continued into the seventeenth century, after the queen's death.

As a result the early colonists included many of the name. In Raleigh's colony, for instance, only 16 women's names were listed, but there were two Elizabeths. Disembarking from the *Mayflower* were 23 women, among them three bearing the queen's name.

But the glamour of that name was perhaps dimming a little among the early colonists. In England itself, Withycombe, for the period 1600–1649, finds Elizabeth the most popular name, with the exceptionally high percentage of 25. In the colonies, however, during the same period, Elizabeth usually took second place to Mary and stood under 20 per cent, but still high.

Being so firmly established in its usage throughout the colonies, and being of the New Testament, Elizabeth resisted fairly well the decline of the biblical names which set in with the late eighteenth century. Nevertheless, the popularity of the name sagged. A Baltimore list of 1840–49 shows Elizabeth barely making the top ten. Later in the century somewhat better standings occur.

With the advance of the twentieth century the name has tended to be viable but to fall below the top ten. Some variant, such as Betty, is often more popular than is the formal Elizabeth.

Elizabeth—because of its length and its two accented syllables—has been prolific in the spawning of variants, as "Good Queen Bess" continually reminds us. Also much favored during her actual reign was the Latinate form Eliza. The classical tastes of the times kept Eliza in a strong position until the nineteenth century, when Lizzie and Liz began to take over.

The other accented syllable was also a rich source of variants. Actually the original Greek spelling is Elisabet, so that there is early justification for the forms Bet and Betty. Actually, however, the *th* (as in "with") seems to have been the standard, since from it Bess would have arisen by the aid of baby-talk.

In the twentieth century Beth has shown some strength, but the most favored form has been Betty. Generally to be considered as an independent name, it has often been numerous enough to make the first ten.

Many variants are foreign imports, such as Elspeth (Scottish), Elise (French), and Lise (German). (*See also* ELSIE, LIB.)

Elkanah ♂ Hebrew, "God-possesses." Occasionally it appears in New England lists during the period of the popularity of biblical names.

Ella ♀ Of Norman origin, occurring in the post-Conquest period but of uncertain etymology and meaning. It is easily confused with Helen and Ellen, and its history is comparable. It passed through a period of popularity in the middle of the nineteenth century, but never attained the status of Helen. Its brevity and easy phonetic quality led to its use in compounds, such as Ellamay.

Ellen ♀ Beginning as a form of Helen, Ellen has come to be considered an independent name. It is particularly common in Scotland. Like Helen, it rose in popularity in the nineteenth century under the influence of Romanticism, reaching its height about 1850.

Elma ♀ Its origin is uncertain, but an English example of 1842 is known to have been formed from the mother's two names, Elizabeth and Mary. Probably no other source need be sought. It is of rare occurrence in the United States.

Elmer ♂ The immediate source is the family name, which is itself from the Old English personal name Aethelmaer, "noble-famous." (Origin from a Norman name, Agilmar, or from a place-name is possible, but less likely.) Elmer appears as an American family name as early as the Revolutionary period, when it was well known in New Jersey as the family name of two brothers who were prominent patriots. The attempt to account for the popularity of Elmer because of these brothers, however, is not well based, since they were very local heroes. Moreover, the center of the popularity of Elmer has been not the Eastern seaboard, but the Middle West.

That in the nineteenth and early twentieth centuries a family name should occasionally be used for a personal name is to be expected. Elmer, however, went further, and in this period was popular to the point of being sometimes considered the typical American name. For instance, Sinclair Lewis used it in the title of what he obviously considered to be a basically American story—*Elmer Gantry.*

To account for the popularity of the name we must suppose other forces than those of the New Jersey brothers. One possibility is that of the highly popular novel *St. Elmo* (1867) by Augusta Jane Evans. St. Elmo and Elmo actually appear as men's names during this period, but were in themselves names of somewhat un-American form and suggestion. They might have served to bring Elmer to mind. The novel, however, cannot be the actual source, since the name was beginning to appear before 1867.

The popularity of Elmer was short-lived—about one generation. Such a once commonly used name, however, is subject to revival.

Elnathan ♂ Hebrew, "god-gave." The idea that the child has been given by God is a common one, and has resulted in many names—*see* e.g. DOROTHY, JONATHAN, NATHAN, THEODORE. Obviously, Elnathan and NATHANIEL are of the same etymology. Elnathan is rare, even during the period of the biblical names.

Eloise, *see* HELOISE.

Elsie ♀ Although commonly taken to be an independent name, Elsie is, like Elspeth, a much-shifted Scottish form of Elizabeth. It enjoyed some popularity throughout the United States in the nineteenth century.

Elvira ♀ It is presumably Spanish, though possibly it goes back to an ancient Germanic root. The meaning is not known, and the frequent use of the name for stage characters even suggests a coinage. In the United States it has been very rare.

Emanuel, Emmanuel, Manuel ♂ Hebrew, "God-with-us!" In general, the name does not appear in English as a personal name, being reserved for Christ Himself. Any appearance of it in the United States can be considered, almost certainly, to be a manifestation of some non-English culture and language. As

Manuel the name is a rather common one in Spanish, and thus occurs, e.g. with Manuel Lisa, who is considered a figure in American history, but of Spanish background, as his Spanish family name would indicate.

Emily ♀ From the Roman family name Aemilius, literal meaning uncertain. The curious circumstance of its being current only in the feminine reinforces the likelihood that the use of Emily primarily sprang from literary sources (Boccaccio, Chaucer). It did not come into common use until after 1800, and its continuing popularity in the nineteenth century is to be attributed partly to its taking over of AMELIA and partly to Romanticism. It is also highly euphonic, and thus is suitable for poetry.

It is subject to confusion not only with Amelia, but also with Emma and Emmeline, with which it shares such forms as Em and Emmy. Its own Latin form, Emilia, is rare.

Emma ♀ The origin is uncertain, but the name is probably of Germanic origin and may be a shortened form of Ermin, "whole, universal." It was a much-favored name among the Normans, and it persisted strongly throughout the Middle Ages. It fell into disuse in the sixteenth century, and hardly existed in the American colonies. With the Romantic interest in the Middle Ages came a revival of Emma, and by the middle of the nineteenth century the name was sometimes making the top ten. By the middle of the century that popularity had fallen off sharply, and the later twentieth century has shown no great interest in it.

EMILY and EMMELINA are not, strictly speaking, to be associated with Emma at all, but on the basis of resemblance of sound Americans have so grouped them for common speech. A girl bearing any one of these names officially may in daily life answer equally well to Em or Emmy.

Emmeline, Emmelina ♀ Germanic, probably with the element *amal*, "work." It was brought into English usage by the Normans. In American usage it is naturally associated with EMMA, but this is questionable. Its more likely association is with AMELIA. It has been a rare name in the United States, chiefly used in the nineteenth century, when similar-sounding names, such as Caroline, were popular.

Enid ♀ Celtic (Welsh), uncertainly taken to be "woodlark." It was probably not used in England before it was popularized by Tennyson's *Geraint and Enid,* and it has been rare in the United States.

Enoch, Enos ♂ The etymology is uncertain, but the language may be Hebrew and the meaning "mortal," the name arising in the patriarchal story at about the point where men take over, as opposed to the semidivine figures.

Though never popular, the name occurs regularly in early New England, and less frequently in the other colonies. It died out about 1850.

The Greek form Enos also appears—especially in crossword puzzles.

Enola ♀ This melodious name was formed by reversal of Alone—probably in the nineteenth century. It occurs also as a place-name as the equivalent of Lone. It has remained very rare as a personal name.

Enos, *see* ENOCH.

Ephraim ♂ The name of a grandson of the patriarch Jacob, from which a tribe took its name. It is of uncertain origin and meaning. Ephraim became one of the more popular Old Testament names in New England, though no good reason for this popularity can be assigned. The name went out of use with the general decline of Old Testament names.

Equally inexplicable is the use of Ephraim as a name for the grizzly bear, necessarily an early nineteenth-century usage, since the Americans first made contact with the animal at that time.

Eric, Erica ♂ ♀ Old Norse. The element *e* is worn down and no longer intelligible; the element *ric* appears in Germanic languages generally, with the meaning "government, powerful."

In the United States, Eric is closely connected with Scandinavian immigration. It begins to make a showing in general lists toward the middle of the nineteenth century. Why should Eric be thus successful, when other Scandinavian names failed? There seems to be no plausible reason. It eventually, around 1975, became sufficiently popular to approach the top ten.

Erica is a feminine form, of approximately the same history.

It is also the Latin name of the plant known in English as heather, and so may be the source of the name occasionally, from the late nineteenth century on, among namers who had taken up the fad of drawing girls' names from flowers and bushes.

Ermentrude ♀ Germanic, "whole-strength." Of rare usage in the Romantic period, chiefly the late eighteenth century.

Ernest, Ernestine ♂ ♀ The name seems obviously to be merely from the German, Ernst, meaning "seriousness, steadfastness." As a name it is primarily German, and probably did not occur in English usage until the late eighteenth century when the Hanoverian dynasty introduced it as a name in the royal family, e.g. for the Duke of Cumberland (born 1771).

In the Harvard and Princeton lists the name begins to appear with students who would have been born about the middle of the nineteenth century. At Princeton the decade of the 1860's shows only one Ernest. The number jumped to ten in the next decade, and then came a sharp decline. The name at Harvard shows a similar history, where Ernest remains a viable but not really popular name. Modern usage has not favored names which are of such moralistic suggestion.

Ernestine, the feminine form, may have been coined in Germany or may merely be a development in England which was transferred to the United States.

Esmé[e] ♂ ♀ The etymology is uncertain. The spelling and pronunciation strongly suggest a French origin, and the spelling (for a man's name) can be traced back to the sixteenth century in Scotland. On the other hand, the connection may be with the medieval English name Ismay, which is still used, occasionally (for women), in England.

The name is scarcely viable in the United States. If used at all, it is commonly in a British context. Though Ismay is feminine, Esmé has been traditionally masculine, but in recent times it has sometimes been feminine.

Estelle ♀ Apparently a nineteenth-century French development as a stage name, using the Old French *estoile,* "star." In American usage it appears occasionally in the late nineteenth century or the twentieth.

Esther, Ester, Hester ♀ In the biblical text (Esther 2:7) the name is given as the Persian equivalent of the Hebrew *hadassah*, "myrtle." In addition, the word resembles the Persian word for star, which might be also applied to the myrtle since "star" is sometimes found in the names of plants because of star-shaped blossoms.

In early New England the name (usually as Hester) was not highly popular. Hawthorne's use of it in *The Scarlet Letter* has tended to make people take it as characteristic of the time, though it can scarcely be so thought on the basis of actual frequency. Its occurrence, however, as the name of the bearer of the scarlet letter accords with the sexual suggestions of the name in the biblical story. In fact, those suggestions may well have worked against the use of Esther in early New England.

The familiar form Hetty appeared in the nineteenth century, but it, too, was not popular. Like Hester, it appealed to novelists, being used, for example, in the *Leatherstocking Tales*. Esther is still a viable name in the later twentieth century.

Ethan ♂ Hebrew, "ancient," originally, perhaps, an honorary name bestowed on an old man. It occurred rarely during the period of biblical names, probably aided by the popularity of the Revolutionary figure Ethan Allen.

Ethelbert ♂ Anglo-Saxon, "noble-bright." It apparently became obsolete after the Norman Conquest, but was revived as a feudal Romantic name in the nineteenth century. *See* HOWARD. It remained very rare, and is probably again to be considered obsolete.

Since the element *ethel* is regularly feminine in the United States today, its presence in a name for a man was certain to work against popular acceptance of that name.

Etta ♀ In the later nineteenth century the Italian diminutive suffix, as in Henrietta, was able to stand alone, but the usage did not develop greatly.

Eugene ♂ Greek, "well-born." Prince Eugene of Savoy was popular with the English in the early years of the eighteenth century, and the name may have been brought into English usage at that time. It became somewhat more popular in the late nineteenth century, and then faded away. It still remains viable, though uncommon.

The shortened form is Gene, as widely circulated during the campaign for the presidency of "Clean Gene" McCarthy. The feminine (also rare) is Eugenia, shortened to Gene, thus leaving only one shortened form for men and women.

Eunice ♀ Greek, "well-[good]-victory," the name of the mother of Timothy (II Timothy 1:15). The name was never a favorite in the United States. Though still in existence, it is, like so many biblical names, tending toward extinction.

American usage seems to be wholly for a two-syllable pronunciation. English usage is divided, with three-syllable pronunciation generally considered to be more "correct."

Euphemia, Effie ♀ Greek, "good-speech." It may be taken as denoting a person of whom people speak well, i.e. a person of good repute. It is the name of several saints. It was rare in the eighteenth century, but gave rise to its variant, Effie, and then, apparently, all but disappeared. Effie, however, remained in use well into the nineteenth century.

Eva, *see* EVE.

Evadne ♀ Borrowed from the character in Greek mythology. It is probably from a pre-Greek language. (Note that *-adne* also occurs in ARIADNE.) It has been scarcely viable in the United States.

Evangeline ♀ This name is apparently the coinage of the poet Longfellow for his title-heroine of *Evangeline* (1847). He used the French form for *evangel,* adding a feminine suffix. The highly popular poem circulated the name widely, and its vaguely religious suggestion was in keeping with the temper of the times. The name, however, has largely faded in the twentieth century.

Eve, Eva ♀ The etymology is not certain, but it is usually given as Hebrew, "life-giving," an appropriate name for the first woman. (It may be based upon the Irish name Aoiffe.) Since Eve was believed to have brought sin into the world, and since her friendship with the serpent was not to her credit, her name was not a popular one. In the Puritan colonies it apparently was not used at all. In other colonies it was rare.

The appearance of "little Eva" in *Uncle Tom's Cabin* (1852) lent some popularity to the name in the latinized form.

Evelyn ♀ In Great Britain it is used for either a man or a woman;

in the United States it is used exclusively for a woman. Dating from the Normans, the feminine usage is the older. The masculine usage dates only from the seventeenth century in England, and is based upon the family name. It apparently did not make the passage to America. The situation, however, is by no means certain. Evelyn, of Germanic origin, is not of well-established meaning.

It is a viable name in the United States, but has never been common. Its identity with -lyn is probably nothing more than coincidental. The feminine Evelina, which flourished in the Middle Ages, may be the original form.

Americans use a pronunciation with a short e for the first vowel; the British use a long e.

Ewen, see OWEN.

Exercise ♀ Occasionally used in early New England. The only biblical text upon which it can be based is I Timothy 4:7, "Exercise thyself rather unto godliness."

Experience ♀ Occasionally used in early New England. The word is rare in the King James Version, and the only text that seems at all apt is Romans 5:4, which lists experience as produced by patience, and, in its turn, producing hope. The name probably did not survive into the eighteenth century.

Ezekiel ♂ Hebrew, "God-is-strong." It is the name of a major prophet and of a book of the Bible. Though not popular, it occurs regularly in the New England lists and less commonly in the other regions, dying out with the general decline of biblical names. Its well-established shortening was Zeke.

Ezra ♂ Hebrew, "help." From the biblical character, whose name stands on one of the books of the Bible. Ezra was never a popular name. Its use began c. 1700 and it began to fade out c. 1800. It was chiefly used in New England.

F

Faith ♀ The meager use of Faith, Hope, and Charity in New England could be a result of their common use in Elizabethan England. To the Puritans they may have become associated with the Church of England rather than with their own church.

Faith scarcely occurred in the seventeenth century. It was revived in the late nineteenth century, and remains viable in the twentieth.

Faith is a very common word in the New Testament. As a name, it can most precisely be derived from the famous thirteenth chapter of I Corinthians—"And now abideth faith, hope, charity, . . ."

Fannie, Fanny ♀ Though the shortening of Francis to Fran is the simplest, the form Fanny is perhaps easier of pronunciation, and it became the established name in the eighteenth century, usually spelled Fannie. (One must also consider the desire to escape from the ambiguity of FRANCIS.)

During the nineteenth century Fannie was one of the popular names, apparently expressing, in some way, an ideal of womanhood fitted to the times.

But with the slang use (c. 1920) of "fanny" to mean "rump," the already failing Fannie went out of use.

As a component of a double name Fannie has been popular, e.g. Fanniemae.

Fay, Faye ♀ Of uncertain origin; probably British rather than American, beginning in the 1890's. It may be a shortened form of Faith, or possibly a Romantic use of the common noun "fay," meaning "fairy." It is rare.

Fear ♀ This strange and humorless name actually occurred in early New England. It was presumably taken as representing some such text as "fear-God," which is recorded as a name in England. The original may actually have been "Fear-not," a form also occurring in England.

Felix ♂ Latin, "happy." It occurs rarely. The feminine, Felicia, is also rare.

Fern ♀ Another of the horticultural names which came into use in the nineteenth century. *See* LILY. It has remained rare.

Fiona ♀ A name which was apparently coined by the Scottish author William McCleod (1855–1905), and which he used as a pseudonym. (Actually some such term as "literary *persona*" might be more accurate, since he did not admit to the identification.) Literally, Fiona is presumably from Celtic, "white." The whole name might be taken, by punning technique, as "white cloud." It has been occasionally used in America, chiefly in the late nineteenth century.

Flora ♀ Latin, "flower." It has appeared occasionally from the nineteenth century on. *See* LILY.

Florence ♀ Derived from one or more of those known as St. Florence. (Actually, the Latin name means "flowering.") In older usage Florence was either masculine or feminine, but in American usage it is wholly feminine. The fame of Florence Nightingale (1820–1912) brought some attention to the name in the later nineteenth century, and it still maintains a mild popularity.

Frances, *see* FRANCIS.

Francine ♀ It appears after 1900, and is very rare. It represents a joining of Francis with a feminine ending, probably under French influence.

Francis, Frances ♂ ♀ The etymology is complicated, being probably dual. First, in the post-Conquest period in England (1066–1300) it appeared as a name or nickname meaning "Frenchman," either as a shortening of Franciscus (Latin) or as a popular adaptation of François (French). Second, after the time of St. Francis of Assisi (1182–1226) the name in English may be from a shortening of his Italian byname (he was actually christened Giovanni).

Ordinarily, in adopting a name from Latin or from one of the Romance languages, such as Italian or French, English-speakers maintained the distinction of gender—e.g. Julius, Julia. Francisco, however, was apparently too long, or some other influence was at work. In any case the name came to be merely Francis, the distinction of gender being lost. Perhaps because of Francis of Assisi, the application was to a male.

Though the names of nonbiblical saints were generally unpopular with the English during the Reformation period, Francis built up, for reasons which are by no means clear. Many of the early colonists bore that name. Among the Massachusetts freeholders (1630–34) who were English-born, Francis stood in tenth place, being comparable to such solid Saxon-Norman names as Henry and Edmund and such popular biblicals as Daniel and Joseph.

Once ensconced in the New World the Puritan namers shifted their practice. Among 675 male children whose births are recorded in Boston in the years 1630 to 1669, the name Francis fails to occur! A similar tabulation for Plymouth Colony shows only two of them in 1288 male births. Obviously, such a cataclysmic shift did not occur accidentally. It may represent the result of a consciously adopted policy to combat "papal" influence.

In the non-Puritan colonies comparable statistics are not available, but there certainly was no such massacre as that of Francis in New England. The New Englanders' prejudice against Francis was remarkably long-lived. Only about 1750 did it become a viable name at Harvard.

Actually, in the non-Puritan colonies also the name was rare. In the colonial period, moreover, it seems to remain exclusively masculine.

In the mid-nineteenth century Francis (so spelled, and masculine in usage) reached the height of its popularity. At about this time, also (in the same spelling), it began to appear as a woman's name. This failure to make the male-female distinction was, we may say, alien to the speech habits of English. Certainly an American boy of the nineteenth century did not wish to be labeled with what he would consider to be a girl's name. Probably for this reason, Francis fell off as a man's name, at the same time becoming more common as a woman's name. Approaching the problem from another direction were the developments of FRANK and even of FRANKLIN.

Toward the end of the nineteenth century began the custom of spelling the feminine with an *e*—that is, Frances. This practice failed to mitigate the oral ambiguity, but was a possibly useful visual distinction. Linguistically, neither the form nor the distinction thus attained can claim much authority, the *e* occurring in the Italian form Francesca being no sign of gender, and also appearing in the masculine Francesco. When linguistic pundits began saying that the *e* form was "right," they lacked any good sanction. Nevertheless, the practice was possibly useful, has in general established itself, and is doubtless approved in some of the many volumes which set themselves up as linguistic cookbooks. One authority to be cited is *The Book of Saints,* compiled by the Benedictine monks of St. Augustine's Abbey. This compilation (3rd ed., 1944) uses Frances as the English spelling for the only female saint and Francis for all the others.

In the later twentieth century the question would seem to be of special interest to the fighters for women's rights. They might declare themselves for either spelling, but hardly for a sex-indicative pair.

Frank ♂ A derivative of FRANCIS. The established Francis became Fran by shortening, and then the addition of the diminutive suffix produced Frankin. By another shortening the name became Frank (cf. HANK, JACK, etc.). A form Frankie may be assumed between Frankin and Frank, but is not necessary, since Frankie can be formed easily by the common diminutive *-ie.* Since the suffix *-kin* has not been much in use since about 1550 the formation of Frank before that time seems likely.

We must, therefore, conclude that Frank came to America

ready-made from England. It must, however, have existed in the nickname status for a long time. The first Frank to be officially so entered in the Harvard list appears in the 1840–49 decade. In the same decade there were 27 occurrences of Francis. We may assume that many of these latter were commonly called Frank. At Harvard in the 1870–79 decade Frank held ninth place. The late nineteenth century was its period of greatest use.

Yonge, writing of England in the mid-nineteenth century, declared Frank to be "exceedingly prevalent." On the whole, however, it seems less British than American. Its rapid build-up in the latter half of the nineteenth century may actually be a result of the feminist raid upon Francis. (*See* FRANKLIN.)

In the twentieth century Frank maintained some of its popularity, on occasion making the top ten. The counterculture, however, has not received it hospitably.

Franklin ♂ From the family name, which in medieval England indicated a free landholder. In the late eighteenth century it began to be used as a given name—largely because of the popularity of Benjamin Franklin. Since boys of this name were commonly called Frank, parents could have the advantages of using that popular name without becoming involved in the uncertainties of Francis. The name fell off during the latter part of the nineteenth century—a decline which may be reasonably attributed to the comparative decline of Benjamin Franklin as a hero, especially because of the bumper crop of heroes which was harvested from the Civil War. Franklin remains in use, but has become rare.

Freda, Frieda ♀ Occurring chiefly in the twentieth century, it is probably a borrowing from German usage, i.e. the manufacture of a feminine form from Friedrich. It may, however, be also a development from WINIFRED or FREDERICK, and from the meaning "peace."

Frederick ♂ Germanic, *frithu,* "peace," and *ricju,* "rule"; in Anglo-Saxon times the name occurred as Freodhoric. Though this name lingered in post-Conquest times, Frederick really entered English usage in the eighteenth century, being brought in from Germany with the Hanoverian dynasty. Enough tradition lingered for the name to take a characteristic English spelling, and not the German Friedrich.

In the American colonies the Hanoverian kings and their names made little impression. For reasons unknown, the name leaped into popularity at Harvard in the 1810–19 decade, and during the 1840–49 decade it stood in tenth place.

The German connections of the name are clear, and it was largely fostered by the heavy immigration from Germany in the years following the Revolution of 1848. It reaches its height of popularity about 1900, at that time rising to sixth place at Harvard. Occasional use of the byname Fritz is useful as showing the German connection, but the almost universal variant in the United States has been Fred. The English have made much use of Freddie and Freddy, and these forms have, rightly, been regarded as slightly anglophile. Because of its German associations, Frederick suffered during the two World Wars. Rather than remaining in the top ten, it now stands in the second ten or lower.

The history of Frederick is a remarkable one—its late introduction, its rise, its tenacious survival.

The spelling Frederic seems to be a matter of personal preference, with no clear origin from a non-English language. The rare feminine Frederica is a late coinage in Germany, and was introduced to the United States in the later nineteenth century.

G

Gabriel ♂ Hebrew, "mighty-God." Though well known in the popular mind for his assignment to blow the last trump, Gabriel has been a rare name, even during the period of biblical names. It had some usage among the French colonists, with Gabrielle supplying a feminine.

Gad ♂ From a son of Jacob, whence is derived a tribal name. Gad is uncommon even during the period of the popularity of Old Testament names, and it approaches extinction in the later nineteenth century. The name may not be Hebrew, and its meaning is uncertain. One influence working against this name is that its pronunciation, especially in certain dialects, is almost the same as that of "God."

Gail ♀ It is from ABIGAIL, but has lost all sense of being dependent and is current as a name on its own. Since its pronunciation is identical with that of "Gael," which has patriotic suggestions among the Irish and the Highland Scots, some connection with that word is possible. One way or another, Gail has shown some activity in the later twentieth century.

Gamaliel ♂ Hebrew, "recompense-[is]-God." Though it was the name of Paul's teacher (Acts 22:3), it is rare even in the period of biblical names.

Gary, Garry ♂ From some Scottish place-name—e.g. Glengarry. It arose from a family name, which came to be used as a given

125

name. In the mid-twentieth century it sometimes has achieved the top ten. Its popularity is based upon its brevity and euphony, but even more upon its use on stage and screen.

Genevieve ♀ Celtic, through French. The first syllable can be taken as "race, tribe"; the third syllable is uncertain. It is a popular name in France. In the United States it is rare, probably a literary name, or else borrowed directly from the French.

Geoffrey, *see* JEFFREY.

George ♂ Greek, "earth-man, farmer."

Whether or not we wish to believe that the original St. George was a Roman soldier who was martyred at Nicomedia in 303, and no matter what our personal convictions may be about dragons, the fact remains that the crusaders of the eleventh century found themselves moved by some of the colorful saints of the Eastern Church, one of these being the valorous St. George, the dragon-slayer. Partly they were thus influenced by a belief that he had come to their help in a hard-fought battle at Antioch. They returned home with an imponderable part of their baggage being the cult of St. George. In particular, the Norman crusaders took him as their patron.

As a result, many English churches were dedicated to the dragon-slayer, and some English children bore his name. More important, King Edward III had a special devotion to St. George, dedicated to him the Order of the Garter in 1349, and thus really established him as the patron saint of England.

Even so, the name did not become common, and with the Reformation (and its hostility to nonbiblical saints) one would have thought that George, like other such saints, would fade away. George, however, held on—probably because of its patriotic connections. Englishmen in battle still shouted "St. George for England!" Among the early emigrants to Massachusetts, George stood high, one count showing him in eighth place. But, as not infrequently happened, the new settlers did not follow the ways of their fathers. The patrician and equestrian St. George may have seemed out of place in a land of wild forests and crude cabins.

By some chance, the decade 1640–49 at Harvard showed a total of three Georges, a number which put the name well behind John and Samuel, in a tie with Nathaniel and William. But in the next two decades Harvard had no George at all! Two of them turned up in 1670–79. Then things bounced along, decade by decade, with one or two or even none. In fact, the years 1720–29 lacked the name, even though the total number of students was 350. You might put it that during Harvard's first century Aleuts and students named George were about equally numerous in Cambridge.

About 1730, however, there came a little stirring of change, because of something that had happened far away. The event was the occasion of the coronation of a new king in 1714, and his name was George. The first decade of students born in the reign of George I would be those who attended college in the decade of 1730–39, and that decade showed a count of three Georges—only a small increase. It should really be taken, however, as the beginning of a trend, and the reason for the trend seems to be, naturally, the accession of George I and the tremendous emphasis which accompanies the royal name. Moreover, four Georges in succession were kings.

The New Englanders in general had little liking for kings, and quite possibly (though countings are not available) George was more popular in the Middle and especially in the Southern Colonies. At least we know of one Virginia baby named George in 1732 (his family name being Washington). Certainly, though he himself echoed the royal name, he affected American naming more than did any king.

Washington became nationally well known and popular in the decade 1770–79. Thirty years later at Harvard George for the first time made the top ten, though only as ninth. But from then on it was roses all the way. In 1810–19 George had jumped to third place. In the next hundred years George varied only from second to fifth. Even after that time it slumped only to eighth.

At Princeton (where the record begins in 1748) things worked out much the same. George made the top ten in 1770–80, thus showing a certain interest in royalty in the Middle and Southern Colonies. Once established in the first ten at Princeton, George has never lost that position in 160 years, and was actually still holding at fifth in 1945, the last year of countings.

In the later twentieth century, George seems finally to have slumped, failing to make the first ten but still remaining a common name.

George, itself monosyllabic, has failed to develop a short form, a count in its favor with people who object to nicknames. The diminutive-feminine, Georgie, has been generally preempted for women. The Scottish Geordie has been scarcely used. Besides Georgie, the chief feminines have been Georgiana and Georgina.

On the whole, George must be put down as thoroughly American—so much so, indeed, as to be almost colorless, once the glamour of Washington had faded with time.

In the early twentieth century "George" became the generic for a Pullman porter, and inspired the more-or-less legendary "Society for the Prevention of Calling Pullman Porters 'George.' " In the same period came the phrase, "Let George do it," another evidence that the name had become workaday.

Gerald ♂ Germanic, "spear-rule." Although the English form Gerald doubtless still exists as an American name, the rather common Jerry (now probably to be considered an independent name) is derived from Gerald and also from Jeremiah. We have thus an unusual situation, with two formal names having become almost extinct, but their familiar forms remaining in common circulation.

The feminine Geraldine is rare, but Jerry (or Gerry) is also in use for women.

Gerard ♂ Germanic, from *gairu*, "spear," and *hardu*, "hard." It has always been very rare in America, but can be a source for Jerry.

Gerda ♀ Probably Scandinavian, but of uncertain meaning. In Norse mythology Gerda was the wife of the god Freyr. The name was popularized by Hans Christian Andersen (1805–75), and has been occasionally used since his time.

Gershom ♂ Hebrew, "stranger." It was in use throughout the period of biblical names. The literal meaning was well suited for an eldest son or for a child born in a new settlement, where the people still felt themselves to be strangers; thus the first-born of Moses and Zipporal bore this name, presumably because he was born in Midian, which was, at least for the father, a new and therefore strange land.

Gertrude ♀ Germanic, "spear-strength." It is the name of two women saints of the Middle Ages. It faded out of use in the colonies, but was revived and became fairly popular (probably as a Romantic development) in the later nineteenth century. It faded again in the twentieth century, but remained viable.

Gertie, the familiar form, unfortunately suggested the coupling "Dirty Gertie," and thus may have aided the decline.

Gideon ♂ Probably Hebrew, "hewer," a descriptive epithet for a notable warrior rather than a name in the stricter sense. It was in use during the period of the biblical names—Gideon being one of the few among the "judges" whose name the Puritans thought worthy of use.

Gilbert ♂ Germanic, from *gisil,* "pledge," and *berhta,* "bright." In the United States it has been fairly common; in many instances it is only a projection of the well-known family name.

Giles ♂ The complicated etymology (usually accepted, but offering some difficulties) is that the Greek *aegidion,* "kid, young goat," became the Latin personal name Aegidius and then the Old French Gide[s]; the *d* then, by an unusual sound-shift, became an *l* and the name ended in English as Giles, chiefly known because of the seventh-century saint.

The saint and his name enjoyed some popularity in the Middle Ages, but suffered in the post-Reformation period along with the other nonbiblical saints and their names. In fact, Giles is so rare in American lists as to be scarcely acceptable as an American name at all.

Gillian ♀ From Julian[a]. The name has scarcely been used in the United States, but its shortening provides the popular JILL.

Ginevra ♀ From GUENEVERE. It is a form borrowed from the Italian in the nineteenth century, and was occasionally used at that time.

Gladys ♀ Welsh, of uncertain meaning. The name is frequently explained as a Welsh rendering of Claudia, a possible explanation that raises more difficulties than it solves.

About 1870 Gladys began to appear in England, and by 1900 it was one of the most popular names. In the United States its popularity began about 1890. It became highly popular about 1900, but faded out about 1910. It is thus a good example of a name which became suddenly fashionable, and by its too great popularity made itself rapidly old-fashioned. It still, however, remains in use.

Glenn, Glen ♂ From the family name, chiefly of Scottish origin, designating a man living in a glen or associated with one. The considerable popularity of the name after 1962 is commemorative of John H. Glenn, Jr., who in that year became the first American to orbit the earth.

Gloria ♀ Latin, "glory." In the United States its use seems to fall entirely within the twentieth century. Although it might be called overemphatic and requiring rather too much of its bearer, it has maintained itself as a viable name.

Gloriana ♀ A poetic coinage of the sixteenth century, applied to Queen Elizabeth, especially by Edmund Spenser, and meaning "glorious one [feminine]." Loughead lists it as an American name. I have not actually found it, but we may assume that it was occasionally used, especially in the Romantic period.

Godfrey ♂ Germanic, from *Guda,* "god," and *frithu,* "peace." It has been a rare name in the United States. Probably working against it has been the fact that its short form would naturally be God, so that even the most callous might feel some embarrassment and the more religious would feel downright antipathy.

Gordon ♂ Celtic, a place (probably meaning "big-hill") in the Border Country of Scotland which gave its name to a notable local family. Gordon begins to appear as a given name in America in the mid-nineteenth century. Being short and euphonic, it has remained in such usage, and is now well established and probably better known as a given name than as a family name.

Grace ♀ The meanings of the word are various. As a name—at least in its earlier usage—it is to be taken in the theological sense, indicating a person who has attained, or is hopeful of attaining, a state of grace, that is, one who is a recipient of

God's favor or mercy. In some instances Grace may be a translation of Hannah or Anna. In the nineteenth century and later, Grace is physical in its suggestion, that is, "a graceful person."

The name was current in the Puritan colonies and, to a lesser degree, in the non-Puritan colonies. Shifted to its later meaning it enjoyed a brief period of mild prosperity in the late nineteenth century. It is still current, but rare.

Gregory ♂ From a late Greek word meaning "watchful." It has been a rare name in the United States.

Greta ♀ German, an adaptation of Margareta, appearing occasionally in American usage in the nineteenth and twentieth centuries.

Griffin, Griffith ♂ Welsh, probably "red," and originally a nickname for a red-haired man. Although there were many Welsh people among the colonists, they apparently gave this name little support, and it has remained rare.

Griselda, Grizel ♀ Germanic, with *hild,* "battle," but the rest uncertain. The story of the patient Griselda was a favorite literary theme, with versions by both Boccaccio and Chaucer. The name was widely used in Scotland, where it still is viable. With its doctrine of the submissive woman, we might expect to find it in use among the Puritans. It makes, however, very little appearance, and can hardly be claimed as American.

Guendolen, Gwendolin ♀ Welsh, with *gwen* meaning "white" and the rest uncertain; occasionally used in the nineteenth and twentieth centuries.

Guenevere, *see* GWENEVERE.

Gus, *see* AUGUSTUS.

Gustavus ♂ Germanic, with *-us* as the Latin nominative ending. The element *stav* means "staff"; the *gu* is uncertain. The name is chiefly Swedish. In particular, it was the name of the great Protestant hero, King Gustaof Adolf (1594–1632), who was usually known in English by the Latin form, Gustavus Adolphus. Though never popular, the name appears over a long time-span, and may not be (even yet) extinct.

Guy ♂ Apparently Germanic, but the etymology is uncertain. Fairly common in Elizabethan times, the name fell into disrepute from being associated with Guy Fawkes and the Gunpowder Plot of 1605. It would thus have been rare among the early immigrants, and there was no reason to revive it.

Not until the Romantic revival of the early nineteenth century did the name become a little active. Romantic poets, such as Scott and Poe, liked it. The name had a slight run of popularity around the end of the nineteenth century and the first two decades of the twentieth. It tended, however, to remain somewhat exotic.

Curiously, for an uncommon name, in its slang use it denoted a person in general, being widely used, and now it is established in dictionaries with no stronger *caveat* than *Informal*. Some aid from the Hebrew *goy*, "Gentile," is possible. Effigies known as "guys" still appear in English celebrations of Guy Fawkes Day, but influence from that source is unlikely, the usage being predominantly American.

Gwendolin, *see* GUENDOLEN.

Gwenevere, Guenevere ♀ Welsh, with *gwen-* meaning "white," and the rest uncertain. The Romanticism of the early nineteenth century (and especially the revival of interest in the Arthurian story) gave a chance to this name to be adopted from literary sources. The character of Arthur's faithless queen, however, must have worked against the name. (*See* JENNIFER.) In recent times Gwen has existed as an independent name, and even developed its own variants, such as Gwynne.

H

Habakkuk ♂ Probably Hebrew, "embracing." Doubtless because of its grotesque spelling it was scarcely used. It is the name of a book of the Bible and of the minor prophet associated with it.

Haggai ♂ Hebrew, "festive[?]." It was known as a book of the Bible and as the minor prophet, its author, but it scarcely appears as a personal name. Undoubtedly Haggai seemed unsuitable because in ordinary pronunciation it was undistinguishable from Hog Eye, and its possible variants (Hag, Hog, and Haggy) were scarcely inspiring.

Haidee, Hedy, Heidi, Heidy ♀ ♂ The origin is not altogether clear, and the name may be from two sources. First, it may be (shown in such forms as Hedy and Heidy) from the Germanic Hedwig, "refuge-war." Second, it appears as Haidee, for a Greek girl, in Byron's *Don Juan,* with no clear source, and perhaps to be considered primarily a Romantic coinage for poetry.

It has been rare in the United States until the mid-twentieth century, when it appears occasionally for women and, less commonly, for men. The variety of spellings suggests a new name for which a standard spelling has not yet developed.

Hale ♂ From the family name, indicating one who lived in or near a *hale,* i.e. a remote nook or valley. Being short and euphonic, the name has become a given one in the twentieth century.

Hall ♂ From the family name, indicating someone associated with a hall, that is, a feudal residence. Being brief and easy to pronounce, it has been somewhat used in the later nineteenth and the twentieth centuries.

Hally, Hallie ♂ ♀ The name may be masculine (from Harry, Harris) or feminine (from Harriet). It occurs chiefly in the feminine, and during the nineteenth century, but is rare. Hattie is the common diminutive.

Hamilton ♂ The family name is from a town in Scotland, of uncertain etymology. In the United States the early popularity of Alexander Hamilton gave some vogue to the name.

Hannah ♀ Hebrew, "grace." (For further discussion of the meaning, *see* GRACE.) Hannah appears in I Samuel as Samuel's mother, herself a prophetess. The name is the same as Anna, thus being spelled in the Greek of the New Testament. As pronounced, the two names differ little, and in an *h*-dropping environment they would be indistinguishable.

A tradition for the use of both Hannah and Anna existed in England at the time of the heavy migration to New England, the latter being common, the former rare. In the Puritan colonies the situation was rapidly reversed. In a Boston list of births for 1640–49 Hannah appears 45 times, topping Elizabeth and Sarah, and barely being exceeded by Mary at 48. On the other hand, Anna, in this list, occurs only three times.

In the non-Puritan colonies Hannah was not highly popular, but it was regularly used. This situation remained throughout the period of the popularity of Old Testament names. As late as the first quarter of the nineteenth century Hannah still could occur among the top ten. Shortly after this time, however, Hannah rapidly disappeared, with Anna becoming correspondingly common. By the middle of the nineteenth century Hannah may be called obsolescent, and in the ordinary list of the twentieth century it fails to appear at all. (*See also* ANNA.)

Hannibal ♂ Phoenician, "grace-of-Baal." Though an African, the great Carthaginian was not a black. The name, however, has been occasionally used for black men, apparently because of the African connection. It occurs both in the period of slavery and later.

Harold ♂ Anglo-Saxon, from *here,* "army," and *weold,* "power." Its use lapsed after the Norman Conquest, but it was revived in the early nineteenth century, probably from Romantic feeling. Beginning about 1850, it enjoyed a period of popularity, reaching tenth on the Harvard list for the decade 1910–19. It is at present much less popular.

The short form is Hal, which was traditionally used for Harry long before the revival of Harold. At present Hal is commonly taken to be for Harold.

Harriet ♀ The French feminine form of Henry. It became established in England during the seventeenth century (*see* HENRIETTE). By analogy, and possibly for patriotic reasons, the English form Harry replaced the foreign Henri in the course of time, to yield Harriette.

But Harriette still looked foreign. Moreover, the *-ette* ending has never been popular in English. A shift of spelling to Harriet solved the problem, though Harriette remained in use.

Although little used in the United States until after 1800, Harriet then became very popular, inhabiting the top ten list at mid-century Mount Holyoke College. It remained a much used name through the nineteenth century. Though it has lost this popularity in the twentieth century, it still remains a viable name in the United States.

During the period of the popularity of Harriet, the diminutive Hattie was much used, functioning as an independent name.

Harry, *see* HENRY.

Harvey, Hervey ♂ The etymology is, probably, that the name is from old Breton *haerveu,* "battle-worthy," being introduced by Bretons who accompanied the Normans in the Conquest. To have a Breton name thus become English is highly unusual. It was also the name of a saint who generally appears in the French form as St. Hervé.

Though fairly common in the Middle Ages, Harvey went out of use for several centuries as a given name, and its reappearance in the early nineteenth century probably owes nothing to the Bretons or the saint, but is merely the adoption of a family name. It has been thoroughly American in its suggestions, having been little used elsewhere in the English-speaking areas. It has not, however, attained great popularity.

Hazel, *see* LILY.

Heather, *see* ERIC, ERICA, and LILY.

Hector ♂ Greek[?], meaning uncertain. The name of the illustrious Trojan of the *Iliad* appears as an occasional name for slaves, in accord with the custom of giving classical names to them. It has also, though very rarely, been used as a name in the general populace.

Hedy, *see* HAIDEE.

Heidy, *see* HAIDEE.

Helen ♀ Attempts have been made to derive the name from a Greek word, "bright," but it is more likely of pre-Greek origin and of unknown meaning. Beginning, in actual(?) record, with Helen of Troy, the name assumed a post-classical Latin form, Helena. This was the name of the mother of the Emperor Constantine. Sainted, and closely associated with the story of the discovery of the True Cross, she passed her name on to the nations of western Europe.

In medieval England (as Helen, Helena, or Ellen) the name had some currency, but with the Reformation, being that of a nonbiblical saint, it nearly disappeared in English.

It survived, chiefly as Ellen, in the non-Puritan colonies. Under the influence of Romanticism Helen became suddenly popular toward the middle of the nineteenth century. Phonetically attractive, it became a poet's word, as in Poe's *Helen*. Around 1900 it was one of the most popular names. By the middle of the twentieth century, however, the popularity had receded, though it remains still a fairly common name.

Heloise, Eloise ♀ From a Germanic form Helewidis, "healthy-wide." Although of very formidable suggestion by modern ideas, the name may indicate what was wanted in a woman by old Germanic standards. The name came into English with the Normans, but died out after a few centuries. It came into use again, probably as a Romantic name and in close association with the story of Heloise and Abelard.

It is still in occasional use, generally with the spelling Eloise. But the full French form demands Héloïse. The spelling -oï-, as indicated by the dieresis in the French usage, is maintained as two syllables in the common use, making possible some confusion with Louise.

Henriette, Henrietta ♀ The French feminine form for Henry became established in England during the early seventeenth century, largely because of the introduction of the name in the person of Queen Henriette Maria, wife of Charles I. This *-ette* form has not been generally popular in English, so that the introduction and the use of the Latin form, Henrietta, is easily explicable.

Imported with the colonization, Henrietta has remained a viable name, but has never been popular. (*See* HARRIET.)

Henry, Harry ♂ Though the name is not recorded in Anglo-Saxon, it is clearly Germanic, meaning "home-rule." It was a favorite name among the Norman conquerors, developing in two ways.

The speech of the Normans was French. In that language the name developed, first, into what was spelled Henri. By further development in ordinary speech the *n* disappeared, and the pronunciation became that which was represented in the English spelling as Harry.

On the other hand, most of the writing of the time was in Latin, and the clerks latinized the name as Henricus. Since official documents were all in Latin, people naturally came to have the feeling that the proper (i.e. official) name was Henricus, and a second pronunciation, commonly spelled Henry, developed from the Latin form.

Through the Middle Ages, these two spellings and the two pronunciations continued to be in use. The name itself was both common and notable, being that of eight English kings.

Even another form developed, when the customary sound-shift "*r* becomes *l*" occurred. The result here was Hal, which was a much-used familiar nickname. (*See* HAROLD.) In his historical plays Shakespeare made use of all three forms, thus being able to indicate different degrees of intimacy between pairs of characters.

In seventeenth-century England the name was not better than moderately common. In early New England it fell off even more. In four decades (1640–79) only one Henry attended Harvard, so that we may consider the name almost obsolete. In the first half of the eighteenth century it grew slowly, and it reached the top ten (though only in tenth place) in the decade 1800–1809.

This return of Henry coincides with the falling off of the biblical names, and may have been thus caused—at least in part. Once again an active name, Henry continued in use—ranging generally from fourth place to eighth for more than a hundred years at Harvard.

Princeton presents the same picture. The rolls of the regiments of the Revolutionary War are similar. From about 1800 onward Henry appears to be nationally well established.

In the mid-twentieth century, however, Henry slumped considerably, and became what may be called a vestigial name.

Not altogether clearly explained is the development of Hank, the ordinary, grass-roots abbreviation or nickname for Henry in the United States. In its formation it shows much similarity to Jack and Frank, i.e. a short form Hann picks up a diminutive suffix to become Hankin (preserved as a family name), and a further shortening then drops the -in. Unfortunately, just where and when all this happened is difficult to determine.

Hank has rarely been used as an official name. It bears with it, indeed, a suggestion of the backwoods and the river-side village. Unlike Jack and Frank, it failed to attain full status. Like Chuck, it is American, but unlike Chuck, it has rarely been granted respectability. There is some evidence—at least for England—that Hank may also have developed from the -hann of a Dutch or German form Johann. In the United States, however, Hank shows itself clearly as from Henry.

The future of Henry (including Harry and Hank) is uncertain. From the point of view of the later twentieth century it has slumped seriously, and suggests a dying name. It may, however, be subject to a revival.

Hephzibah, Hepzibah ♀ Hebrew, "My-delight-is-in-her." She is mentioned once in the Bible, as being the wife of Hezekiah, and again as a figurative name for Jerusalem (Isaiah 62:4). The name has sometimes been held to be a favorite among the Puritans, but in my own actual listing it is scarcely to be found at all. Doubtless the strangeness of the name made people more likely to notice it.

Herbert ♂ Germanic, *harja,* "army," and *berhta,* "bright, famous." The family in England has been both ancient and honorable. As a given name, Herbert became suddenly popular about 1850, reflecting a similar popularity in England. This name continued to be much used for more than half a century. Although having much in common with the feudal names (cf. SIDNEY), Herbert became wholly americanized. In some lists it appears in the second ten. After 1925 it faded, reverting to occasional use.

The short form is commonly Herb, though Bert may be used. As opposed to most of the feudal names, Herbert has escaped being considered namby-pamby and foreign—to some extent, doubtless, because of President Hoover, who was born (1874) at the height of the Herbert boom.

Hercules ♂ Greek[?], containing the name of the goddess Hera, but otherwise of uncertain meaning. It occurs very rarely, as the name of a slave, in accordance with the custom of giving classicial names to blacks. Hercules would have been an appropriate name for a gigantic man, but in that case we must suppose that the name was not applied, as was customary, shortly after birth.

Herman ♂ Germanic, from *harja,* "army," and *mana,* "man." It has occured rarely, and usually in families having some German background.

Hester, *see* ESTHER.

Hetty, *see* MEHETABEL.

Hezekiah ♂ Hebrew, "strong-[is]-God." Although never numerous, the occurrences of Hezekiah are sufficent to indicate a name regularly used in early New England. In the Bible it is borne by an outstanding king of Judah—enough to make it a name of good omen.

Hilda ♀ Anglo-Saxon, probably a short form of which only the element *hild,* "war," is preserved. It died out in the Norman period, but was revived in the nineteenth century as a part of the renewed interest in the Middle Ages.

Hildegard[e] ♀ Germanic, from *hild,* "war," and probably *gardan,* "know." It was the name of a famous German abbess who attained sainthood. Her name became a popular one in Germany. In the United States it is generally to be considered an evidence of German influence.

Hiram ♂ The name is probably Phoenician, but the meaning is uncertain. Hiram was the king of Tyre who was on friendly terms with both David and Solomon. Like CYRUS, the name may be considered counterbiblical. It came into use about 1800, when the biblical names were falling off. It enjoyed certain runs of popularity in the nineteenth century, but has scarcely survived in the twentieth.

Holly, *see* LILY.

Homer ♂ Ordinarily we may suppose it to be from the family name rather than from the poet. Curiously, the name appears as that of a slave in a Virginia list of 1726. This may be taken as an early example of the giving of classical names to blacks, and a Scipio appears in the same list.

Once Homer had been given a start, it could the more easily come into general use by namers, without any need for a knowledge of the classics. It has been a viable name from the nineteenth century on, but has never been common.

Honor ♀ Probably Latin, meaning "honor." It was current in the Middle Ages, but fell into disfavor at the Reformation because it was a saint's name. With the use of abstracts among the Puritans it revived a little, and was sometimes borne by men. With the decline of abstract names Honor became so rare as scarcely even to be considered viable.

Hope, Hopestill, Hopefor ♀ ♂ The common English word furnished an occasional name in early New England—ordinarily for women, but occasionally for men. Curiously, indeed, the members of the famous triad "faith, hope, and charity" are so rare as names in the seventeenth century that one searches for some special reason for their disbarment (*See* FAITH.) Hope, like Grace, survived, however. It is to be found down to the present, though it is always rare.

The form Hopestill was about equally as popular in early times as was Hope. We must suppose "still" to be merely the common adverb, the name indicating that we should continue to hope. Hopefor appears occasionally.

Contrary to usual practice, Hope and Hopefor appeared not only for women, but also for men—e.g. Hope occurred in the Harvard list for 1650–59.

Horace, Horatio ♂ The name is from the Roman clan, Horatius. In the Italian form, Horatio, it apparently was introduced as a given name in Italy during the Renaissance, and by the middle of the sixteenth century it had spread to England. (The audience at *Hamlet* would have accepted it as a current name.)

Actually Horatio may, in the highly literary and classics-directed atmosphere of the time, have been commemorative of the Roman poet Quintus Horatius Flaccus, who was commonly called Horace in England. The name actually naturalized itself as Horace, Horatio eventually dying out in the later nineteenth century.

Horace enjoyed some popularity in the mid-nineteenth century. In the twentieth century it has become rare. It seems to have preserved a suggestion of middle class solidity and righteous industry, perhaps thus crystallized by the image of its two chief American examples—Mann and Greeley. Both men were sufficiently popular in the nineteenth century to ensure at least a moderate crop of babies who were christened in their honor.

Horatio, *see* HORACE.

Hosea ♂ Hebrew, "God-is-help," the name of a minor prophet and of a book of the Bible. It was viable but not common in early New England. It disappeared with the ending of the period of biblical names. About 1850 James Russell Lowell chose "Hosea Bigelow" for his typical New Englander of the mid-nineteenth century.

Howard ♂ From the family name, the Howards being one of the foremost English noble families. Early (pre-1800) uses of the

141

name may be for actual Howard families in America. In the mid-nineteenth century, however, the name built up with a rush, indicating that it is another case of a feudal name, such as Clarence and Sidney, by which certain citizens of a democracy ape an aristocracy. Howard may be considered the most successful of these names. By being so numerous it lost its snobbish suggestions and became merely another solid American name. It still remains moderately common.

Howell ♂ Welsh, probably from the family name in most American usage. It could, however, be directly from the Welsh *hywell,* "lordly." It is rare.

Hubert ♂ Anglo-Saxon, Hygebeorht, with *hygu,* "heart, mind," and *beorht,* "bright, famous." It was common in the Middle Ages, to some extent because St. Hubert was the patron of hunting, a highly popular medieval sport. Like so many names of saints it faded out in the Renaissance. It was scarcely (if at all) used during several centuries. It then enjoyed a slight revival in the later nineteenth century, probably beginning in England as a literary name reflecting the renewed interest in medieval studies. One student at Harvard in the decade 1870–79 is the earliest evidence in my lists. The name has remained very rare in the United States.

Hugh, Hugo ♂ Germanic, a short form of some name containing the element *hugu,* "mind, heart." It was popular in the Middle Ages, partly because of the two saints of the name who were associated with the city of Lincoln. Along with the names of other nonbiblical saints, Hugh went out of favor with the growth of Protestantism. It gradually returned to a modest usage, and has remained a viable name in modern times.

The German form Hugo appears occasionally—probably because of direct German influence.

Humphrey ♂ Germanic, probably from a tribal name, Huni, and *frith,* "peace." It has been little used, but has had some build-up because of the popularity of Humphrey Bogart, the actor, and perhaps also because of the triple-aitched Hubert Horatio Humphrey.

I

Ian, Ion ♂ The Scottish forms of JOHN, usually treated as independent names, but never common in the United States.

Ichabod ♂ Hebrew, "where-is-the-glory?" The question is rhetorical and the passage can be read, "The-glory has-departed." On hearing of the catastrophe in which the Philistines had captured the ark, the (unnamed) wife of Phineas went into labor, and died after giving birth to a son and naming him with references to the disaster.

The name is rare, but is of interest in showing that those who drew their names from the Bible would sometimes use a pessimistic one (cf. BENONI).

For associations with Ichabod many Americans would be influenced by Irving's character Ichabod Crane in *The Legend of Sleepy Hollow*. Obviously Irving chose the name because it had become old-fashioned (and therefore grotesque) by his time, and because its meaning supplied a touch of satire. (*See* PRESERVED.)

Ida ♀ Germanic, probably a short form of some name built up with the root *id-*, "work." Introduced by the Normans, it became common for several centuries, but eventually died out. It was revived in the nineteenth century along with so many other medieval names, and it has been moderately used in the twentieth century. It has no demonstrable connection with Mount Ida of early Greek origins.

Ima ♀ Through much of the nineteenth and twentieth centuries Miss Ima Hogg was a well-known citizen of Texas, respected and even loved for her good qualities. The name is one of the few that can be credited to hostility toward a child. When urged to change her name, however, Miss Hogg refused.

Imogen[e] ♀ As Innogen, it appears in the work of Geoffrey of Monmouth, but is there of unknown origin and meaning, though a Celtic etymology may be suspected. On the other hand, Geoffrey himself was quite capable of coining the name. From Geoffrey we have the name taken by Shakespeare for his heroine in *Cymbeline,* with the spelling Imogen.

Two ideas about the shift are held. First, it was a mere slip of spelling or typography. Second, it was a conscious reworking of the name, presumably by Shakespeare himself. As Imogen, according to a recent theory, the name assumed an English form based on a hypothetical Latin rendering—i.e. *imus,* "last, lowest," and *gen,* "born." This ingenious explanation loses some credibility in view of the fact that in the play Imogen is neither "last born," nor "lowest born." On the other hand, another character in the play is Posthumus, Imogen's husband, usually called Leonatus, "lion-born," and his name certainly involves the problem of birth. At this point, however, the question becomes one of Shakespearean criticism rather than of a name.

The prestige of Shakespeare and the sympathic qualities of the heroine led to borrowing for actual use, probably in the early nineteenth century, and this adoption can be put down as part of the Romantic revival. Imogen has, however, always remained a rare name.

Ina ♀ It is probably a coinage, formed by using the ending from such names as Melvina, Nina. It was in use especially in the nineteenth century.

Increase ♂ There is every reason to accept this as the common English word, and it may have been used, like Hope, Recompense, and other such words, as a term of good omen in a country which needed "increase" in nearly every respect. Quite

possibly, however, the namers knew that Joseph was translated as "increaser," and they thus gave further circulation to
that name.

Though well known because of the prominent Increase
Mather (1639-1723), the name was actually very rare and
scarcely viable.

Inez ♀ This is the Spanish form of AGNES. It has been occasionally
used from the early nineteenth century on.

Ingrid ♀ Old Norse, from Ingir, the name of an ancient hero,
and *rida,* "ride." Originally limited to Scandinavian immigrants, since the mid-twentieth century it has become more
generally used, being borrowed from "stage and screen."

Ion, *see* IAN.

Ione ♀ It may be a development from John (as are Ian and Ion),
but the pronunciation is regularly *aye-own,* and suggests a
connection with the classical Ionia, or with the famous Scottish island Iona. It has been a rare name since the mid-nineteenth century.

Ira ♂ Hebrew, "watcher." It is the name of three men in the Old
Testament, none of them being of any great importance. The
brevity of the name may have appealed to some American
namers. It occurs as a rare name from the later eighteenth century on. It did not fade out with the general lapse of biblical
names, but enjoyed its greatest use in the late nineteenth century, when namers may not even have recognized it as biblical.
It became less used in the twentieth century.

Irene ♀ Greek, "peace." The name made its appearance in the
later nineteenth century, on both sides of the Atlantic. The
trisyllabic pronunciation which the British use is pedantically
close to the classical Greek, suggesting that the name was
brought into English self-consciously and at the sophisticated
or learned stratum—that is, by someone who had studied
Greek. The name may then have entered American usage by
transition through non-oral means, that is, by writing or printing, so that the pronunciation became that which the spelling
suggested. British usage pronounces the name in three syllables; American, in two.

Irene enjoyed a mild popularity in the earlier decades of the twentieth century, and is still current. A highly popular song of the 1950's gave the name much publicity.

Iris, *see* LILY.

Irma ♀ Probably a shortening from Ermengarde or Ermentrude. It is very rare, but appears occasionally in modern usage.

Irvine, Irving ♂ From the family name, which is derived from a town (or towns) in Scotland. It occurs chiefly in the twentieth century, and in Jewish contexts.

Isaac ♂ The name is usually given as Hebrew, "laughter," the reason for the naming being told in Genesis 21. The story of the laughter, however, is probably an attempt by speakers of Hebrew to give Hebrew meaning to an unintelligible name. Like many others of the names in Genesis, this one is probably from some language other than Hebrew, and its meaning must be considered uncertain.

Isaac was a well-established name in England during the Middle Ages. Being biblical, it did not suffer from the Reformation, but might even have been stimulated by the vacuum which was left by the abandonment of the names of the non-biblical saints. The early immigrants brought the name with them to America. Among baptisms in Boston (1630–69) Isaac appears as fourteenth, and among Plymouth baptisms it is ninth. Since Isaac was a well-known figure of the Old Testament, no special reason for the use of his name need be sought.

The Harvard list (for New England) and the Princeton list (for the Middle Colonies) both show Isaac to have been an especially active name for men born about 1740 on, during the period of the next full hundred years. Toward the end of the nineteenth century, however, the name definitely slumped—almost, indeed, disappearing from both lists.

What little use of Isaac remained was likely to show Jewish connection. Undoubtedly, the disapearance of the name from general Amrican usage indicates a self-consciousness about Judaism and a dislike of seeming to associate a child thus—though actually the name might have been used for several generations in the family.

The unusual short form, Ike, is difficult to explain. Apparently such forms as Iz and Izzy lacked dignity.

Isabel, *see* ISOBEL.

Isador[a] ♂ ♀ Probably Greek, of a dithemic structure, meaning "equal-gift," but other translations are possible. It has not been traditionally used in the United States, but occurs occasionally in a Jewish context, along with its diminutive (masculine) Izzy.

Isaiah ♂ Hebrew, "helper-[is]-God." In spite of its importance as the name of a major prophet and a book of the Bible, Isaiah was not much used, though it made steady appearances at Harvard during the period of the use of biblical names.

Ishmael ♂ Like so many names in Genesis it may not be Hebrew. The Hebrew meaning is clear ("God-hears"), but the application is artificial, and does not lead on to the prophecy, "His hand will be against every man." Though strikingly used in Melville's *Moby-Dick,* it otherwise is very rare.

Isobel, Isabel ♀ The French form for ELIZABETH, but tending to independent usage—especially from the nineteenth century onward.

Israel ♂ Hebrew, "ruling-with-God." It was the name given to the former Jacob (Genesis 32); it was also given to the twelve tribes as a whole. It was never very common as a given name, and it faded out with the general decline of biblical names in the mid-nineteenth century. General Putnam (born 1718) has been the chief American hero to bear the name.

Issachar ♂ The name of a son of the patriarch Jacob and of an Israelitic tribe, of uncertain meaning, possibly non-Hebraic. It occurs, but rarely, in the name rosters of early New England.

Ivan ♂ Though it is the Russian form of John, it has been an independent name in English. It appears, rarely, in the period following 1870, and we may consider it a literary name, developed from the reading of the novels of Tolstoy, Turgenev, etc.

Ivy ♀ This very rare name may be from the family name or may be another horticultural one (*see* LILY).

J

Jaazaniah ♂ Hebrew, "God-hears." Four persons so named in the Old Testament are of little note, but the literal meaning may have been taken as indicating an answer to prayer. The name is very rare.

Jabez ♂ Probably Hebrew. The only biblical passage in which the name occurs is I Chronicles 4:9–10. A note in the King James Version (an authoritative source in early times) gives the meaning as "sorrowful." The passage runs, ". . . his mother called his name Jabez, saying Because I bare him with sorrow." The text goes on to give Jabez's calling upon the Lord and the prosperity that the Lord granted him.

In a minor way, therefore, Jabez was a natural name with which the colonists could associate themselves—all the more so because he was associated with sorrow (as childbirth often was), and a mystery.

Although never popular, Jabez appears regularly in the lists, especially in New England, down to the middle of the nineteenth century, when the biblical names were falling into disuse.

Jack ♂ Its development from John is clear, but it is beginning to be used as an independent name, and is better so considered. (The resemblance to the French form Jacques, meaning James, is coincidental.)

The definite development of the name begins in the later

Middle Ages, when the common diminutive -*kin* was suffixed to John, thus providing Johnkin, which soon came to be spelled Jankin, as in *The Canterbury Tales*. The dropping of the first *n* soon followed, and the -*in* was clipped off for shortening with the resulting Jak, commonly spelled Jakke, and, as the spelling normalized, finally producing Jack.

The derivation of Jack from John is thus clear on the basis of preserved transitional forms and also because of the association of John and Jack. As early as Shakespeare's time (and probably a century or so earlier) anyone named John could expect to be called Jack when familiarly addressed, as with Sir John Falstaff, who is regularly Jack to his comrades.

James, on the contrary, has nothing to do with Jack, and, in spite of the French rendering as Jacques, becomes Jim or Jimmy in intimate talk. The Scottish form, Jock, has been little used in the United States.

Jackson ♂ One of the more frequent surnames, Jackson is also fairly common as a given name, partly because of the hero-status of Andrew and of "Stonewall."

Jacob ♂ The biblical text attributes the name to the Hebrew, "heel," and gives a highly implausible story of its origin (Genesis 26). As with so many others of these early and difficult names, we do better to consider it to be borrowed from some unknown language, and thus to be of unknown meaning. (For the relationship of Jacob to James, *see* JAMES. *See also* ISRAEL.)

Although the story of Jacob is more fully developed in the Bible than is that of Isaac, the name Jacob was somewhat less popular in the American colonies, quite possibly because the patriarchal Jacob seemed to lack heroic qualities. From early colonial times, moreover, the name was associated with two quite distinct groups, viz. the Jews and the Germans. The former, very small in numbers, were concentrated in New York and Rhode Island, and the latter, much more numerous, settled chiefly in southeastern Pennsylvania. Since these "Pennsylvania Dutch" largely maintained the German speech, their retention of Jacob in place of James was natural. In one group of these German immigrants, Jacob stood in third place, exceeded only by Johann and Hans.

As a general rule, the association of a particular name with a particular group tends to make the name avoided by other groups, even when no prejudice is involved. The only moderate use of Jacob may thus be the result, partially, of the feeling that the bearer of the name would be judged as belonging to a special minority.

After thus dragging through the period of the popularity of Old Testament names, Jacob had (so to speak) no reserve against the general decline, and was ready by 1800 for what amounts to a collapse. By the mid-nineteenth century heavy German immigration and the beginnings of anti-Semitism worked toward a near extinction of the name, except in its special groups. In the twentieth century the anti-German feeling, inevitable in a period of two wars, kept Jacob at the verge of extinction.

The short forms Jake and Jakie, in particular, came to have Jewish associations, and even led to the use of Jack as a substitute.

Jacqueline, Jacquelyn ♀ Apparently a French diminutive-feminine of Jacques—that is, James. Usage in the English language, however, naturally refers it to Jack. Jackie exists primarily to provide a feminine form for the name. Jacqueline has never become common, but it remains active in the later twentieth century, sometimes in the alternative spelling, Jacquelyn.

Jael ♀ Commonly translated as "chamois, female wild-goat," Jael may actually, like Elijah, couple the two words for divinity and thus be taken as "Jah-is-God."

Jael treacherously violated the sanctions of hospitality and killed Sisera. She had, however, the patriotic justification for raising her hand against the enemy of her people, and the biblical text declares her "Blessed above women."

Nonetheless, her name was not commonly used among the Puritans, in spite of statements to the contrary by modern scholars. In my own fairly extensive records of Puritan names I cannot find it listed at all. I should not be surprised, however, to have some instances turn up.

The history of this name (or its lack of history) is an interesting case of Puritan attitudes, especially of their unwill-ingness to use names of questionable moral suggestion.

Bardsley was in such straits for examples of Jael that he used the same one twice—an English christening of 1613! He seems to have found no other instance.

Jair, Jairus ♂ Hebrew, "God-enlightens," is the name of several biblical characters of little note. Jairus is apparently the same name, with a Greek-Latin ending. In Mark 5 the name is that of a man who was involved with an early miracle performed by Christ. In America Jair had only occasional use as a name.

James ♂ The history is one of peculiar complication. James and Jacob are actually the same name in the Hebrew text of the Bible. In the Greek text the original Hebrew name appears as Jakob for the patriarch and as Jakobos for the five persons (including the two Apostles) bearing it in the New Testament. The modern name Jacob thus clearly descends from this Hebrew form, passing through the Greek and thence into Latin. The regular Latin form is Jacobus (with a long o).

At some point, however, a colloquial variant developed with a short o and an m for the b—Jacomus. This form took hold in Spain (Jaime), France (Jacques), and Great Britain (James), becoming the vernacular form, with Jacobus remaining as the Latin form, Jacob appearing occasionally as the name of an individual, and generally known as the name of the patriarch.

The history in the Anglo-American tradition is also highly complicated. The popularity of James rested upon several circumstances. It was the name of two Apostles and of three other persons who are prominently mentioned in the New Testament. The great pilgrimage to St. James (Santiago) at Compostela in Spain was a kind of major institution in the Middle Ages. Among New Testament names for men, James is, in most English lists, usually exceeded only by John and Thomas.

In Scotland the name was even more popular, since it was the royal name for over a century. This Scottish influence was sufficient to make a showing in America. At Harvard in the later eighteenth century James regularly shows up less strongly than it does at Princeton in the same period, a situation doubtless arising from the fact that Princeton's students were drawn largely from the Scottish and Scotch-Irish settlers of the Middle Colonies.

James maintained its popularity throughout the nineteenth century and the earlier part of the twentieth. In the counter-culture it suffered severely, along with most of the other traditional names.

The colloquial variants are commonly Jim and Jimmy in England and in the United States, Jamie in Scotland. But down until the middle of the nineteenth century the English used Jem and Jemmie, forms which seem to have been uncharacteristic of America.

The name's literal meaning in Hebrew is "following-after, supplanter," and it was given to the patriarch (according to the story) because he managed to supplant his twin brother, Esau. Its frequency of use in the New Testament suggests that it had become, by that time, a common name, possibly indicating a second son.

Jane ♀ The commonest feminization of JOHN. It apparently developed from the French. (After the Norman Conquest the upper classes in England were French-speaking for several generations.)

For the other adaptations of John, *see* JOAN, JOHANNA, JEAN. All of these have come to be considered independent names, and have thus kept Jane (the most numerous of them) from attaining first place, as John has done. It has often, however, stood in third place, following Mary and Elizabeth.

In the early New England colonies Jane (along with the other feminizations) was not much favored, being nonbiblical. Elsewhere, it flourished in the eighteenth century, and declined in the nineteenth. At this time, however, it was much in use as a kind of auxiliary in such double names as Mary Jane and Sally Jane.

About 1900 Jane again became popular—so much so, indeed, that "jane" became a slang term for "girl." Since such a usage tends to make a name commonplace, or even vulgar, Jane fell off in the mid-twentieth century, and ceased to be in the top ten. Some of this decreased popularity, however, was the result of the increasing use of variants, particularly Janet.

Janet ♀ A diminutive of Jane, of French origin. It developed a strong Scottish usage, and has become highly popular in the twentieth century.

Janice ♀ It is apparently another feminization of John, but its background is uncertain. It may be Scottish or from some Scandanavian language. It has not been much used, but has enjoyed a little popularity in the twentieth century.

Japhet[h] ♂ Usually taken as Hebrew, "extender." This etymology, however, is doubtful, and (like some other names in Genesis) the name may be of non-Hebrew derivation. It is of very rare occurrence, even in the period of biblical names.

Jared ♂ Like many other names occurring in Genesis, Jared is probably not Hebrew, and its meaning is uncertain. The character is chiefly notable for having lived to the age of 962, thus providing a good second to Methuselah's 969. Jared might have been used for its suggestion of long life, or it may be another name chosen by luck.

Except in the Ingersoll family it may not have existed. Jared Ingersoll and his son of the same name were prominent in public affairs in the late eighteenth century, and the name lingers still in that family (cf. ADLAI).

Jason ♂ A biblical name (Acts 17:5). In the Greek text the name is Eason, and the rendering in English may have been influenced by the name of the Greek mythological hero. It is rare as an American name, though given some fictional currency by its use in Faulkner's novels. In the mid-twentieth century it has enjoyed a mild boom, probably set in motion by its use by TV personalities.

Jasper ♂ The "wise men" who came to adore the child at Bethlehem are nameless in the biblical text, but later imagination remedied this lack, and they became Caspar (Gaspar), Melchior, and Balthasar. These nonbiblical names made little impression upon England, but Caspar/Gaspar was sufficiently used to develop the English form Jasper, which appeared also in America. Balthasar (Balser) and Melchior also appear occasionally in colonial lists, but probably among German-speaking colonists, or those under strong German influence.

The language of these three names is uncertain. Melchior suggests the widespread Semitic word for "king," and *bal* may have some tie to *bal, bel,* which suggests a widely used word for "god," also Semitic.

Jean ♀ The French form for John, which in England developed into the feminization Jane and became Jean in Scotland. Together with other Scottish forms, it was hospitably received in the United States along with the poems and novels of Sir Walter Scott in the early nineteenth century. *See* JOHN, JANE.

Jedidiah ♂ Hebrew, "friend-[is]-God." In the King James Version the passage (II Samuel 12:35) runs: "And he [Nathan] called his [Solomon's] name Jedidiah, because of the Lord." An explanatory note renders Jedidiah as "Beloved-of-the-Lord." Although the name fails to occur elsewhere in the Bible, its aptness for naming was clear, and it became, even before 1700, an established name, though never highly popular. Its use, however, was chiefly in New England, where its shortening, Jed, became a characteristic American form. The name lasted, in some degree, through the nineteenth century.

Jefferson ♂ From the family name, "son of Geoffrey." The name had some currency in the early twentieth century because of the hero-status of Thomas Jefferson. Its short form is Jeff, the handiness of which somewhat compensated for the awkward length of the whole.· Jefferson is, however, scarcely viable in the later twentieth century. Its most eminent bearer as a first name has been Jefferson Davis, president of the Confederacy.

Jeffrey ♂ The modern American spelling seems to have become dominant in the United States, but the older spelling, Geoffrey, maintains itself in Great Britain. Aside from its being Germanic, little is surely known about the etymology. Several names may have become mingled during the Middle Ages. The element *-frey* is quite possibly from the Germanic *frithu,* "peace."

Jeffrey in itself has been rare; its shortening, Jeff, has been commoner. Actually, Jeff may be from Jeffers, Jefferson, or some other family name, and may be to some extent a tribute to Thomas Jefferson or to Jefferson Davis (known as "Jeff").

Jehiel ♂ Hebrew, "God-lives." The name of eleven persons in the

Old Testament, none of them of any note. This very rare name may have been used because of the literal meaning.

Jehu ♂ Hebrew, "Jah-is-he." As a king of Israel, Jehu was both good and bad. His name became a conventional one for coachmen because of his furious driving. In colonial New England the name was occasionally used, probably in commemoration of Jehu's good deeds, which outweighed his bad.

Jemima, Kezia, Kerenhappuch ♀ In the last chapter of Job we are informed that that once-again-proposperous Uzzite had seven sons and three daughters. Curiously, considering the common attitude toward women in those benighted times, the names of the sons were not listed, while those of the three daughters were carefully recorded. And a strange trio they were—Jemima, Kezia, and Kerenhappuch!

We can consider it only as a fine manifestation of what Canon Bardsley termed as one of *The Curiosities of Puritan Nomenclature* that in the early New England records we find all three of these names. Just why they so appealed is difficult to ascertain, or even to guess at. The meanings are uncertain, though the Puritans, assuming the language to be Hebrew, probably took them as Jemima, "pure, fortunate"; Keziah, "cassia"; and Kerenhappuch, "horn-[receptacle]-for-eye-paint." Yet all three appear in the lists—even the grotesque and over-long Kerenhappuch.

This last, indeed, was rare. But Kezia was occasionally used clear down into the nineteenth century, and Jemima was an even better-established name.

One possibility is that the triad of names helped out at a time of that rare happening, a birth of girl triplets. From that point on Jemima and Kezia, having once got into the process of naming, could make it on their own, though Kerenhappuch could not.

Jenny, Jennie ♀ Diminutives of JANE. In an earlier period they were usually pronounced and even spelled Jinny. Jenny has come to be so completely an independent name that Jane has developed a new diminutive in Janey or Janie. The height of Jenny's popularity was around 1870, when it sometimes approached the top ten, or even reached it.

Jennifer ♀ The resemblance to Jennie is coincidental. The name is actually an English variant of Guenevere. It became suddenly popular in England *c.* 1950, probably because of its use by actresses. In the United States a similar but not so striking popularity occurred in the same period.

Jephthah ♂ Hebrew, "opposer." The literal meaning suggests that we have here a kind of nickname or descriptive epithet, such as appears with others of the judges (cf. GIDEON). Jephthah occurs, though rarely, among colonial names.

Jeremiah, Jeremias ♂ Hebrew, "high-[is]-God." As a major prophet and the name of one of the books of the Bible Jeremiah was well known, and the name was used during the period of biblical names, especially in New England. The English form Jeremy scarcely appears in America. Instead, the common shortening is Jerry (*see* GERALD). Jeremias is the Greek form.

Jeroboam ♂ Hebrew, "enlarger[?]." It occurs occasionally in America. The fact may be significant that the name of a successful rebel against a legitimate king had some appeal to the American colonists.

The large wine-jug known as a jeroboam may have been named with reference to the literal meaning or because Jeroboam himself was described as "a mighty man of valor . . . who made Israel to sin" (I Kings 11:28; 14:16).

Jerome ♂ The Greek-Latin form is Hieronymus, from which the English form has evolved. The name is chiefly associated with St. Jerome (5th century). As a nonbiblical saint he was not cherished by the Protestants, and his name has been rare in the United States.

Jerry, *see* GERALD, JEREMIAH, GERARD.

Jerusha ♀ In the Old Testament the name (possibly meaning "possession") occurs twice in colorless passages, but with clear reference to a woman. It was occasionally thus used in the United States during the period of biblical names.

Jessamine, Jessamyn ♀ The name is French, but as an alternate form for "jasmine" it goes back to Persian. Like most flower names (*see* LILY) it came into use in the later nineteenth century. It is a possible, though unlikely, source for JESSIE.

Jesse ♂ Hebrew, "God-is." Being the father of David, Jesse was a well-known biblical character, and his name was steadily used, though never attaining great popularity. Its usage seems to have arisen late, after 1750. As if in compensation, it remained in use at a later date than most of the biblical names, being still current as late as 1875.

Jessica ♀ Shakespeare used the name in *The Merchant of Venice*. Apparently it was his own coinage, perhaps aided by the analogy of such Hebrew names as Jesse. Not being truly Hebrew (and originally borne by a renegade), it makes little appeal to the Jewish community. But it carries Jewish connotations with the non-Jewish community. It has been little used in the United States. (*See* JESSAMINE.)

Jessie ♀ It is of uncertain origin, but with Scottish associations. It could be a diminutive of Jessica, or of Jesse, or of some other biblical name beginning with *jes-*. Withycombe gives, for England, no citation earlier than 1770, and some literary use; from then on she suggests a Romantic background. The situation is additionally curious in that we here have an apparent diminutive without a main form to which to refer it with confidence.

Jessie has never been common in the United States, but it enjoyed some mild popularity about 1880.

Jesus ♂ In the Anglo-American tradition of naming, Jesus is not used. Its occurrence may confidently be put down to the use of some other language, most commonly Spanish.

Jethro ♂ Hebrew, "preeminence." Quite possibly Jethro is a title, such as "Excellency." Such a meaning seems the more likely in that the same man (the father-in-law of Moses) is definitely mentioned as a priest, and is also called Raquel (or Reuel), "a-friend-is-God," a name of common Hebrew construction. In colonial New England Jethro occurred, but very rarely.

Jill ♀ A shortening of GILLIAN. The name has become much more popular than Gillian ever was, and exists as a moderately common independent name in the twentieth century.

Joab ♂ Hebrew, "God-is-father," the name of David's chief military commander. It occurs rarely in the period of biblical names.

Joachim ♂ Hebrew, "God-has-set-up." In the Apocryphal writings this is given as the name of the father of the Virgin Mary—whence St. Joachim. The name was not popular in England even before the Reformation, and it scarcely appears to have made the passage to America, where its few occurrences may be in foreign context. *See* JOAQUIN.

Joan, Johanna ♀ A feminization of John. It was popular in the Middle Ages, and may have been the original form of the adaptation, being from the northern French form Jehan. It remained popular throughout the sixteenth century, but by 1600 had apparently become commonplace, as Shakespeare's derogatory "greasy Joan" would suggest.

Though remaining current in the colonies and later, it has not been a popular name in the United States.

Joaquin ♂ The Spanish form of JOACHIM. It occurs in a Spanish context, and was adopted as a pseudonym by the nineteenth-century poet Joaquin Miller.

Job ♂ Various "suggested" meanings show themselves, rather too obviously, to be coined from the nature of its original bearer, e.g. "hated, persecuted." Rejecting such guesses, we must write the all-too-frequent gloss on Old Testament names, "Language and meaning uncertain."

Although the general suggestion of the name may be unpleasant, its brevity was a point in its favor, and it was viable during the period of biblical names.

Jocelyn, Joscelin ♂ ♀ Of Germanic origin, meaning uncertain. It was a common name among the Normans, but fell out of use in the fourteenth century. Originally it was a man's name, and it is so preserved in Great Britain. In the United States it is more commonly feminine, perhaps because of the analogy of Jacqueline. It is, however, a very rare name.

Jody ♂ ♀ Of uncertain, but recent, origin. It is sometimes feminine, and in such instances is to be conceived as a variant and diminutive of Judith. More commonly it is masculine, from Joseph or possibly Jude.

Joel ♂ Hebrew. Joining the two commonest terms for "God," the name could be translated as "God-is-God," or "Jehovah-is-God." Joel was viable in the period of biblical names and it still survives, its brevity and euphony counting in its favor. It is generally not abbreviated, probably so as to avoid confusion with Joseph in the form Joe.

John ♂ Hebrew, "God-is-gracious." In the Hebrew (Old Testament) form Johanan, and the Greek (New Testament) form Ioannes, it is the name of fourteen men mentioned in the Bible. With the advance of Christianity the name spread to many different languages, assuming different forms by phonetic development. Merely to list these variants would be beyond the scale of the present work. Those which have chiefly affected English (in addition is those of the classical languages) are Ian (Scottish), Evan (Welsh), Sean (Irish), Jean (French), Ivan (Russian), Hans (German), Juan (Spanish), Giovanni (Italian).

John passed readily into Christian use, but was much less popular in the Western Church than in the Eastern. The Anglo-Saxons, even after their conversion, retained their old names, though an occasional churchman took the name John. The early Crusades reestablished contacts with the East, and thus may have brought John back into usage. More likely, the more highly organized Church of the Norman period, by steady pressure, succeeded in building up the biblical names in contrast to the Anglo-Saxon names, with their partially pagan suggestion. By 1200 John had become a much used name.

This popularity sprang largely from the circumstance that two prominent saints (the Baptist and the Evangelist) bore the name, and that each of them also had a day of special festival. A child therefore had twice the ordinary chance, on a purely numerical basis, of being born on or near a festival of St. John. (Moreover, the Baptist was one of the most colorful of all saints.)

John came to lead the list. Thus, of 427 baptisms of males in London during the decade 1540–49, John is decisively in the lead with a quarter of the total—Thomas standing in second place, with only half as many. Since the English Puritans accepted biblical saints in some fashion (though rejecting their nonbiblical associates), the Reformation really aided the hegemony of John, since it cut down the competition. As a result, John is the usual leader of any English or American list.

In the early period as many as a fifth of all American men may have borne this name. In the last century, John has generally maintained leadership, though the percentage has declined, since there has been a tendency, because of larger population units, to keep away from very popular names.

The middle of the twentieth century, with its so-called counterculture, has seen some displacement of John in America. Even so, I have not actually seen it below fifth place.

The contrast with Britain is interesting. John has not led the list there since 1925, and in 1971 it was 17. In an Australian list for 1971 John sinks to its lowest point—25.

John is also remarkable in having well-established feminine forms—JANE, JEAN, JOAN, JOHANNA. The diminutive Johnnie (or Johnny) offers no difficulty. For the short form Jack, see the individual entry.

Johnson ♂ Though second only to Smith in its frequency as a surname, Johnson has not been much favored as a given name. For one thing, no notable American hero has borne it—though two unlucky Presidents have done their best. On the whole, moreover, there seems to be some prejudice against using one of the -*son* names as a given name.

Parents, indeed, probably think twice before labeling a child with a name that is already exceedingly common as a family name.

Jonah, Jonas ♂ Hebrew, but of uncertain meaning. Though a well-known biblical character, Jonah was inevitably linked to the whale, and was a somewhat humorous, unlikely, and grotesque figure. Understandably, namings for him were rare. When occurring, parents were likely to use the New Testament (Greek) form, Jonas.

Jonathan ♂ Hebrew, "God-gave." The name has essentially the same meaning as Nathaniel, Nathan, Theodore, etc. Known from the gallant prince, the son of King Saul, and as the friend of David, Jonathan entered English nomenclature shortly after the Reformation. In New England, however, it became much more popular, and in the summations that are available for the seventeenth century the name stands in the top ten. Its popularity continued to rise in the eighteenth century. In the Fourth

Regiment of the Connecticut Line (1781) Jonathan is in third place, exceeded only by John and William in the list of enlisted men and privates. Among officers, however, the name failed to make the top ten, a possible indication that it was already being considered as socially on the down side.

From contact with this regiment or others like it (which may even have harbored still larger proportions of Jonathans) the British at the siege of Boston applied the nickname "Brother Jonathan." The term "Brother" doubtless originated from the ideas of the basic brotherhood of the two English-speaking entities. There was nothing especially derogatory about the nickname, and it might even have been half affectionate, but any such term applied by the enemy in wartime is sure to be resented. Apparently the Americans showed their resentment, in one way, by ceasing to name their sons Jonathan. The use of the name fell off, and it did not again make the top ten at Harvard (allowance being made for a two-decade lag, while the new generation grew up).

The name fell, along with the general decline of the Old Testament names, and by 1840 it was almost extinct at Harvard. It has enjoyed some rise of popularity in the mid-twentieth century. The term Brother Jonathan, having lost its aptness, has also fallen out of use.

Some of Jonathan's popularity may spring from its resemblance to John, to which it can readily, in speech, be shifted.

Joscelin, *see* JOCELYN.

Joseph ♂ It is commonly explained as Hebrew, "increase, increaser." Quite possibly, however, it may be a word of unknown language, like many other names in Genesis. The name is borne by other biblical characters, notable among them the husband of Mary.

Since this latter Joseph was not especially of interest to the Puritans, we can assume that the numerous namings before 1900 have the patriarchal figure in mind. Afterward, as Joseph was falling in popularity among the Protestants, it began to receive Catholic support, especially from the important segment of population with Italian background—Giuseppe being readily shifted to Joseph.

There is no simple explanation for the popularity of Joseph among the colonists, eclipsing, as he does, the other patriarchal figures—Abraham, Isaac, and Jacob. The most famous incident of his life is probably his rejection of Pharaoh's daughter.

There is about Joseph a sometimes unpleasant holier-than-thou attitude. His exploitation of the people in favor of Pharaoh can be termed callous, and is certainly nondemocratic. Nonetheless, from the very beginnings of the Harvard lists the name stands high. Down to 1750 (a full century), Joseph made the top ten, regularly as fifth, fourth or third, and once reaching second place.

After 1750 Joseph began to decline at Harvard, and after 1820, still more. This was natural in a period when the biblical names were falling off in general. It frequently could not make the top ten, though it still remained active. It was, thus, one of the half-dozen biblical names continuing through that period to maintain some degree of popularity.

After 1900, in fact, the name had a revival at Harvard, reaching fifth place in 1915. The counterculture, however, has not adopted this ancient creature of the Establishment, and the name scarcely shows in their list.

The regular short form is Joe, with the not-much-used Joey being the diminutive. (Jo—indistinguishable in pronunciation—is the feminine form from Josephine, and its diminutive is Josey.)

An interesting testimony to the continuing popularity of Joseph is the use, in World War II, of G.I. Joe as the name of the ordinary American soldier, the equivalent of the British Tommy Atkins.

Josephine ♀ A French feminine-diminutive of Joseph, popularized in the nineteenth century by the Empress Josephine, Napoleon's wife. As with most of the feminine forms, it gained only enough vitality to keep it current.

Women so named are usually called Jo, and the name is thus spelled, leaving Joe as the masculine, though the reverse arrangement would be more closely analogous to usage with other names.

Joshua ♂ Hebrew, "God-saves." As the conqueror of Canaan (and a book of the Bible), Joshua was well known to the colonists, and the name was in use from the beginnings. Like most of the biblical names, its chief flourishing was in the hundred years from 1750 to 1850. It lingered in use, however, and turns up occasionally even now.

Josiah ♂ Hebrew, "God-supports." The Greek form Josias also appears. As the name of an unusually "good," though unfortunate, king of Judah, the popularity of the name during the period of biblical names requires no further explanation. Possibly, however, Josiah borrowed something from the vogue of Joseph, becoming a kind of substitute for that name, which was becoming very common.

    Josiah was increasingly used from 1750 onward, until the use of biblical names began to lapse about 1850—Josiah Royce, the philosopher (born 1855), being one of the later bearers of it. By 1900 it was nearly extinct.

Jotham ♂ Hebrew, "God is perfect." The three persons so named in the Old Testament are of no great importance. The actual meaning may well have been attractive enough to make the name viable in the colonial period.

Joy ♀ It seems to have been simply the English word applied as a name. It has been so rare as scarcely to be considered viable.

Joyce ♀ Germanic, but exact origins and meaning are uncertain. It was a much-used name in the Middle Ages—for either a man or a woman. By 1400, however, it had become restricted to women. It then went almost out of use, until a revival in the early twentieth century. Throughout this century it has remained current. The existence in the name of the word "joy" has probably been of service in establishing Joyce, since "joy" is a word of favorable suggestion.

Juba ♂ ♀ As *jub,* Puckett/Hiller give the word as West African, Hansa, meaning "anthill." In America it is a name for either a man or a woman, with numerous variants, e.g. Jubah, Juby. It occurs with some frequency until the decline of African names in the later nineteenth century—being, apparently, one of the names which were used by blacks only. Juba is also the name of two kings of North Africa, both of whom are mentioned in

Roman history. Slave-owners, who were in some instances familiar with the classics, may have retained the name because of this resemblance (*see* JUPITER).

Juba is also one of the "day-names" which occur widely in West African usage. As such it could be applied to a female or male child born on Monday. On the whole, however, these day-names seem to have had rather little influence in the United States. Possibly the system was decadent in Africa even before the time of slave trading. At best, being limited to seven names for each sex, the system called for supplementary names of some sort.

In practice we have Quash or Quashee (male, Sunday); Cudjo (male, Monday); Juba (primarily female, but sometimes male, Monday); Cuffee (male, Friday). Perhaps Phibba (female, Friday) merged with Phoebe. (See those names in the present book.)

Judah, Judas, Jude ♂ The name of the son of Jacob from whom a tribe and an Israelite kingdom took their names. In spite of this prominence in the biblical story, Judah appears so rarely in the American roster as to be almost nonexistent— a lack of popularity which may be attributed to a tendency to associate this name particularly with the Jews. It was also recognized as the Old Testament equivalent of Judas, the chief villain of the Christian story, and so was shunned. The short form Jude is equally rare.

Judith ♀ Hebrew, "Jewish woman," the chief character of the Book of Judith in the Apocrypha. The use of Tobias and of Susannah among the Puritans would show that they had no objections to names from the Apocrypha. Judith, however, was unused (as far as the available records show). Possibly Judith represented too strikingly the type of the aggressive woman to appeal to the Puritan mind.

Judith, for reasons unknown, showed some popularity in the South around 1800. In the rest of the nineteenth century and in the early twentieth, Judith scarcely was current.

Its popularity in the mid-twentieth century (often as Judy) may be in large part the result of the use of the name by the actress Judy Garland. In a list (Lawson's) of the 1970's Judith holds eighth place, and is thus a leading name.

Julius, Julian[a], Julia, Juliet ♂ ♀ Julius is the name of a Roman clan, especially known because of the historical prominence of Julius Caesar. Julian is from Julianus, a form current in the later Roman period.

As the name of a number of saints, Julian was well used in English during the Middle Ages. The more classical Julius appeared in the Elizabethan period. In the colonies these names made little showing before the later eighteenth century, at which period the classical influence worked in their favor, and they became current.

The usual feminines are Julia and Juliana (*see* GILLIAN). Juliet, based upon Shakespeare's heroine, appears rarely.

June ♀ The name probably originated from the suggestion of MAY—that is, from the idea of the name of a month being conceived as a fitting name for a girl, just as girls might bear the names of flowers or of gems. It is chiefly of the twentieth century in its use, and has never become common. *See* MAY, APRIL.

Juniata ♀ Though very rare, it appears in Loughead's list, and is remarkable for being a personal name taken from a natural feature—i.e. the Juniata River in Pennsylvania. The name was known from its use in a popular song of the nineteenth century. *See* ALFARETA.

Junius ♂ Latin, from a personal name, particularly in commemoration of the Roman revolutionary hero M. Junius Brutus. It occurred occasionally in the period of the popularity of classical names.

Jupiter ♂ Of the major Roman dieties only Diana and Minerva came into common use in America. Jupiter appears to have been used exclusively for blacks. Its origin may be tentatively ascribed to the use of JUBA, which frequently appeared as Jub and thus easily became Jup or Jupe which could, in turn, be taken as a shortening of Jupiter.

The name is a common one in early slave lists, but went out of use gradually after 1800.

Justin[e], Justina ♂ ♀ Latin, "just." This is a late Latin name, based upon St. Justina. It is very rare in the United States.

K

Karen ♀ A Scandinavian form of Katherine. In the twentieth century it has shown spectacular growth in the United States. At the opening of the century it was very rare, but among children born around 1950 the name stands high, often in the top ten. No particular reason is in evidence to account for such growth. It is probably somewhat influenced by the usage of the numerous Scandinavian immigrants. It is also a short and euphonic name.

Karl, *see* CARL.

Kate, *see* KATHERINE.

Katherine, Katharine, Catherine, Catharine ♀ The name goes back to a Greek form, Aikaterine, of which both origin and meaning are unknown. The Russian form, Ekaterina, is indebted to the Greek for its first letter. Latin rendered the name as Katerina or Katharina, thus making it a derivative of the Greek adjective *katharos,* "clean, pure," an apt and meaningful name for a virgin martyr. Though six saints bear the name, its popularity in western Europe rests upon the story of St. Catherine of Alexandria, which narrates the circumstances of her martyrdom c. 310.

The western nations inherited the Latin form, but early spellings differ greatly, the most common probably being Katerine. The use of *K* instead of *C* probably indicates that the name was brought into English by returning crusaders directly from the Greek, and not by way of the French, since that language scarcely uses *k*. The early use of *t* (instead of *th*) might, however, be taken to suggest French influence. Indeed, although details and exact dates are lacking, the use of C for K and of *th* for *t* apparently arose from the pedantic urge for "correctness" during the eighteenth century. The surprising fact is that this movement was successful in establishing the *th* pronunciation. (The actual pronunciation in Shakespeare's time is doubtless indicated by the spelling "Katrin.")

St. Catherine's cult can be traced in England from 1100. The name itself rapidly took root, and its shortened form Kate became one of the stalwart English names. The baptismal lists soon reflected that popularity by showing the name to be one of the most used. In particular, Kate became a characteristic name among the English.

Catherine survived the Reformation better than did most of the nonbiblical saints. Among the more vehement Protestants, naturally, her name could find no favor, since her very existence rested only upon dubious legends. Less fanatical English Protestants, however, refused to surrender Kate—one of them being William Shakespeare, who seems to have had a liking for the name.

With the multiplication of the Puritans in America, Katherine lost much ground, being really abandoned by that large segment of the speakers of English. In most of the birth records of New England in the seventeenth and eighteenth centuries, Katherine is simply missing. In the other colonies the name survived, although it was not very common. Kate began to be used as an independent name.

Then, in the nineteenth century, the situation began to improve. In a Vassar College list of 1868–73 Kate appears six times, and Katherine/Catherine stands also at six, a number sufficient to approach the top ten.

As the twentieth century has advanced, the popularity of Kate has fallen off, but Katherine/Catherine has continued to stand high.

Indeed, some of the popularity of Katherine undoubtedly

springs from the richness of its by-forms. In addition to the greatly favored Kate, the diminutive Kathleen (originally Irish) has come into such favor as often to exceed the original. So also it has gone with Karen (originally Scandinavian). Somewhat less numerous is the spelling variant Kathryn. Kitty, a favorite colloquial diminutive of the eighteenth century, has declined. On the other hand, Kay and Kathy have developed considerably.

In a high school list of girls born about 1955, the combined spellings of the name actually hold the number one position. The continuance of Katherine in one form or another—or several—thus seems highly probable.

Kathleen ♀ An Irish form of Katherine, it has become highly popular in the mid-twentieth century, and must be considered an independent name, in many lists outnumbering the basic Katherine.

Kathryn ♀ This is a variant of Katherine which became popular in the twentieth century, in some lists being more popular than Katherine itself.

Katina ♀ This variant of Katherine has become popular in the late twentieth century. Its detailed history is uncertain, but we should note that it is unusual in dropping the *r*-sound. It may be an American coinage.

Katrina ♀ A variant of Katherine, possibly of Slavic origin. It has become somewhat popular in the twentieth century.

Kay ♀ The name is a man's in the King Arthur story, but its modern use is as a shortening of Katherine. It has enjoyed some popularity in the twentieth century, and has tended to become a name in its own right.

Kenneth ♂ Celtic, "good-looking, handsome." A popular name in Scotland, it began to appear in America toward the end of the nineteenth century, enjoying a slight burst of popularity about 1880. It is still something of a favorite.

Kerenhappuch, *see* JEMIMA.

Keturah ♀ Hebrew, "fragrance." As the second wife of Abraham she was considered to be the ancestress of numerous tribes. Since suitable names for women are rather rare in the Bible, we need not be surprised that Keturah was occasionally used during the period of biblical names.

Kevin ♂ Irish, from Caoghin, "comely-birth." Long used in Ireland, it has been introduced into Irish contexts in the United States during the twentieth century, and has become moderately popular.

Kezia, *see* JEMIMA.

Kim ♂ ♀ Its origin is uncertain, but it fails to appear in lists which are currently available and date before the publication of Kipling's *Kim* (1896). That book was of some popularity. In it, as if to indicate that the name calls for explanation, Kim is noted carefully as a shortening of Kimball (a family name) the whole name being Kimball O'Hara. Kim, thus named, is a boy. In later usage Kim is a woman's name.

It showed some popularity about the middle of the twentieth century, even getting into the top ten. This popularity is probably due to the Hollywood cult, especially to the actress Kim Novak.

On the other hand, some recent lists give the name as Kimberly, which is basically a place-name, "Cynelwig's-clearing," Cynelwig being an Anglo-Saxon name for a woman.

Kitty ♀ As a derivative of Katherine, Kitty was popular in the sixteenth century, went out of fashion in the seventeenth, and was in again in the eighteenth, only to fall off a second time in the nineteenth. Though still viable, Kitty in general failed to return to popularity in the twentieth century.

L

Laban ♂ Like other names in Genesis, Laban is probably not Hebrew, but of some other language and of unknown meaning. In the story of Jacob, Laban occupies an important place. He was, however, a lumpish and unlovable person, and there was little in him to inspire naming. Still, for some reason, a few children of early New England bore that name.

Laetitia, Letitia ♀ Latin, "gladness, joy." This is apparently an abstract name, though names of that kind were rare in the Norman period, when this one developed. It was used in the thirteenth and following centuries, and was common enough to develop the shortened form Lettice. It lapsed in the seventeenth century, but enjoyed something of a revival in the Romantic period. It has always been rare in the United States, but Letty had some currency in the eighteenth and nineteenth centuries.

Laila, *see* LEILA.

Laura ♀ The etymology is uncertain, but the name is probably to be taken as a feminine of Laurence. The actual origin in modern English may be from its literary use in Petrarch's poetry, which was largely addressed to Laura.

Short, euphonic, romantic in its associations, Laura has been a well-established and active name in United States during the last two centuries, and so remains.

Laurel, *see* LILY.

Laurence, *see* LAWRENCE.

Lavinia ♀ It is of Latin form, but the etymology is uncertain. It is really of literary origin, being the name of Aeneas' second wife in the *Aeneid*. During the period of great classical interest, in the later sixteenth century, the name appeared in England. It was brought to the United States, but remained a rare name.

In the *Aeneid* the city of Lavinium is represented as having been named for Lavinia. More likely, Lavinia is to be conceived as deriving her name from that of the city, by a fictional process at some point.

Lawrence, Laurence ♂ Latin, from *laurus,* "laurel, bay tree," from which the ancient Latin town of Laurentium took its name. The medieval use of the name, however, sprang from St. Laurence of Rome, martyred, by being broiled on a gridiron, in A.D. 258.

Along with the other nonbiblical saints Lawrence was shunned by the Puritans, though the name was used a little in the Middle Colonies. In the twentieth century it increased in popularity considerably.

Older diminutives maintained the long vowel sound, and have resulted in family names such as Laurie and Lowry. In the twentieth century the form, with a short vowel, has become Larry.

Both the name itself and the diminutive Larry have been popular in Ireland, and part of the American usage is the result of Irish influence.

Lazarus ♂ A Graeco-Latin form of the Hebrew name ELEAZAR. In the United States it has been very rare and has probably been always used in a Jewish context.

Leah ♀ Like many other names in Genesis, this one may be of non-Hebrew origin. It can, however, be rendered in Hebrew as meaning "weary."

Leah was the first wife of Jacob. We are informed that she was "tender eyed," whatever that may mean.

There seems to be little reason to have used this name, but it had a continuing usage in early New England and lingered on into the nineteenth century until the general decline of biblical names.

Lee ♂ ♀ From the family name, which is derived from the Anglo-Saxon *leah,* meaning "meadow, glade, clearing," and signifies a dweller at such a place.

In the United States the given name is from the family name. It began to appear in the early nineteenth century, but its chief vogue arose after Robert E. Lee had become the heroic symbol of the Confederacy. Since Southern usage allowed a family name to be bestowed on a girl, many women were called Lee. As the memory of the Civil War dulled, the name spread to other parts of the country, used chiefly for men.

Leigh ♂ ♀ Pronounced identically with Lee, this name is actually derived from the Anglo-Saxon form *leah,* from which Lee also descends. On account of the identity of sound, Leigh has been, to some extent, identified with Lee. It is, however, in most lists, a minor name compared with Lee.

Leila, Laila ♀ Persian, etymology and meaning uncertain. Byron used this name for the heroine of his poem *The Giour* (1813), so that it is of clear literary origin. It has remained rare, but viable.

Lemuel ♂ Hebrew, probably "God-is-bright." The name occurs twice in Proverbs as that of a king, not further identified. Lemuel was viable throughout the period of the biblical names.

Lena ♀ A shortening of Helena, it had some use as an independent name in the nineteenth century. It may also be a shortened form of Pauline and other names ending in *-ina.*

Leo, Leon, Lionel ♂ Latin, "lion." The name scarcely exists in the United States before 1850, but shows some increase in the late nineteenth century, probably because of Jewish influence. It remains rare. Lionel is from a French diminutive form, but has become an independent name. Leon can possibly be in some instances from Eleonora.

Leonard ♂ Germanic, "lion-bold." The name was established as that of a fifth-century saint. Like those of other nonbiblical saints, the name went out of favor with the Reformation. Around the middle of the eighteenth century it began to make a reappearance, and it has continued to be viable down to the present, along with its diminutive, Lenny.

Leonor, Lenore, Leonora, Leonore ♀ Probably the name was derived from Eleanor. Its various spellings suggest borrowing from different languages—e.g. Leonora being Italian, and Lenore being German. The name apparently is a poetic borrowing in the Romantic period (early 19th century). Two famous poets who made much of it were Poe and Bürger. Though always rare, the name has remained viable, even through the period of the counterculture.

Leopold ♂ Germanic, "people-bold." It has been very rare in the United States, appearing in a German context.

Le Roy, Leroy ♂ French, "the king." It occurs as a rare family name, and thence was adopted as a given name in the mid-nineteenth century. It remained viable through the rest of that century, but has tended to decline since 1900.

Leslie, Lesley ♂ ♀ From the family name (especially Scottish), in literal meaning probably to be distantly connected with Latin *laetitia,* "gladness." In the United States it began to be used as a given name in the later nineteenth century. It soon became a woman's name, perhaps because the endings suggested a feminine in American usage. It has remained viable, but not common, in the twentieth century.

Lester ♂ From the family name, which is from Leicester, the English city and county. It developed somewhat as a given name in the twentieth century.

Letitia, *see* LAETITIA.

Levi ♂ The name of a son of the patriarch Jacob, and the tribe thus designated. It occurs rarely in the name rosters of early New England. Going out of use with the general decline of Old Testament names, it maintained some special popularity in Jewish use throughout the later nineteenth century.

Lewis, Louis ♂ Germanic, from *hlu,* "hear," and *viga,* "fight." As a royal name it enters the record with the Frankish king (466–511) whose name commonly appears in English as Clovis. From Clovis it soon became shifted in French to Louis. It was brought to England after the Norman Conquest, at first

173

appearing in numerous spellings, but eventually being standardized as Lewis.

As representing the English pronunciation, Louis and Lewis are about equally good, but the spelling with the w is more characteristic of English (the French lacking a w in common usage).

The American colonists were not especially fond of the name, but a few instances occur, nearly always spelled Lewis. After 1780, however, the name became commoner, and the Louis spelling also occurred more noticeably. Naturally, we would tend to ascribe such shifts to the French alliance in the Revolution and the cultural drift away from England after Independence. But these conclusions must be left as general inferences, not statistically founded facts.

In time, however, the shift became more notable—e.g. at Princeton in the period 1900–1906 there were 21 occurrences of the name, of which only seven were of the w spelling.

In the same list, we should notice that the number of the combined figures for the two spellings puts Louis/Lewis only a little below the top ten. Again we may suspect the influence of France, so often the dictator of style. We do not find, for example, Ludwig, the German form.

In the end, however, we must admit to an anticlimax. In the last generation no one has paid much attention to the name and the question of spelling merely vanishes along with the near-vanishing of the fine old name itself.

Lib, Libbie ♀ Although ordinarily taken to be an independent name, Lib is a variant of Elizabeth. The unusual sound-shift (z becoming b) is doubtless to be attributed to baby-talk, with Lizzie being the first stage. Lib was a fairly common name in the nineteenth century.

Lillian ♀ Probably a derivative in baby-talk from Elizabeth. It occurs in England in the sixteenth century, and so can have come to America with the earliest immigrants. It has enjoyed some popularity, standing 23 in Smith's list for the early twentieth century. It was known from the actresses Lillian Russell and Lillian Gish. The former, however, had adopted it as a stage-name before herself becoming well known.

Lily, and the flower-names. ♀ Except for the special cases (*see* ROSE, DAISY), the naming habits of the speakers of English did not include the giving of flower-names to women. The custom began about 1850, and by 1900 had spent what little vigor it had possessed. One difficulty was that many of the possible names were already preempted and could not well be used for women, e.g. Poppy and (while Greek dictionaries lasted) Orchid. As followers, came Iris, Violet, Viola, and also the flowering bushes, such as Heather, Azalea.

Individually, the flower-names were negligible; as a group, they gave a touch of variety to the later nineteenth century.

Lincoln ♂ From the family name, which originally indicated a man from the town or county of that name in England. General Benjamin Lincoln was one of the heroes of the Revolutionary War, and a few names may thus have arisen. Of much greater importance as a hero has been Abraham Lincoln.

Since Abraham was disappearing in the general decline of biblical names, anyone wishing to name a child after the chief Union hero of the Civil War would be likely to use the name Lincoln. Though not highly popular, Lincoln remains a viable name.

Linda ♀ Probably from Spanish, *linda,* "beautiful [feminine]." Withycombe derives it from Germanic *lind,* "serpent," from which we have Rosalind and other names. The Spanish origin, however, seems more likely.

Linda has had, in any case, a strange history. It began to show in America only in the last decades of the nineteenth century. It advanced in a remarkable thrust, and in the decade 1940–50 can be found—on one list, at least—as the commonest name. The reaction, however, hit sharply, and Linda became rare.

The rise and fall of Linda shows similarly in the British lists. In 1925 Linda did not show in the list of *The Top Fifty First Names for Girls.* In 1950 it was in second place. By 1971 it had fallen to fortieth.

Linus ♂ From the name of the saint, a first-century Pope. It has scarcely been viable in modern times, except as made known by the comic strip Peanuts.

Lisa ♀ It is obviously from Elizabeth, but its more detailed history is not clear. English handling of the situation should give us Liz, so we may consider it likely that Lisa is taken from some other language. Yonge, in her tabulation, shows Lisa in Portuguese, and very similar forms in the Slavic languages and German. It was scarcely in existence before the nineteenth century, and its chief usage has been in the twentieth. At the present time it is within the top ten in most lists.

Lloyd ♂ Welsh, "gray." In the beginning it may have been applied to a gray-haired man. Its use in the United States is probably from the family name. It can be traced from the eighteenth century, but has never been common.

Loammi ♂ Hebrew, "not-my-people." This is a fictitious name coined by Hosea, the prophet (see Hosea 1:9). The clear and unusual meaning may account for its usage, since it could identify a family which wished to attain separateness. It appears rarely in the period of biblical names.

Lois ♀ Probably Greek, meaning not known. Lois, Timothy's grandmother, is mentioned only once in the Bible (II Timothy 1:5), where she is commended for her faith.

The name occurs in New England lists as early as the 1680 decade, but it was not popular. A revival of the name occurred in the early twentieth century, for unknown reasons. It remains an active name—one of the few biblical names for which that connection seems to be wholly forgotten.

Lola, Lolita ♀ The Spanish form Lola arose by the use of *dol-* from Dolores with an *l* substituted for the less euphonic *r,* an uncommon practice in Spanish, though common in baby-talk transformations in English. It has been in rare usage in the twentieth century. *See* DOLORES.

Lorane, *see* LORRAINE.

Loretta ♀ The *-etta* is the Italian feminine-diminutive ending, and *Lor-* is probably to be taken as an Italian abbreviation of Lawrence. It was probably introduced as a stage-screen name in Hollywood in the early twentieth century. In the Smith list (1941) it was 50, but it quickly declined from that high point, and in the later twentieth century it has been little used.

Lorna ♀ Coined (1869) by R. D. Blackmore for the heroine of his novel *Lorna Doone*. The novel became highly popular. He himself apparently borrowed from Lorne, used as a place-name and for a title (Marquess of Lorne) in Scotland. The name was not much used in the United States, but is still viable.

Lorraine, Loraine, Lorane ♀ The origin is uncertain, but may be from the French province, used as a given name by Romantic poets to whom the euphonic quality of the *l-r-n* structure would have been highly appealing.

Its connections are American, and it shows an occasional example as early as 1820. The first spellings were Loraine. The double-*r* spelling became predominant in the twentieth century, possibly because Alsace-Lorraine became well known in connection with the wars of 1870–71 and 1914–18. (The province itself is from a French version of the name of its ninth-century ruler, Lothaire.)

Possibly stimulated by the "Alsace-Lorraine problem," Lorraine grew more popular toward the end of the nineteenth century. In Smith's list of 1941 it is 26, borne by more than half a million American women. Since then its popularity has fallen off sharply, but it still remains viable, sometimes with the Loraine spelling.

The thoroughly American nature of the name is shown by its failure to appear in such exhaustive British lists as those of Yonge (1863) and Withycombe (1945).

Not to be altogether rejected is the possibility of a name manufactured from Laura and Anne.

Lottie ♀ To arrive at Lottie, Charlotte (already with the French diminutive *-lotte*) was further altered by the English diminutive *ie*. Thus, finally, all that was left of the original name was one letter! The name was fairly popular during the nineteenth century.

Louis, *see* LEWIS.

Louisa, Louise ♀ The names are, respectively, the Latin and French feminines of Louis. They came into English usage during the seventeenth century, a time of strong French influence.

Louise became the prevailing form in the eighteenth century and later. It then became a fairly popular name, and so remains.

Lucille ♀ In form the name is French, but it is derived from the Latin form Lucilla, the name of an obscure third-century saint. Actually, Lucilla may well be a diminutive of Lucy, and, like Lucy, Lucilla was the head of a band of martyrs. *The Book of Saints* makes the practical suggestion that the records may have "somehow in ancient times got mixed up together."

Lucille has been rare, but has remained viable in the twentieth century.

Lucinda ♀ It is apparently a seventeenth-century poetic coinage from Lucy and one of the names ending in -*inda*, e.g. Belinda. It had some currency in the nineteenth century.

Lucretius, Lucretia ♂ ♀ Latin, the name of a sub-tribe, is to be connected with *lux*, "light," or *lucrum*, "profit." The masculine has scarcely been used, but the feminine has been viable, though rare.

Lucy ♀ The Graeco-Latin element *luc-* or *lyk-* appears in several names, and has itself a considerable range of meaning, e.g. "light," "wolf," "Lucanian" (from a tribal name). It also supplies various personal names, e.g. Lucy, Lucius, Lucia, Luke, Lucian.

Lucy was a martyr of the fourth century whose cult became popular in England during the Middle Ages. With the Puritan antipathy to nonbiblical saints, Lucy went out of common use in the sixteenth and seventeenth centuries. It had a revival in the nineteenth century, but has fallen off in the twentieth. In Smith's list of 100 in the early twentieth century, Lucy holds the last place.

Ludmilla ♀ Of Slavic origin, "people-love [?]." Although a recognized saint's name, Ludmilla has been used almost entirely in a Slavic or Baltic context and is scarcely viable in American usage.

Luke ♂ Greek, from the word for "wolf," or else from the place-name Lucania.

Though universally known to the colonists as the name of the third Evangelist, Luke was little used. It seems to have been somewhat more common in the country than in the towns, and there has thus been a suggestion of rusticity about it. Unlike MARK, Luke has failed to show a twentieth-century popularity. A suggestion of this rusticity may linger in the rhymed nonsense-saying, "Shoot, Luke! And give up your musket," possibly a Civil War product.

Lulu ♀ Probably a reduplicated form of Louise in which a baby-talk term of affection has been carried across into maturity. It was fairly common in the late nineteenth century.

Luther ♂ From the family name of Martin Luther, the Protestant reformer. The name may mean "lute-player," though one hesitates to ascribe such frivolous activities to the ancestors of such a serious figure.

As a commemorative, the name was particularly cultivated among those of the Lutheran Church, who in the colonies were nearly all Germans and were strong in the Middle Colonies. Understandably, therefore, the name is much commoner at Princeton than at Harvard. Though showing no special popularity in the twentieth century, it still remains viable.

Lydia ♀ Greek, "Lydian woman." In ancient Greece a slave was often named from the country of origin, and Lydia was apparently thus derived. A certain Lydia is mentioned once in the Bible (Acts 16:14). Since women's names in the New Testament are rather rare, this one was readily adopted.

Lydia was a popular name among the Puritans, often rating in the top ten, generally as seventh or eighth. Even after the decline of biblical names it remained viable, and a certain usage of it still survives.

The short form Lyde may be from Lydia, but in actual practice seems more likely to be from Elizabeth.

Lyndon ♂ The history of the name is not certain, but it may be from a family name which has been derived from the name of a village, "linden-hill." *See* BARRY.

Lynette ♀ Celtic (Welsh), of uncertain meaning. Made familiar in the mid-nineteenth century by Tennyson's *Idylls of the King*, it appears occasionally, and was probably conceived of as being a diminutive for Lynn. It may have slightly aided the development of LYNN.

Lynn, Linn ♂ ♀ In its curious history Lynn can be traced down through many centuries. It appeared first as the Celtic (ancient British) word for "pool." Various places thus took their names, and the Anglo-Saxons and Normans preserved them— notably in the town of King's Lynn. In turn, various people (presumably those who went to some other town) adopted the surname Lynn, or had it thrust upon them. A few of these Lynns came to America, though they were never a large family. Nevertheless, in the nineteenth century the name began to turn up as a given name for a man.

In the twentieth century, however, Lynn not only became much more numerous, but also became a woman's name. The manner of this development, though unusual, seems to be clear enough.

In the early twentieth century the language included many names ending in *-line*. Notably there was Caroline, which was formed by *Carol* with *-ine* as a French suffix. Not many Americans, however, knew or cared about the historical origin of the name, and they apparently took it to be *Caro* and *-line*. Moreover, the *i* of *-line* was usually pronounced as a short vowel, and so suggested the spelling *-lin*.

Several other things then happened.

First, the spelling with a *y* became the common one. It represented, perhaps, only a fancy for something new. Or it may have been an idea that *-lyn* was the better spelling to represent a short vowel. Or it may have been because the family name was often spelled Lynn.

Second, Lynn (or Linn) became in itself a given name, borne by women. At the same time it went out of use for men. But this name did not attain much popularity.

Finally, *lyn* (and sometimes *lin*) came in most people's understanding to be conceived not so much as a name in itself, but more as a name-element, a suffix, which could be a kind of building-block for new names. By this time (the earlier part of the 20th century) many of the great names such as Mary and Katherine had been so often used over the years that people were apparently becoming tired of them. The suffix *-lyn* therefore gave a touch of novelty.

Caroline (where the idea most likely began) was the first of the new names to develop—as Carolyn. Marilyn soon caught up with it, and passed it—standing at 42 in the Smith list (1941) as against Carolyn, which was 86. Less popular but still in good evidence were such names as Kathalyn, Donnalyn, Bonnylin, Jaquelyn, Judylynn. Names which already had the *-ine* ending were especially easy to shift, so that Madeline gave rise to Madelyn.

An associated movement, but one working in an opposite way, resulted in names which used the long-vowel pronunciation, such as Norahlene, Michaelene, and Saralene. Sometimes a desire for new spellings seemed to run away with things, so that Charlotte yielded Sharlene.

From a rather conservative beginning Lynn thus came into alliance with the strong twentieth-century tendency—actually to coin names.

M

Mabel ♀ From the Latin *amabilis*, "lovable." The name is probably a post-classical usage. It appeared in England after the Conquest. It must have been much used, since it was worn down to the much shortened Mabel. It thus ceased to be meaningful, though some people took it as "my beautiful one" in French.

The name fell into disuse after the fifteenth century, but was revived toward the end of the nineteenth. In a list of the decade 1890–99 Mabel stands in fifth place but, as often happens when a name thus becomes suddenly popular, the reaction was quick, and Mabel after a decade or two again became a rare name.

Madel[e]ine, Magdalen ♀ Hebrew, "woman of Magdala," known in medieval usage as St. Mary Magdalene, who was closely associated with Christ in the Gospels. Madeline represents the French form. Magdalen[e] is closer to the Greek, and is the traditional English form.

The name reached some popularity in the later Middle Ages, and developed the short form Maudlin, which in its turn became a common adjective, meaning "excessively affectionate," probably reflecting the traditional manner in which the part was rendered in the miracle plays.

The Protestants, though on the evidence of the Scriptures

they might accept her penitence, saw no reason to name their daughters after one who in earlier life was recorded as a flamboyant sinner. Nor, indeed, did the English-speaking Catholics, either, do much for the name.

Its revival is essentially literary, and particularly to be connected with the revival of medievalism in the Romantic period of the early nineteenth century.

The name had some circulation in the mid-twentieth century counterculture, even appearing in such variants as Madelyn. Some use of the name of the sinner-saint seems natural for those who so often seem to go by opposites.

Madison ♂ The fourth President was not widely popular and scarcely attained a hero's reception, but his name came handily to the tongue. It has furnished a moderately popular name.

Magdalen, *see* MADEL[E]INE.

Mahalah ♀ Hebrew, probably "tenderness." It appears once in the Bible, there referring to a man. In its rare modern usage, however, it is a woman's name, probably because the ending *-ah* is more commonly so used.

Mahershalalhashbaz ♂ Hebrew, occurring only in the first three verses of Isaiah 8. It is a symbolic name for a "son" of Isaiah, and was written at the time of a threatened invasion. Translated, it is "hasten the spoil, rush upon the prey."

It "is said" to be, with its 18 letters, the longest name in the Bible. Who established this fact we do not know, but no one is likely to challenge it.

Obviously the name has qualities (beyond its length) that are mysterious, grotesque, and even poetic, and such names may appeal to an occasional parent who is looking for a name for his child.

At least one American (in 1668, a citizen of Rhode Island) bore this name. One wonders what he was called in ordinary speech—Hash, perhaps, or Buzz. Bardsley records several examples in England, extending into the nineteenth century. (Cf. SHEARJASHUB.)

Mahlon ♂ Probably Hebrew, "mild[?]." He was the first husband of Ruth, and the name was occasionally used in early New England.

Maisie ♀ A Scottish variant of Margaret, usually being conceived of as an independent name.

Malachi ♂ Hebrew, literally "My-messenger," often expanded as "messenger-of-God," the title of the last book of the Old Testament. It is chiefly used in Ireland, where it replaced some of the native names. By the time of the great Irish immigration to the United States in the mid-nineteenth century the tradition had been lost, and Malachi is scarcely used as an American name.

Malcolm ♂ Celtic, "disciple-or-servant-of-[St.]-Columba." This favorite Scottish name began to be current in the United States about 1800. It has remained steadily in use, though never reaching heights of popularity. At the present time it appears to be comparatively out of favor.

Malvina, Melvina ♀ The name appears as that of a character in the so-called Ossianic poems (1760–63), and was presumably coined by James Macpherson, the author of those works. He may have modeled the name upon an Irish original, such as *maol-mhin*, "smooth-snow."

   Although the name never became popular, it appears occasionally, most commonly in the Romantic period, i.e. the earlier nineteenth century.

Manasseh ♂ The name has been rendered in English as "causing-forgetfulness," but this is upon the assumption that is Hebrew. Quite possibly, like so many names in Genesis, it is of some language other than Hebrew. It was never popular in America, and with the decline of the biblical names Manasseh seems to have vanished.

Manfred ♂ Germanic, *mana*, "man," and *frithu*, "peace." It was a Norman name, but never popular in England. It had a slight revival in the nineteenth century as a Romantic name, e.g. in the poem by Byron.

Manuel, *see* EMANUEL.

Marc ♂ *See* MARK. The form represents a variant which has become somewhat popular in the twentieth century.

Marcia ♀ From the Latin form *marcius*, having to do with the tribe of that name; probably the tribal name is from the name of the god Mars. In common thought, Marcia is regarded as the feminine of Mark or Marcus. In recent times when Mark has increased in popularity, Marcia also has shown consider-able growth. In modern usage it is sometimes spelled Marsha.

Margaret, Margot, Marguerite, Margery ♀ Greek, *margarites,* "pearl." The popularity of the name derives from St. Margaret of Antioch (3rd century) who became (along with Barbara, Agnes, and Katherine) one of the four great virgin martyrs. In a colorful apocryphal biography she is made (like St. George) a dragon-slayer. She was known in England even in Anglo-Saxon times. Equally early, she seems to have become es-tablished in Scotland, where she was extremely popular. A clear evidence of her popularity is to be seen in the myriad of abbreviations and diminutives, both English and Scottish— Marge, Madge, Maisie, Maggie, Meg, Peg, Mamie, and others.

As a nonbiblical saint, Margaret almost disappeared with the Reformation, and even in the nineteenth century it was not a common name in the United States. A strong revival, how-ever, occurred in the early twentieth century.

The French form Margot has become somewhat popular in the mid-tenth century, sometimes being spelled Margo to cor-respond more closely to the pronunciation. Marguerite, also a French form, was popular in the nineteenth century but has declined in the twentieth. A third French form, spelled Margery or Marjorie, dates from the twelfth century and has, over most of the time, been considered an independent name.

Variants which are formed from the end-sounds occur chiefly in German, e.g. Gretchen and Greta. These forms have been used in the United States chiefly in German context.

Maria ♀ It is the Latin form of Mary, and also occurs in Span-ish, Italian, and several other languages. The eighteenth cen-tury was notable for its cultivation of the classics, and this Latin form became popular at that time. Its popularity has fluctuated, but Maria has always remained a viable name.

The traditional pronunciation in English has called for the *i* to be pronounced as is the sound in "high." In recent times, probably because of Spanish analogies, the *i* is often pro-nounced as is the double -*e* in "see."

Marian, *see* MARION.

Marie ♀ The French form of Mary. Down to the nineteenth century it was not much used except in French context. It has become merely another variant of Mary, however, and since the opening of the nineteenth century it has been a well-used name in wholly American situations.

Marilyn ♀ A twentieth-century coinage from the familiar MARY and LYNN. Its growth was certainly influenced by the popularity of the actress Marilyn Monroe.

Marion, Marian ♂ ♀ The history of the name is complicated. In the Middle Ages, English made much use of diminutive suffixes, one of which was -*in,* also appearing as -*on, -un.* Thus with Mary, it yielded Maryon—or, as commonly spelled, Marion. Both Robin Hood and Maid Marion, those basic popular characters, bore names formed with this diminutive. The family name Marion also was so derived. Early spellings indicate -*on* as the normal form.

In the early nineteenth century Marion (referring regularly to women) became more common. From the pronunciation the idea developed that the name was really Mary Ann, one of the doublets which were increasingly popular at that time. Apparently by this route the form Marian developed, being restricted to women's names. The status of the -*on* ending thus suggested a new name for men.

In the later nineteenth century the situation was highly confused. The woman's name was generally -*an,* but might retain the tradition of -*on.* The man's name was regularly -*on.* Such man-woman name pairs have not, however, been popular in English, and this (we may say) attempt of the men to invade women's territory made little advance, and seems to be now of small moment.

Insofar, however, as Marion gave the original suggestion of double names, such as Mary Ann, it may be held of much importance.

Mark ♂ From Marcus, a Latin name which is probably derived from Mars, the name of the war-god. Of the four Evangelists, Mark has traditionally been the least used as a personal name. Indeed, it scarcely appears before 1800. It had, however, a sudden run of popularity beginning in the early twentieth century. In one list of children born *c*. 1955 Mark stands in a three way tie for fourth place.

There is no clear reason for this popularity. In a changing social time, we may suppose, many namers viewed with favor the fact that Mark (well known but little used) could be taken for something new without actually being any decisive break with the past.

Marlene ♀ German, probably a manufactured name from Mary or Margaret or Martha, combined with Lena, from Helen or Helena. In the United States it has developed chiefly from the publicity accorded the actress Marlene Dietrich. It is a fairly popular name in the later twentieth century. The pronunciation varies: it can be of two or three syllables.

Marmaduke ♂ Probably Celtic, from Maelmadoc, "servant-of-Madoc." This name, rare in England, began to make an occasional appearance in the United States at the end of the nineteenth century. It is probably to be classed with the feudal names—Howard, Percy, etc. It never caught on, and is probably now extinct in America.

Martha ♀ The derivation is from the local (Aramaic) speech of New Testament Palestine, meaning "woman" or "lady." (Cf. SARAH, DONNA, etc.)

The biblical Martha (Luke 10; John 11, 12) is represented at housewifely duties, such as preparing meals ("cumbered about much serving"). With a touch almost of modernism she complains that her sister does not help, and Martha herself is therefore gently rebuked by her Lord.

The Puritan father, who was largely concerned with the naming of his children, was thus in an ambivalent position with the name. He approved Martha's devotion to family duties, but he could not escape the rebuke.

Martha was in use from the earliest colonization, after showing up as fairly common and reaching low positions in the first ten. It was about equally used in the Puritan colonies and in the South, where Martha Washington gave it almost regal status.

Throughout the new nation the name was common enough to allow the by-forms Matty and Patty to assume independence. Less used in the nineteenth century, Martha was one of the few biblical names to throw off the suggestion of being out-of-date and to attain, in the twentieth century, a moderate popularity.

If its by-forms were included, the popularity of Martha would be considerably enhanced. Besides the already mentioned Matty and Patty, the influence of Martha is probably to be seen in the enigmatical Marsha and in the common diminutive Marty (also a family name). Martha may, moreover, have influenced Marcia (actually to be connected with Marcus) and Patsy (also to be taken as from Patricia).

Martin ♂ From the Latin form Martinus, a diminutive of Martius, "of-Mars." Much used in medieval England, it scarcely survived the prejudice against the names of nonbiblical saints. It gradually came into use again, with President Van Buren (born 1782) being one of its prominent bearers, though he was commonly known as "Little Van." Martina is a modern adaptation for a woman's name.

Mary ♀ The name arose from an unusual development of the same name that is elsewhere given as Miriam, occurring in the early Hebrew texts as M-R-Y-M. The Greeks (e.g. in the Septuaguint) rendered this as Mariam. Speakers of Latin, however, apparently took the final *m* as the sign of the accusative case, and then assumed a nominative, Maria.

The Vulgate followed this course, inconsistently rendering the name of the mother of Jesus (and of those others of the New Testament) as Maria and the name of the sister of Moses as Miriam. The tremendous authority of the Vulgate assured the adoption of that usage in the languages of western Europe. In English the accent shifted to the first syllable, in accordance with the usual practice in that language.

The name was not in general use before 1200, partly—it would seem—because it was considered too holy. The development of the so-called "cult of the Virgin" apparently brought Mary into common use, however.

The Reformation, in the first half of the sixteenth century, deemphasized the role of Mary, and the popularity of the name suffered somewhat. The Protestants did not actually reject it, but its use fell off during the later sixteenth century—partly because of the unpopularity of "Bloody" Mary and of Mary Queen of Scots.

By the time of the English colonization of America, Mary had again risen in popularity, and it generally shows up in any American list as the most used name. In the later twentieth century, however, it fell off sharply, though usually still remaining in the first ten.

Generally speaking, modern usage accepts as "independent" the names Miriam, Maria, and Marie, together with a few other "foreign" forms. The diminutives are less certain, but Marian and May seem to be established on their own. The *l*-form was originally Mal or Mally, but eventually became Molly, from which Moll developed naturally. Poll and Polly represent still further variations, probably arising from babytalk. In general, these *l*-forms of Mary have not become independent. (*See* MIRIAM.)

Matilda, Maud[e] ♀ Germanic, "strength, battle." The Latin form was Matilda; Maud is a French development. Matilda was the name of the wife of William the Conqueror. From that time on, Matilda (and, later, Maud) flourished as English names, though declining in popularity in the fifteenth to eighteenth centuries. Matilda enjoyed a slight revival in the later eighteenth century, as Maud did in the nineteenth. Tennyson's popular poem *Maud* probably helped to increase interest in that name.

Matthew ♂ Etymology uncertain, but presumably a Greek rendering of some Hebrew or Aramaic name. It was universally known among the Puritans as the name of the first Evangelist, though the early colonists were not fond of the name. From 1700 on, however, it is steadily viable at Harvard, and rather more favored at Princeton and in the non-Puritan colonies generally. The alternate form, Matthias, also occurs—probably being especially favored among colonists of German background.

Chiefly as Matthew, the name has remained viable. In the mid-twentieth century it even appears in the first ten.

Maureen ♀ Irish, Mairin, a diminutive of Mary. It began to appear in the twentieth century, but has never attained popularity.

Maurice, Morris ♂ Latin, *Moor*. The name enjoyed a considerable vogue in the Middle Ages because of the cult of the saint. As the name of a nonbiblical saint, it went out of favor with the Reformation.

It has never regained much popularity, but the English-American form Morris has been commonly used in Jewish contexts.

Mavis ♀ The capture of ROBIN opened up the possibility of using other birds' names for women. In spite of our feathered friends' many indications of a vigorous love life, the smaller birds have generally been conceived, linguistically, as feminine. Quail has appeared in modern lists. So have Mavis and Merle, but, curiously, neither of these names is used as a common term in the United States, and the origin is probably literary, both of these songsters being used in Scott's line, "When mavis and merle are singing."

On the whole, ornitholatry (as it might be called) has made little progress, and seems to offer equally little chance for the future—few parents, we may conclude, caring to call a daughter Ostrich, Flycatcher, or Turkey.

Max ♂ The Emperor Frederick III coined the name Maxmilian from those of two classical Romans whom he admired—Fabius Maximus and Scipio Aemilianus. Thus originating in the fifteenth century, the name became a popular one in Germany, usually shortened to Max. In the United States it has been a rare name, regularly Max. Its occurrences can usually be ascribed to German influence.

Maxine has been coined for a feminine, with occasional variants such as Maxime, Maxima, and Maxa.

May ♀ The name is a rendering of Mary in baby-talk. It indicates another method by which a child escapes the difficulty of *r* (as in Molly). Also as possible origins may be Margaret, Mabel, and even other names.

May carries with it the pleasant suggestions of spring. The name flourished chiefly in the nineteenth century, but failed to become numerous.

The remarkable feature of May, however, is not as an independent name, but its great popularity as a middle name or a combining unit. Thus we have very commonly in the later nineteenth century the appearance of such forms as Idamay or Ellamay. (*See* JUNE.)

In Middle English *may* was a common noun, meaning "maiden, girl." Whether this usage influenced modern speech is uncertain. May also is fairly common as a family name. Then, too, it must sometimes have been used with reference to the month, and thus have encouraged the usage of June and April.

Mehetabel ♀ Hebrew. Translations vary between "God-is-doing-good" and "God-makes-happy." The first of these seems more likely among the Puritans. First listed in 1650, the name remained steadily in use. What its appeal was is hard to specify. The people bearing that name in the biblical text are altogether unimportant. The name is moderately euphonic, but the Puritans were not greatly impressed by euphony. Possibly the literal meaning was sufficient.

During more than a century Mehetabel was popular enough in New England to stand frequently in the lower part of the top ten, or just below it.

Instead of dying out as the biblical names became unpopular, Mehetabel continued for a while by shifting to its short form Hetty, which served as an independent name. The spelling Mehitabel also occurs.

Melanchthon ♂ From the family name of Philip Melanchthon, Protestant leader and associate of Luther. The name was originally Schwartzerd, "black-earth," in German, which was translated into Greek, as was sometimes done during the time of the enthusiasm for Greek studies during the Renaissance.

The name makes only an occasional appearance in the United States. (Cf. LUTHER.)

Melanie ♀ Greek, "black." It has never become popular, though made known from its use for a character in *Gone with the Wind*. It is also the name of two saints.

Melchizedek ♂ Hebrew, "king-holy." In Genesis, where the names are generally of doubtful Hebrew origin, we have here a name which is clearly of that language. It was of rare usage in early New England.

Melinda ♀ Probably a coined name of the twentieth century, fusing Linda with *mel-*, which appears in such names as Melanie and Melody. Belinda also could serve as a model. Melinda is fairly popular in the later twentieth century.

Melissa ♀ Greek, "bee," a name known in classical Greek. It has been traditionally of rare occurrence in English, but is to be considered viable. In the mid-twentieth century it became suddenly popular, for no easily determined reason.

Melody ♀ No source of the name is known except the ordinary English word. It occurs sporadically in England from 1800 on. In the United States, in the mid-twentieth century, it has shown some activity, perhaps as a part of the counterculture, and aided by the popular song, "A Pretty Girl Is Like a Melody."

Melvina, *see* MALVINA.

Mercedes ♀ Spanish, "mercies," derived from *Maria de Mercedes,* an epithet of the Virgin. The curious history is that the name originated (as the language indicates) in Spain, then passed to France, and finally (probably in the early nineteenth century) to England. At more or less the same time the name MERCY was common in the colonies. We may even think that Mercy, in rare instances, sprang from Catholic piety.

On the other hand, Mercedes maintains only a loose connection with Catholicism, and is more likely to owe its usage to Romantic poetry. It still remains a viable name. The accent is usually upon the second syllable.

Mercy ♀ In the seventeenth century Mercy was the most commonly used of the abstracts. In the Plymouth list of 1130 names, Mercy occurred 74 times (6%). It thus must be rated a popular name in that period, sometimes making the top ten and once reaching fourth place.

Probably the name was used as a declaration of God's mercy. The word is so common a one in the King James Version that the name can scarcely be associated with any particular passage.

Meriel, *see* MURIEL.

Merle ♀ The name for the European blackbird. (*See* MAVIS.)

Some other etymology is possible for Merle, since it originally was used as a man's name, thus occurring in the later nineteenth century. It has always been rare.

Micah, Micajah ♂ Hebrew, variant forms which are of the same meaning as MICHAEL. They were in steady use until the biblical names declined.

Michael ♂ Hebrew, "who-is-like-God?" A common name in medieval England, it became unpopular with the Reformation, probably because St. Michael, though securely biblical, was also an angel, and angels had a rather uncertain status with the reformers. Both at Harvard and at Princeton the name was rare, clear down into the nineteenth century. It was somewhat commoner in the Continental Army, sometimes listed merely as Mike.

Michael (like Patrick and Bridget) reflected the presence of the Irish. With the heavy growth of Irish immigration in the mid-nineteenth century, Michael became commoner. Toward the end of the century, as the Irish also increased in wealth and social status, Michael increased correspondingly.

By 1950 the change had become striking. Michael was one of the most popular of men's names, not only making the top ten, but going well into it. In one list (1955) Michael and David stood in a tie for first place.

Although the Irish influence was still important, much of the use of Michael must be attributed to the general workings of a fashionable trend. Parents of a conforming type follow the lead and name their boy Michael because they are aware that Michael is much used and therefore should be a "safe" name—as indeed, it may well be, though it can scarcely at the same time be a distinctive or a distinguished one.

Michelle ♀ This French form for a feminine of Michael became popular in the mid-twentieth century. It is another of the numerous cases in which the failure of the English language to develop a feminine led to taking one from the French.

Mildred ♀ Anglo-Saxon, from *milde*, "mild," and *thryth*, "power." The name displays the unusual history of being a pre-Conquest one that maintained itself through the later periods, probably because Mildred was an Anglo-Saxon saint. It has been a rare name, except for some revival in the twentieth century, but it is still viable.

Miles ♂ Probably Germanic, but of uncertain meaning. It is sometimes from the Latin form, *miles,* "soldier." Because of Miles Standish, many people think of this as a typical Puritan name. Actually it scarcely occurs in American usage, the redoubtable Standish being an oddity.

Millicent ♀ Germanic, from *amal,* "work," and *swintha,* "strong." From France, it was brought to England about 1150. In the United States, though it has enjoyed some revival in the nineteenth and twentieth centuries, it is now so rare as scarcely to be rated even viable.

Milton ♂ From the family name, originally indicating a village with a mill. It began as a given name in the mid-nineteenth century, and attained some popularity which has carried on into the twentieth century. The reasons for this use are not clear. We cannot assume that the poet could have been of great influence.

   The name has entered American usage to the point of having a regular shortening, Milt.

Minerva ♀ The names of the Graeco-Roman deities (except for Diana) have not been much used. Minerva suggested a middle class figure of virtue and wisdom. During the nineteenth century her name occurs sporadically. *See* MINNIE.

Mingo ♂ One of the commoner African names, used for slaves, in the period of slavery. Its meaning and connections are uncertain. It went out of use early, perhaps by 1800.

Minnie ♀ It could have been formed as a diminutive of various women's names, e.g. Minerva. It was actually, however, a Scottish rendering from Mary. In the nineteenth century it was fairly popular on its own, and is to be considered an independent name.

Mirable ♀ Latin, "wonderful." As is possible elsewhere, the-*bel* has been misunderstood as "beautiful." It existed in England during the Middle Ages, but went out of use later, until it was revived in the nineteenth century. It is very rare.

Miranda ♀ Latin, "to be admired," coined by Shakespeare to be the name of the heroine of *The Tempest.* It is very rare.

Miriam ♀ The name occurs in Hebrew, but is uncertain. Meanings are offered ranging from "rebellion" to "fat"—none of them being at all convincing. Probably the solution is that the name is not really Hebrew, but is of some other language, and (as is common) was merely taken over as a name, without reference to meaning. Since Miriam was the sister of Moses, an Egyptian origin would be possible, or even likely.

Miriam is a rare name, and in most American lists it fails to appear at all. (*See* MOSES, MARY.)

Moira, Moyra ♀ An Irish name, connected with Celtic *mor,* "big." It is viable in the later twentieth century. It is also used as an Irish variant of Mary.

Molly, *see* MARY.

Mona ♀ Celtic (Irish), the diminutive of a name meaning "noble." It occurs rarely in the later nineteenth and the twentieth centuries, commonly in Irish context.

Monica ♀ Language and meaning are uncertain. It was the name of the mother of St. Augustine, herself sainted. The name may be of African origin. In the twentieth century it has become somewhat popular.

Montgomery ♂ From the family name, which is from a place in Normandy. The popularity of the name (cf. WARREN) springs from the hero-status of General Richard Montgomery, the American commander killed in the attack on Quebec in 1775. It is commonly shortened to Monty.

Mordecai ♂ One unnotable man of this name appears in both Ezra and Nehemiah, and a notable one appears in Esther. Since the Babylonian and Persian connections of these books are close, the name Mordecai may be a Hebrew rendering of Marduk, one of the figures of the mythology of that area. It has been very rare in America, and usually appears in a Jewish context.

Morgan ♂ Welsh, with *mor* meaning "sea" and the rest perhaps "dweller." In the sixteenth century it was a given name in Wales, much used. It became a family name, and in the colonies was primarily so regarded, e.g. General Daniel Morgan of the Revolution. It is still used to some extent as a given name, but in such cases is ordinarily considered to be the family name thus used.

Mortimer ♂ From the family name, a feudal usage of the late nineteenth century. *See* HOWARD, etc.

Moses ♂ The second chapter of Exodus tells the story of the Hebrew baby whose life was saved when Pharoah's daughter drew him out of the river—"And she called his name Moses: and she said, Because I drew him out of the water."

Moses is here taken as the Hebrew word meaning "to draw." A little reflection, however, suggests that the situation is reversible—that is, that the name Moses suggested the incident, not that the incident led to the naming. Why would an Egyptian princess be speaking Hebrew?

We can even go further than mere probability. Egyptian names, such as Rameses and Thothmes, show an *m-s* element, thus suggesting that Moses also is to be so taken. The *m-s* element, indeed, means "son" in Egyptian.

In the period of the popularity of Old Testament names, Moses carried with it no especial Jewish suggestion and appeared regularly, if not commonly. With the decline of the Old Testament names, Moses went out of general use, but maintained itself for some time as a Jewish name.

Moyra, *see* MOIRA.

Muriel, Meriel ♀ Probably Celtic, but of uncertain meaning. In the Middle Ages it was associated with Brittany, a Celtic-speaking area. An Irish name is Muirheal, "sea-bright." Much used in the Middle Ages in England, Muriel lapsed in the early modern period until it was revived in the later nineteenth century, perhaps from some literary source. It has moved toward extinction in the twentieth century.

Myra ♀ Apparently coined by Fulke Grenville as a name for the lady to whom he addressed some love poems in the late sixteenth century. It is, we may suppose, an anagram of Mary.

Myrtle ♀ From the name of the ornamental shrub, a flower-name (*see* ROSE, LILY, etc.) introduced as a woman's name in the late nineteenth century.

N

Naaman ♂ Hebrew, "pleasant[?]." The name of several biblical characters, notably the Syrian captain whom Elisha cured of leprosy. It occurs, very rarely, in America.

Nahum ♂ Hebrew, "comforter." The name of a minor prophet and the title of a book of the Bible. Nahum occurred rarely in the period of biblical names.

Nancy, Nan ♀ The origin of Nancy seems surely to be Agnes, though many have supposed it to be Anne, and such a derivation is certainly possible for Nan.

We can start with Annes, the common spelling of Agnes in the sixteenth century, with the pronunciation roughly represented by a spelling "Annyess." From Annes we can have a short form Ance or a diminutive Annesy. These forms would inevitably have developed *n*-forms—Nance and Nannesy. At this point, by a natural shortening, we arrive at Nancy, and (by some further shortening) at Nan.

The difficulty of deriving Nancy from Anne is that there is no reasonable place from which the *c* or *s* can develop, whereas the sound was there from the beginning with Agnes. Nan, however, is easily developed as an *n*-form of Anne. In modern times Nan and Nancy are generally considered to be variants of the same name. The older diminutive of Nan, however, was Nanny.

Nancy, for reasons by no means clear, became a highly popular name in the twentieth century, often attaining a place in the top ten.

In general, Nancy has been more used in the United States than in Great Britain.

Naomi ♀ Hebrew, "pleasant," used in contrast to Marah, "bitter." The name of a character (the mother-in-law of Ruth) in the biblical Book of Ruth, Naomi was used by the Puritans, but did not attain the popularity of Ruth. It has survived, and is still viable in modern usage.

Naphtali ♂ From a son of the patriarch Jacob, whence is derived a tribal name. If taken as Hebrew, Naphtali may be translated as "wrestling," and the occasional use in early Puritan settlements of Wrestling as a personal name may spring from this beginning, with the implied expansion into a pious phrase, such as "wrestling-with-sin."

Natalia, Natalie, Natasha ♀ Latin, a feminine form from *dies natalis*, "birthday," that is, Christmas. It is thus related to NOEL.

A diminutive form in Russian yields Natasha, a popular Russian name, and that name may thus appear by literary transfer, e.g. from Natasha, the heroine of Tolstoy's *War and Peace*. The name shows some increase in the twentieth century, doubtless because of general interest in things Russian.

Nathan ♂ Hebrew, "He-gave." The meaning is presumably to be taken as "God-gave," and the name would be the equivalent of a shortening of Nathaniel. Nathan has been the preferred form in Jewish usage, but it also was popular in colonial usage generally. During the middle years of the eighteenth century, among students at Harvard, Nathan exceeded Nathaniel (which then varied in its spelling), and in the decade 1750–59 it stood in eighth place. The patriot Nathan Hale serves as a notable example of the usage of the name in the Revolutionary period. Except for Jewish usage, the name is vestigial after the decline of the Old Testament names in the mid-nineteenth century. *See also* NATHANIEL.

Nathaniel, Nathanael ♂ Hebrew, "God-gave, gift-of-God." Cf. NATHAN. This name was a particular favorite during the period of Old Testament names, often appearing in the top ten in New England lists. Actually Nathaniel is a name of the New Testament, borne by one of the Twelve, generally supposed to be an alternate name for Bartholomew. This unusual linguistic situation (a Hebrew form with Christian associations) may have had something to do with the popularity of the name—the actual Nathaniel making only one brief appearance in the Gospel text, Nathan, however, being the name of one notable character of the Old Testament and of ten less notable ones. In its apt meaning for the expression of thankfulness for the birth of a child is doubtless to be found the chief reason for the popularity of the name.

Nathaniel is one of the few Hebrew names to be adopted into English usage before the American settlements were begun. In the colonies, however, it grew rapidly in popularity. Among Harvard students for the decade 1690–99 (births 1670–79), of a total of 128 there were nine students named Nathaniel. Comparable figures hold throughout the eighteenth century, keeping Nathaniel in the top ten, ranging from fifth to tenth. In the nineteenth century this popularity fades, along with that of the Old Testament names in general. The Civil War roughly marks the period at which Nathaniel ceased to be a current name, and by 1880 it had become vestigial.

Nat and Natty are the regular abbreviations. Our most notable historical example is General Nathanael Greene. Even more widely known is Natty Bumppo of the *Leather-Stocking Tales.*

Neal, Neil ♂ Probably Irish, being derived from a word meaning "warrior, champion." In America it begins to appear in the nineteenth century, and is probably of Romantic origin, with Irish and Scottish background. It has never been popular.

Nehemiah ♂ Hebrew, "God-is-comfort." A regularly used name in the Puritan tradition down through the eighteenth century and the first decades of the nineteenth. The name was chiefly known, we may suppose, because it is that of one of the books of the Bible.

Neil, *see* NEAL.

Nellie ♀ Originating as a *n*-form and diminutive of Ella (or

Helen or Ellen), the name became independent. It flourished in the later nineteenth century, but faded rather quickly in the twentieth. Nell, also common in the same period, is the *n*-form without diminutive.

Nelson ♂ From the family name, "son of Neil." Nelson is a major hero in Britain. Some of this enthusiasm apparently spread to the United States, so that Nelson has been a favored name.

Nicholas ♂ Greek, "victory-people" The name derives from Nicholas, Bishop of Myra, whose relics were brought west by the Normans of southern Italy. His cult became immensely important throughout western Europe (especially in the Low Countries) and his name was highly popular in England during the late medieval period.

Like the other names of nonbiblical saints, Nicholas suffered severely at the Reformation. So many Englishmen had already been named Nicholas, however, that the name had established its own tradition and could not easily be wiped out.

From 1700 onward Nicholas continued as a moderately popular name in the colonies. An important influence must have been the special interest of the Dutch colonists in the name. It was also used freely among the numerous German immigrants. In more recent periods the name has been especially associated with Greek immigrants, as in the phrase "Nick the Greek." It remains in use, though scarcely more than a rare name.

St. Nicholas has become the patron saint of Christmas, and from Dutch usage he has become Santa Claus, in a common form making use of the latter part of the name instead of the first part. This form, however, has not become current as a name for individuals.

Nina ♀ Russian, a diminutive for Anne, related to Ninon in French. It has been used occasionally since the mid-nineteenth century.

Noadiah ♂ Hebrew, "God-assembles." A rare name.

Noah ♂ As with many other early names which are recorded in Genesis, the language and meaning of Noah must be considered uncertain.

As the divinely appointed builder of the ark and the re-founder of the human race, Noah seems to have been held in well-justified honor among early Christians. However, in the English tradition (especially in the miracle plays) he became something of a buffoon, from being associated with all those pairs of animals, from being caricatured as a henpecked hus-band, and from being a man who definitely could not hold his liquor.

Nevertheless, he was not without honor among the Puritans, and his name occurred sporadically at Harvard in the eigh-teenth century, but soon afterward dropped to the vanishing point. The most famous of the name, Noah Webster, was born in 1758.

Though the name still occurs rarely, it may be considered no longer active.

Noel ♂ French, from the Latin *natalis,* "having-to-do-with-birth," i.e. with Christmas (cf. NATALIA). It occurs so rarely as scarcely to be held viable, except in a French context.

Nora[h] ♀ It is most simply explained as an abbreviation of Honora. Its popularity in Ireland, since at least the time of the Norman Conquest, suggests that it was originally used because of its similarity to some Celtic name.

In the United States the name retained its Irish associations, but, like Bridget, suffered a loss of social status. By the later nineteenth century it may be classified as rare. It is, however, a likely name for revival.

Among Arabic-speaking peoples the name Nura (and other spellings) is common, but its resemblance to Nora is probably accidental.

Noreen ♀ The *-een* suffix (as in KATHLEEN, MAUREEN) indicates an Irish diminutive—here a diminutive of Norah. It is rare in the United States.

Norma ♀ The origin is uncertain, but there is probably no con-nection with Norman. It appears as the name of a character (and the title) of Bellini's opera (1831), and it may have been coined on that occasion. American usage is subsequent to that time. The name has not been common; it appears as 81 on Smith's list of 100.

Norman ♂ Anglo-Saxon, "northman," a name applied to Scandinavians during the Middle Ages. Norman seems to have been first a given, individual name, though a family name developed. The given name went out of use, but the family name survived. The modern use of Norman as a given name is based upon the family name being again so used.

Norman is associated with the feudal names (*see* HOWARD). It appears chiefly around 1900, and is 71 in Smith's list (1941) of 100.

O

Obadiah ♂ Hebrew, "servant-of-God." Known as a book of the Bible and its author, Obadiah occurred as a name, though rarely. It was, however, at some time well enough a part of the American heritage as to have supplied the heroes for the drinking-song, "Said the Old Obadiah to the Young Obadiah."

Olaf ♂ From Old Norse, "ancestor-relics." In the United States it has been rarely used except in a Scandinavian context.

Olga ♀ Of Scandinavian origin (from *helga*, "holy"), but in modern usage, Russian. It generally appears in a Russian context, dating from the later nineteenth century or the twentieth. During periods of friendship with Russia several such names have developed some popularity—e.g. Ivan, Sonia.

Olive ♀ From the Latin, *oliva*, "olive," the name of a saint of uncertain date. In the United States it probably does not appear before the later nineteenth century. Since the adoption of the name of an obscure saint seems unlikely at that time and place, the name may be connected with the use of plant names which arose at that period. *See* LILY.

Oliver ♂ Among the traditional twelve peers of Charlemagne, Oliver was highly conspicuous, and his name became commonly used in England during the later Middle Ages. The actual origin of the name is uncertain. It can be derived from the Latin *olivarius*, "olive tree," but this origin makes little sense.

More reasonable is some connection with the Scandinavian name Olaf ("ancestor-remains"). Or it may be from some other Germanic form.

In the period of American colonization, the name Oliver was chiefly associated with Oliver Cromwell, and such an association (after the Restoration in 1660) meant that the name was tabooed. (By the aid of a prefixed *n,* the short form of Oliver is Noll, which was used as a derogatory for Oliver Cromwell.) The popular Dickens novel *Oliver Twist* (1840) and a twentieth-century stage version of it made Americans conscious of the name, but it has not found much favor.

Olivia ♀ It is probably a Latin or Italian form of OLIVE. It lingered into the sixteenth century in England and was used by Shakespeare in *Twelfth Night.* In the United States it has been very rare, though known from the Shakespearean use.

Onesimus, Onesiphorus ♂ Greek, but of strange meaning. Onesimus may be translated "profit, profitable," and *-phorus* has the same meaning. Onesiphorus is thus "profit-profit."

Onesimus was a slave; Onesiphorus may have been a freedman. This ancient meaning may have been significant, but we must leave to Greek specialists its further study.

In America the name appeared occasionally, whether in use especially for slaves is not certain.

Ophelia ♀ Spelled Ofelia in an Italian text, it appeared in Sannazaro's *Arcadia* (1504) and was probably his own coinage, though perhaps suggested by the Greek word *ophelia,* "help." Shakespeare's use of it in *Hamlet* has preserved the name, and it has appeared occasionally, though rarely and perhaps not even enough to be considered viable.

Oriana ♀ The name is a doubtful one, and is probably to be considered a coinage from *or,* "gold," and a feminine (Latin) suffix. Poets applied the name to Queen Elizabeth. Stevenson mentions it as one of the common names in backwoods America, but actual countings fail to vindicate his observation. It was probably taken as a feminine of ORION.

Orion ♂ The name is from the constellation more likely than from the character of Greek mythology. Stevenson, in his *Silverado Squatters,* listed this as one of the prevailing names among the frontier people of the United States around the year 1880. But it was not common in the country generally. It was regularly accented on the first syllable.

Orlando ♂ The Italian form of ROLAND. It was introduced into England in the sixteenth century during a period of strong Italian influence. It has occurred rarely in later centuries in the United States.

Osborn ♂ Anglo-Saxon, "a god," and "man." In Norse *born* would be "bear [the animal]." After being commonly a personal name, Osborn gave rise to a family name, and died out, around 1500, as a personal name. Later still, the family name appeared as a personal one.

Oscar ♂ The element *os* does not occur as a word in Old English, but stands in a number of names. It has been generally translated as "god," or "a god." The element *car* is from the common word *gar,* "spear." Oscar was a name in Anglo-Saxon, but died out after the Conquest.

James Macpherson gave the name Oscar to a character in the Ossianic poems, which were widely read, even more on the Continent than in English-speaking regions. The name thus came into use on the Continent, and was scarcely introduced into the United States until it came with Scandinavian and German immigrants in the mid-nineteenth century. It has remained viable, but has never gained popularity in America.

Other names in *os-* are Osbert, Osmond, Osborn, Oswald, Oswin. These names have been revived in Great Britain, but (except possibly for Osborn and Oswald) scarcely have currency in the United States.

Oswald ♂ Anglo-Saxon, "god-power." In England it had remained in use from the Anglo-Saxon period on. Like most of the names in *os-,* it has been more popular in England than in the United States.

Otto ♂ Germanic, "rich." Though introduced into England by the Normans, the name died out. It appears in the United States in the nineteenth century, generally in a German context. It established itself sufficiently to stand as 81 in Smith's (1941) list.

Owen, Ewen ♂ These are variants of a Welsh name, probably of

Celtic origin. A Latin origin from Eugenius has also been suggested. They have been viable in the United States, but have never attained popularity.

Ozias ♂ Apparently a Greek rendering of UZZIAH. It occurs only in the genealogy of Matthew 1, and it may in America have been a name selected by lot.

P Q

Pamela ♀ Coined by Sir Philip Sidney for the name of a character in his *Arcadia* (1590). What suggested the name to him is unknown, but its general form indicates a Latin influence.

The name made little impression upon the world until Samuel Richardson took it for the heroine and title of his novel *Pamela* (1740). The great popularity of that work led to the use of Pamela as a personal name, but its popularity died out, and the name may never have crossed the Atlantic in the colonial period. In the mid-twentieth century, however, Pamela became popular in the United States, for no reason that can be suggested.

As a coined name, Pamela presents no rule by which its pronunciation can be determined. By custom it is Pámela, but if anyone wishes to say Paméla, there is no authority by which he can be declared wrong.

Pansy, *see* LILY.

Patience ♀ Job being the chief biblical exponent of patience, we might expect the name to be borne by men, and Withycombe notes it as so applied in seventeenth-century England. In America I have found it only applied to women. It is one of the commoner of the abstracts. In the Plymouth list of 1131 names it occurs 25 times, standing second to Mercy.

Patience (appearing only in the New Testament) is not common in the King James Version, but the general idea of the word was one that was much urged—as, for instance, in the nonbiblical story of GRISELDA.

Like most of the abstracts Patience fell out of favor in the eighteenth century. It has not been revived.

Patricia ♀ Latin, "patrician" (feminine form). In England the feminine of Patrick came into general use after the birth and naming of Princess Patricia (1886); its use in the United States developed in the twentieth century (probably from this English usage). Unlike Patrick, the name has not had close associations with the Irish. It had, however, the advantage in the United States which a name for women seems to possess when closely associated with a name for men.

Its by-forms are Patty, Pat, and Patsy—with the first of these the favorite. Pat offers no differentiation from the masculine form, a situation which seems to tend to the general decline of the masculine (*see* FRANCIS). Previous to the later nineteenth century Patty is to be taken as the irregularly formed variant of MARTHA.

Patrick ♂ From the Latin *patricius,* "patrician." A certain Sucat took this name, *c.* 425, when he was consecrated as a missionary to Ireland. Presumably he knew its meaning, though it seems a curiously snobbish name for a missionary. The bearer of the new name became St. Patrick, and one result of his conversion of Ireland was that his name came to be widely used among the Irish. It also was used in Scotland, but made little penetration into England.

It was thus a rare name among the New England immigrants, and, being the name of a nonbiblical saint, it was under the general suspicion of that type of name. Patrick failed to occur at Harvard until about 1820, and even after that it remained very rare.

In the United States the name has been especially associated with the Irish immigrants, who became numerous after 1840, and remained a definable class until 1900 at least. In the middle of the twentieth century this association became less strong, and Patrick has enjoyed some modest popularity.

The standard short form has been Pat. Paddy has not been

much used in the United States and suggests the stage Irish-man. (*See* PATRICIA.)

Patty, *see* MARTHA, PATRICIA.

Paul ♂ The Latin *paulus* means "small," and must have been originally a descriptive personal name. For practical purposes, however, it originates with Saul of Tarsus, who took the name Paul after his conversion.

It was not much used in England until the seventeenth century, when it had a mild popularity, and was carried to the colonies. It remained steadily in use clear down into the twentieth century, without any great vogue. Its typical usage at Harvard down through the nineteenth century was one or two occurrences in a decade. Only with the twentieth century did Paul become somewhat more popular—in 1945, in one list, rising to sixth place. In a list of births *c.* 1950 it is in eighth place, and it seems to have had some use in the counterculture.

Considering the importance of Paul as reflected in the New Testament and in the development of Christianity, as well as the handiness of the name, we must be somewhat surprised at its generally rare use. One possible reason may be that Paul supplies neither a short form nor a diminutive—any attempt at Paulie running counter to Polly. With Paul you must be, so to speak, formal—even when addressing a baby in the cradle.

As feminines, Paula, a German form, has been occasionally used, and Pauline enjoyed some vogue in the nineteenth century.

Pearl ♀ The nineteenth century, a highly experimental period for women's names, may be said to have inaugurated the use of the names of precious stones for women, but the practice did not go far. Hawthorne, needing a name of special significance, used Pearl in *The Scarlet Letter,* and that occurrence of it may have done much to establish it. Of the others, Ruby, Beryl, and Opal have remained in use, though they are not common.

Pelatiah ♂ Hebrew, "God-delivers." It occurs in the Bible four times as a personal name, though never of anyone of importance. During the period of biblical names it appeared, but rarely.

Peleg ♂ Like those of other characters in Genesis, Peleg may be a non-Hebrew name. It is, however, one of the few biblical names to be honored with a biblical translation: in I Chronicles 1:19 the author writes, ". . . the name of the one was Peleg; because in his days the earth was divided. . . ." From a modern point of view, however, one can object to this name of unusual meaning (division) and believe that the Hebrews of many centuries later merely made this name intelligible by a translation based upon accidental similarity of sound, one of the biblical words for "division" being "pelaggah" or "peluggah."

Peleg appeared occasionally in American usage during the period of biblical names.

Penelope ♀ Greek, the name of Odysseus' wife, who devoted much of her time to weaving. The name, with some stretching of etymological data, seems to reveal in both parts a meaning associated with weaving—roughly, "woof-cloak." But like so many of the Homeric names, it may actually be of non-Greek origin.

The English-American tradition of naming has made little use of the Homeric epics (or indeed, of Hellenic mythology in general) as a source for names. (HELEN is from Helen of Troy only at second hand, through St. Helena.)

Penelope appeared as an English name in the late sixteenth century, but did not become common. The Homeric lady was a paragon of domestic virtues, and almost set an ideal for the Christian housewife. But the Puritans never really adopted her name. Such vogue as Penelope has attained dates from the late nineteenth century, and is chiefly of the twentieth.

The attractive variant Penny has sometimes appeared as the official form, and has established some tradition for itself.

Penuel ♂ Hebrew, "face-of-God." In the Bible it occurs both as a place-name and as a personal name. It appears very rarely during the period of biblical names.

Perceval, Percival ♂ French, probably a twelfth-century coinage by the poet Chrestien de Troyes for the hero of his poem of the same name. Literally, the meaning would be "pierce-valley," which fails to make good sense—but poets, to be sure, are not held by the bonds of good sense. There is also a French place-name, Percheval, which might have helped to suggest the name, and to convert it, superficially, into *cheval*, "horse," a connection which is an apt one for a hero of chivalry. Etymologically, it has no connection with Percy, merely sharing coincidence of sound.

In the United States the name appeared in the later nineteenth century, a period in which Arthurian names were popular. Perceval, however, remained always a rare name, and in the later twentieth century is scarcely viable.

The occurrence of a single Perceval at Harvard in the 1680–89 decade seems to be the only one until the 1890–99 decade. This occurrence furnishes a good example of the way in which 100 per cent generalizations about names are dangerous. His naming may have been based upon some family tradition.

Percy ♂ The famous family name is from the village of Perci in Normandy. It occasionally appears as a given name in families connected with that one. Included here must be the poet Percy Bysshe Shelley, his family having a remote connection with the great one.

In the United States the name began about 1850, and it seems thus to tie up with the snobbish use of feudal names which began about this time (*see* HOWARD). Percy enjoyed a boom in the period 1870–90, but since that time has declined, and it is probably no longer viable.

The short form has curiously developed, with the pronunciation *perse* but the spelling Perc.

Perez ♂ Probably Hebrew, "bursting-through." It has only one mention in the Bible, and may be a choice by luck. It occurs rarely in the period of biblical names.

Persis ♀ Greek, "Persian woman." But by the time of the New Testament the name was apparently being used without reference to its original meaning. The comparative lack in the New Testament of women's names made the namers use some of them, such as Persis, to which no appropriate meaning could be attached (cf. LYDIA). Although St. Paul referred to Persis as "the beloved," hers has remained a very rare name.

Peter ♂ From the Greek form *petros*, "stone, rock," itself a translation of the Aramaic *cephas,* of the same meaning. (*See* CEPHAS.) Not only is it a biblical name, but it even might be considered the most deeply biblical of all names, because of the naming being credited (John 1:42) to Christ Himself: "Thou art Simon, the son of Jonah: thou shalt be called Cephas, which is by interpretation, a stone."

The association of St. Peter with the Roman Catholic Church led to the name's being a common one throughout western Europe in the Middle Ages. By the same token, the name suffered a reaction with the Reformation. Though Peter was certainly a biblical name, it suffered much, as did the names of the nonbiblical saints. Its use in England fell off sharply in the sixteenth and seventeenth centuries.

It scarcely existed among the early immigrants to New England. In one list of 452 it occurs only twice. As this prejudice died out with time, Peter became somewhat commoner, but failed to attain popularity, partly because of the lack of a large pool of early bearers of the name from which later namers could draw. Outside of New England Peter was somewhat more used, in New York and Pennsylvania drawing strength from established use in Dutch and German. But the New Englanders took to the name very slowly. Even as late as the decades of 1820 and 1830 there were no Peters listed at Harvard.

In more modern times—to some extent reflecting the increased Catholic population—Peter has grown stronger, and has at least been regularly viable. It remains in current usage, and has even displayed some vigor among the challengers of the old name-pattern—for instance, a California list (*c.* 1940) shows Peter in third place. It thus gives some evidence that it will maintain itself in the future.

Phebe, *see* PHOEBE.

Philander ♂ Greek, "love-man." It has had very little currency in the United States, but an example is the eminent political figure Philander C. Knox (1853–1921).

In English usage (reflected in America) the name in the eighteenth century was less common in practice than in literary usage. Philander appeared often (to quote Yonge): "He was the amiable gentleman in philosophical dialogue, or the affectionate shepherd in Arcadian romance." Curiously, this association with amiability and affection (neither word suggesting depth of character) led to this uncommon name becoming the verb "to philander"—a term suggestive of triviality.

Philemon ♂ Greek, with the common name-element *phil-*, "loving," and the rest uncertain, though sometimes rendered as "mind." Though it is the name of a book of the New Testament, it was not much used as a personal name, and it appears rarely in the period of biblical names.

Philip ♂ Greek, "lover-of-horses." Though biblical, and borne by one of the Apostles, the name's associations were apparently secular, and it was scarcely used in New England during the period of the popularity of the biblical names. In the non-Puritan colonies it was commoner, even standing as ninth in a Virginia regiment of the Continental Army.

Its popularity increased during the later Romantic period, from 1850 on, but it never became extremely common, and has a slight English or "learned" suggestion, possibly because of its "ph" spelling. Similarly, the short form, Phil, has failed to become wholly American.

Philip is, however, viable in the counterculture.

Feminine forms (Philippa, Philipine) are used, but without much vogue.

Phine[h]as ♂ Hebrew, "oracle." As the name of three biblical characters, Phineas occurred regularly in early New England. It died out in the nineteenth century.

Phoebe, Phebe ♀ Greek, "shining, shining-one." The name is well known in ancient Greek mythology—being among other things, as Phoebus, a common term for Apollo in the Homeric poems. The actual source of the name for the American settlers, however, was the passage in Romans 16:1, in which the writer commends "Phebe our sister." Not only in New England, but in other colonies too, the name (often spelled Phebe), though never really popular, maintained itself as viable down through the nineteenth century.

The usual development through Latin would result in a form Phoeba, but this fails to appear, further evidence that the source of the name is its occurrence in Romans.

The accepted pronunciation is of two syllables, though the spelling Phebe would suggest a monosyllable.

Phyllis ♀ Greek, "leaf." It was the name of a girl in Greek mythology, one of the few examples in modern English of names thus derived. It makes little appearance in early American lists, but enjoyed a mild popularity in the later nineteenth century, and remains viable.

Polly, *see* MARY.

Pompey, Pomp ♂ There is no discernable reason for the frequent use of Pompey as a name for slaves. The common use of Pomp suggests that the name developed from an African form which was associated with Pomp, but no such name has been discovered. Far-traveled though he was, the great Pompey had little contact with Africa, except for some philandering in Egypt, which hardly counts as Africa.

Preserved ♂ A rarely used name in early New England, it is like the other "meaningfuls" in its suggestion of a biblical text. It differed from them in being conferred on men. It would scarcely be worth being listed except for the fact of its becoming somewhat famous by being adopted by the Fish family. Preserved Fish was well known in the mercantile world for two generations. Naturally, such a suggestive name drew fire from humorists, e.g. Washington Irving.

The various stories fashioned around the name are mere fabrications, some of them elaborate and ingenious, for example, that the name was given to a baby, the sole survivor of a shipwreck. Actually, the most famous Preserved Fish was born in ordinary circumstance and conventionally named after his father.

Prince ♂ Occasional uses in recent times are from the family name, which arises from someone in the service of a prince or in other ways thus associated.

The greatest usage of the name is as one for blacks during the slave period. Why it should have been so used is uncertain;

possibly it was first applied to men who had been chieftains in Africa.

According to Puckett/Heller, free blacks did not use the name Prince.

Priscilla, Prisca ♀ Latin, a diminutive and feminine form of *priscus*. A Priscilla is mentioned in Acts 18:2, and a Prisca (probably the same person) appears in II Timothy 4:19. Priscus had a number of meanings, among them "old, primitive, strict."

The use of the name in the United States was probably not directly influenced by those meanings, the name rather being taken directly from the biblical text. Priscilla appeared chiefly in the period of biblical names, with a New England background. It was rare, and Prisca was even rarer.

The diminutive was Prissy, and the adjective "prissy" may have arisen from this name, some of whose meanings point in that direction.

Prudence ♀ Because it maintains the ordinary meaning, the tendency must be to class Prudence as merely one of the abstracts. Its history, however, seems to be somewhat different.

Since it occurs before the Reformation, it is probably from St. Prudentius. Apparently because of this association with a nonbiblical saint (albeit a very minor one), the Puritans rejected it, and it was not much used in early New England. The eighteenth and nineteenth centuries gave it some use—enough for the shortening Prue to become well known. At the same time the likeness to "prude" was too close for comfort, though actually the two words are totally distinct. Putting everything together, we may consider Prudence to have little hope of future popularity.

Quash, Quashey ♂ One of the "day-names" traditionally given, in many African tribes, to a male baby born on Sunday. It was one of the commoner African names in the period of slavery, but it went out of use early, probably by 1800.

Quentin ♂ From the Latin *quintus,* "fifth," to indicate a fifth-born child. Namings in medieval England are from St. Quentin, martyred in A.D. 290.

In America the name was close to being extinct in the eighteenth century, but then it was used a little in the nineteenth century as a Romantic revival. Scott's *Quentin Durward*, a popular book, was published in 1823 and exerted some influence.

It is probably to be grouped with HOWARD, etc., among the feudal names, although there is no prominent English family of the name.

Quincy ♂ From the family name, which is derived from various French villages of that name. Since those villages were named after a man named Quintus, "fifth," we can establish a whole process—from given name back to given name.

Quincy is chiefly known as the middle name of President John Quincy Adams, and it has been rarely used as a personal name.

R

Rachel ♀ The name means "ewe, lamb" in Hebrew, and it may be so taken, although (like so many names in Genesis) it may not actually be Hebrew.

Rachel bore a sweetly poetic name, was "beautiful and well-favored," and was the subject of a romantic tale of her wooing by Jacob; in short, she had a good press, and rounded things off by pathetically dying young in childbirth. Yet her name was never greatly favored, being regularly much below her counterpart Rebecca in spite of the latter's harsh-sounding name. The reason for Rachel's lack of popularity is inexplicable in our present state of knowledge.

In the Boston births of 1630–69 Rachel stood far down, in eighteenth place. Used during the period of biblical names, Rachel almost died out in the general passing of those names. It had something of a revival in the late nineteenth century, but has become very rare in the twentieth.

Perhaps because of the prominence of the great French actress Rachel, there has been a tendency to re-spell the name to indicate the French pronunciation, e.g. Rachelle. Rashel is another variant.

Rachel has developed neither a common short form nor a diminutive. These limitations may have adversely affected its usage.

Ralph ♂ Germanic, from *raed*, "counsel," and *wulf*, "wolf." A common name in medieval England, it failed to become popular in the colonies, and (much like Roger) nearly disappeared. It revived around 1800, and has been viable from that time onward. It had a period of prosperity in the earlier twentieth century.

The older spelling was with an *f*, the *ph* representing a pedantic spelling of the eighteenth century, apparently in an attempt to indicate a Greek connection of the name. Rafe, the older spelling, also indicated the pronunciation. Like Paul, Ralph is a name with no short form and no well-established diminutive, and may have suffered in popularity because of this enforced formality.

Raoul is a French form of the name, but it can scarcely be considered American, though somewhat used in Britain.

Ramona ♀ The feminine form of Ramón, which occurs in American usage only in Spanish context. Ramona furnishes the feminine, but is taken merely as a name from the popular novel *Ramona* (1884) by Helen Hunt Jackson. It was a common name in the late nineteenth and early twentieth centuries.

Randal[l], Randolph ♂ Old English, from *rand*, "shield," and *wulf*, "wolf." It remained viable during the Norman period, and probably never went completely out of use, though it has never been popular in the United States.

Randolph is one of its variants. Randy (or Randie) has been at once a short form and a diminutive. At the present time Randal[l] is to be considered primarily the family name.

Raymond ♂ Germanic, *raed*, "counsel," and *mund*, "protection." Though brought into England with the Normans, its use declined, and it scarcely occurred in the colonial period. About 1800 it reappeared. Probably we can maintain that the personal name died out entirely, but was replaced (after a lapse) by the family name used as a given name. In the twentieth century it is generally considered to be primarily the family name. Ray has developed as the short form.

Rebecca ♀ Like many of the other names in Genesis, Rebecca is probably not Hebrew, and its language and meaning must be considered unknown.

Brought to America by the earliest immigrants, Rebecca at once became established in the colonies generally, and especially in New England, where it was commonly in the first ten, often ranking as fifth or sixth. Going into a long decline with the other biblical names, Rebecca recovered in the twentieth century, becoming again a viable name.

The reasons for this popularity of Rebecca are not easy to determine, aside from the fact that she was a prominent character in the story of the patriarchs, and was one of the few biblical characters to show regard for animals. She was, however, by no means wholly admirable. For example, she was underhanded in her aid to her son Jacob. Her great moment is that of her blessing: "Thou art our sister, be thou the mother of thousands of millions," to which is added the belligerent note, "let thy seed possess the gate of those which hate them."

The New Testament spelling, Rebecca, was regularly employed in America, as opposed to the Old Testament spelling, Rebekah. Becky is the common diminutive.

Reggie, *see* REGINALD.

Regina ♀ Latin, "queen." It serves as the feminine of Rex, but has never been as much used, and is rare.

Reginald, Reggie ♂ The Anglo-Saxon Regenwald (from two elements, each meaning "strength") developed in various ways after the Norman Conquest, amalgamation with a similar Norman name, Reginald, being the most common result.

This name went out of use in the sixteenth century but was revived in the mid-nineteenth, becoming somewhat popular in England, commonly in the familiar form as Reggie. The revival did not take hold in America, and Reggie became in fact the prime example of a over-pretentious, decadent, or un-American name.

In the mid-twentieth century, however, it has been triumphantly borne by Reggie Jackson, the baseball hero. Whether his career will lead to a revival of the name is a detail of history which remains to be watched with interest. *See* RONALD.

Reliance ♀ The word does not occur in the King James Version, and the verb "rely" appears only four times, in unnotable passages of Chronicles. The name is probably to be taken in some

219

general sense, e.g. "God-is-my-reliance." It occurs rather rarely in the seventeenth century, but went out of use and has not been revived.

René, Renée ♂ ♀ French. In French the forms are commonly Réné and Rénée, English prefers René and Renée.

It was originally a Germanic name, brought into France by the Normans as Rayner or Rainer. The present forms were taken over in modern times from the French.

The name is rare, and may even be rejected as an English name, since it maintains a French spelling and pronunciation.

Repentance ♀ In England this was sometimes conferred upon illegitimate infants, presumably because the mother had expressed repentance. It was possibly so given in New England, but this is questionable. The name was very rare.

Reuben ♂ From the oldest son of Jacob; also a tribal name. The *ben-* may be Hebrew, "son," and therefore appropriate for the name of a tribe. The conventional rendering, "Behold-a-son!" cannot be sustained, but may on occasion have led to the bestowal of the name upon a male baby. The name is uncommon, and approaches extinction after 1850.

By some unkown associations, Reuben, in the later nineteenth century, became symbolic of rusticity, so that a "reuben" or (more commonly) a "rube" came to carry that suggestion.

Rex ♂ Latin, "king." Withycombe classes it as an adaptation of the Latin in its literal and commendatory meaning, and dates it as "modern"—apparently meaning from about 1900.

It occurs, however, in a Pennsylvania regiment of the Revolutionary War, where it might be a form of a longer name—Richard, perhaps. Some trace of this older usage may have given an impetus to the slight activity around 1900. The popular writer Rex Beach (born 1877) made the name widely known.

Rhoda ♀ Greek, a feminine form from *rhodon,* "rose." It is the name of a woman mentioned in Acts 12, and was adopted as a personal name in the seventeenth century. It remained rare, however, and did not replace the simple English form, Rose.

Richard ♂ Germanic, with the elements *ricja,* "rule," and *heard,* "hard." The elements (and possibly their combination into a name) occurred in Anglo-Saxon. The popularity of Richard, however, springs from the Normans, among whom it was much used. Three kings of England bore the name.

In Elizabethan England the typical stand of Richard (yielding to the three great leaders, John, William, and Thomas) was fourth place. The same situation displays itself among the early immigrants to New England. But among the children of those immigrants (675 males born in Boston in the decades 1630–69) Richard fell to tenth place. In Plymouth Colony during the same period a list of 1288 males shows only a vestigial remnant—five Richards.

In trying to explain such a shift, we may maintain that Richard was simply unable to stand against the enthusiasm for biblical names. We find, however, that even in the non-Puritan colonies Richard was not much used. The situation here may be partly explained by noting that apparently Richard was English in the narrower sense, and thus drew little support from the numerous Scottish, Welsh, and Irish settlers. Richard was somewhat more popular in the more English colonies, such as Virginia and South Carolina.

"Every Tom, Dick, or Harry" was an oft-quoted phrase, but over a period of centuries Richard (including Dick) held no such place in the colonies. The Continental Army offers some evidence: out of 1697 enlisted men and officers from Connecticut, Virginia, South Carolina, and Pennsylvania, only sixteen were named Richard. And in Virginia the name tied for tenth place with five, while in South Carolina it tied for fifteenth. There were no Richards at all among the soldiers from Pennsylvania. Richard thus continued through the eighteenth and most of the nineteenth centuries—generally in the second ten; occasionally rising to a low place in the top ten.

A definite change began with namings around 1890–1900. Richard began to appear in the top ten, sometimes even as high as fifth. By 1950 it showed up occasionally as high as third. No definite causes are assignable to this change.

The regular short form is Dick, although Rick also occurs. No feminine form has developed, perhaps because until 1900 Richard itself has been comparatively little-used.

The name supplied Franklin with his pseudonym, "Poor Richard." It has also furnished the bit of rhyming slang, "Tricky Dick." Few prominent Americans happen to have borne the name, however. We may mention "Dick" Ewell, the Confederate general, and President Nixon.

Rita ♀ A shortening of Margarita in Italian or Spanish. It has been used as an independent name in English in the twentieth century, and has become fairly common.

Robert ♂ Though Hreodbeorht is an Anglo-Saxon form used before the Conquest, the name is essentially to be classed as Norman, being one of the two-element Germanic formations, with the meaning "fame-bright." One of the half-dozen favorites among the Normans, the name continued in favor as the English language reasserted itself. In fact, Robert has shown remarkable stability in the Anglo-American tradition, appearing generally in about fifth place. Because of the heroic King Robert the Bruce, the name could count upon Scottish support. Likewise providing a name-hero was Robert E. Lee. Largely, one would think, from this special support Robert survived the general breakdown of the traditional names that occurred in the mid-twentieth century, and maintained its traditional popularity.

The variations of Robert are numerous, and some of them are difficult to explain. From the obvious Rob, a common Middle English diminutive was joined to produce Robin, the most used early by-form, from which we have the folk-hero Robin Hood (but *see* ROBIN).

The origin of Bob, the prevailing modern short form, is obscure. The shift of an *r*-sound to a *b*-sound is unusual. It may be possibly explained as being "attracted" by the *b*-sound already in the name. Other much used early forms were Hob and Dob. On the other hand, Robert has shunned the *r-l* shift which is common in so many names. The explanation may be that an *l*-shift would have been a derogatory, since *lob* in Middle English meant a foolish or slovenly fellow.

In Roberta we have an excellent feminine form, but it has actually been little used.

Robin ♂ ♀ It consists of the shortening of Robert with the addition of the common diminutive -*in*. It was much used in the Middle Ages, as is shown by its use for a folk-hero in Robin Hood, and by the commonness of the family name Robinson. In the seventeenth and eighteenth centuries it was not much in use as a given name.

In America the name was applied to a bird, though not the same bird as that so called in Britain. At some point, probably in the early nineteenth century, the name was conceived as being a feminine. It was then applied to women, and a small movement toward birds' names was thus inaugurated. As happens, the feminine form largely displaced the masculine, and other birds' names were applied to women (*see* MAVIS).

Roderick ♂ Germanic, "fame-rule." Its chief usage was traditionally in Scotland, though it is not of Scottish origin. What scattered usage it has attained in America has largely sprung from literary appearances, e.g. in Scott's *Lady of the Lake*.

Roger ♂ Germanic, *hrothi*, "fame," and *gairu*, "spear." It was a common name in medieval England. It was well represented among the early immigrants, but failed to establish itself in the colonies, scarcely appearing in the seventeenth and eighteenth centuries. In the later nineteenth century it enjoyed a slight revival, which has been passed on to the twentieth century.

Roland, Rowland ♂ Germanic, "fame-land." Among the traditional twelve peers of Charlemagne, Roland became the most famous. Introduced into America at the time of the colonization, the name failed to become popular, but has lingered as barely viable. The common early spelling was Rowland. (*See* OLIVER, ORLANDO.)

Ronald ♂ The name is the Scottish development from Regenwald (*see* REGINALD), but has escaped the decadent suggestions of Reggie. Not much in evidence in America before the twentieth century, it came to be moderately popular by 1975. The divergence of the two forms of the same name provides us with a curious bit of name-history.

Rose ♀ To American namers the assciation with the flower has been an obvious one. In actual history, however, Rose apparently originated in such names as Rosalind. (One may note that the Rosalind of *As You Like It* is familiarly called Rose.)

Rosalind is a typical two-element Germanic name, to be analysed as *ros,* "horse," and *linda,* "serpent." Equally possible of originating *rose* is Rosamond, "horse-protection." Though never common, these names appeared in the English name-pool during the Middle Ages. Being of non-Christian origin, they existed in spite of the Church rather than with its aid. After the thirteenth century, however, the name could be favored as being derived from St. Rose of Viterbo.

The pleasant suggestion and the brevity of Rose have led to its use in compounds, e.g. Rosalie, Roseanna, Rosemary, Rosabel. The Latin form Rosa also exists, and may in fact be one of the sources from which the English form is directly taken. (*See also* SHARON.)

Rosemary ♀ The name came into use in the late nineteenth century. Withycombe took it as the adaptation of a plant name— Latin *rosmarinus,* from which the name of the condiment obviously developed. In general usage as a name, however, it is to be considered a compound of Rose and Mary, developing some popularity along with other such compounds in the early twentieth century.

Ross ♂ The family name is Scottish, from a place-name. Like so many other Scottish names (especially the short ones), Ross has become a well-established given name in the twentieth century.

Rowena ♀ It occurs in the twelfth-century writings of Geoffrey of Monmouth. Since those writings are essentially fictional, the name may be considered his coinage. Withycombe suggests a connection with Old English Hrothwyn, "fame-friend." Sir Walter Scott used Rowena for the Anglo-Saxon heroine of *Ivanhoe.* From that very popular novel it was adopted for real women, and thus it enjoyed some use in the middle nineteenth century. It is a good example of what we may call a "Romantic" name.

Rowland, *see* ROLAND.

Roy ♂ Gaelic, from *rhu,* "red," often applied in Scotland to a red-headed man—curiously so, since red hair is common (and therefore not distinctive) among the Gaels. The form can also be considered the archaic form of the French *roi,* "king." As Le Roy ("The King"), it occurs once in a Virginia regiment of the Continental Army. Not until 1870, however, did it become regularly used, even developing a slight boom, which, in turn, was dying out by 1920. It has also been something of a favorite with the counterculture.

Ruby, *see* PEARL.

Rudolf, Rudolph ♂ Germanic, "fame-wolf," a modern German rendering of the older Hrodolf. In the United States it occurs rarely, usually in a German context.

Rufus ♂ Latin, "red-haired," but a well-established Roman name. It is the name of two people who are mentioned in passing in the New Testament. It was not in favor in the early Puritan period, when the Hebrew names were being exploited. Rufus enjoyed some favor, however, in the eighteenth and nineteenth centuries. It was an American, not a British, usage, and has been tending, in the twentieth century, toward oblivion.

Rupert ♂ The Old German Hreobert (*see* ROBERT) developed in German into Rupert. Partly because of the popularity of Prince Rupert of the Rhine, the name came into use in England during the later seventeenth century.

The New England colonies were on the opposite side from Rupert during the British civil war and its aftereffects, and the other colonies had no great involvement. As a result, Rupert failed to become viable in America. Its present occasional appearance can be attributed to German influence.

Russell ♂ Though Russell is a common family name, in the Smith list of 100 commonest given names its standing (72) is far above what would be expected. Russell apparently was introduced in the late nineteenth century as a feudal name, being that of a notable English aristocratic family. (Cf. SIDNEY, HOWARD, *et al.*)

Ruth ♀ Since the biblical test specifies (more than once) that Ruth was a Moabitess, she presumably had a Moabite name, thus rendering futile the attempts to decipher it as Hebrew.

About all that can be said etymologically is "Language and meaning, unknown."

The name was already in use among the first white immigrants to America, and it seems to have increased in popularity. In Boston births (female) of the period 1630–90, Ruth stood in seventh place. In the long period of the eighteenth and nineteenth centuries, the name suffered some vicissitudes, and during much of that anti-biblical period Ruth cannot be considered a popular name. Toward the end of the nineteenth century, however, it became common. Much of this popularity has remained in the twentieth century. Ruth has no short form, but it lacks austerity by the easy use of the diminutive Ruthie.

More than with most names, we can make some appraisal of the causes of this continuing popularity. Ruth is not only a book of the Bible, but also the name of its chief character, highly eulogized and sympathetically conceived. As a common noun, the word means "compassion," and this coincidence may have been a factor in its popularity as a name.

One detail of Ruth's story came especially close to that of the early American women. Like her, they had migrated, and they faced the problems of being "strangers in a strange land," and along with all this they faced the heartbreaking dilemma of "to go or to stay" when families had to be forever divided. An occasional man, as merchant or seaman, might visit England, but a woman had no such hope. Not as empty rhetoric would the emigrating woman read the words: "whither thou goest, I will go; and where thou lodgest, I will lodge: thy people shall be my people, and thy God my God."

S

Sallie, Sally ♀ On the *r-l* shift, see the Note on Shifting. We have here an example of the shift, though the basic Salah is missing. We may assume, however, that it actually once was in use. The shift must have been accomplished in England before the colonization of America. The Puritans favored the *r*-form, probably because it was closer to the biblical text. Sallie, however, was common elsewhere in the colonies.

Sallie remained definitely a secondary or derivative name down until the decline of the biblical names. It was, however, very popular in this secondary use. In the twentieth century Sallie began to stand as an independent name, and by the middle of this century it had become approximately as much used as Sarah. Both of them have remained popular.

Salmon, Zalmon, Salma ♂ Probably Hebrew, but of uncertain meaning. It may be another name from the idea of "peace" (cf. SOLOMON), but it also may be from *salma*, "strength," or from *zalmon*, "ascent." The name was in use during the period of biblical names.

Salome ♀ Hebrew, to be associated with *shalom*, "peace," perhaps with its special meaning, "perfect." The form is a Greek adaptation.

From nonbiblical sources Salome is known as Heroidas' daughter, who danced before her stepfather Herod and asked for the head of John the Baptist. In the Bible itself this "damsel" is not named. There is, however, a follower of Jesus bearing the name Salome (Mark 15, 16). She was the mother of James and John, and was made a saint as Mary Salome. Conceivably, indeed, the Evangelists avoided mentioning the name of the daughter of Herodias in order to avoid confusion. From the modern point of view, however, Salome is associated with lascivious dancing and the head of John on a platter.

Canon Bardsley, in his *Curiosities of Puritan Nomenclature* (1880), devoted a section to which he gave the title "Objectionable Scriptural Names," and in it he charged that the Puritans loved to select for their names those of characters from the most unsavory stories of the Bible. He is, however, unable to make a good case. We certainly must consider that Salome may have been selected in ignorance, but not in fascination with a lewd and evil character. Indeed, we might argue from the rarity of Salome that the connection with the daughter of Heroidas was known generally and led to the name being avoided.

The name would naturally have developed in English into a trisyllable, and the spelling Salomy probably originated thus, rather than as a diminutive. The French form Salomé is common, but there also exists in English a dissyllabic form accented on the second syllable.

Sambo ♂ In its origin the name has no connection with Samuel. The meaning is uncertain, though similar words occur in several African languages, and the name itself was planted in America by African-born slaves.

In the long run it became the most common of the African names, and even came to stand as a generic name for a black. The influence of Samuel (often, Sam) was undoubtedly a factor in this popularity. Like Samuel, Sambo declined in popularity toward the end of the nineteenth century.

Samson ♂ Hebrew, apparently containing the word for "sun" joined with a suffix to indicate a male. (Several incidents of his career suggest that Samson was originally a kind of sun-god.)

The name was popular in English during the Middle Ages but had less appeal after the Reformation, probably because the violent and melodramatic career of the biblical strong man was not admirable to the Puritans. The name occurred but rarely in the colonies.

The occasional appearance in later times is probably to be attributed to the family name used as a given name.

Samuel ♂ Hebrew, "heard-by-God," with reference to Hannah, wife of Elkanah, who had vowed (I Samuel 1:11) that if God would "give unto thine handmaid a man child" she would dedicate him to God. The birth of Samuel thus showed that Hannah had been heard by God.

More than with most names we can give some suggestion for the immense popularity of Samuel. In most societies many women have an intense desire to bear a child—especially a male child. The story of Samuel's birth and the significance of his naming thus made a particular appeal to wives who were under social pressure to provide population for an empty land.

Before the American settlement Samuel had already become a common name in England. (In France it had become a specially favored name among Protestants, so that anyone bearing it may be supposed to have some Hugenot connections.) In America the relative use of Samuel increased, perhaps for the reason already suggested. From a position usually around fifth or seventh, Samuel, in the Boston birth list of 1630–69, rose to second place, yielding only to John. At Harvard, except for two minor variations, Samuel stood in second place for a century and a half, from 1640 to 1790. During the same period at Princeton the situation was roughly the same, though Samuel was never so popular there as it was at Harvard.

From 1800, however, Samuel began to feel the general decline of biblical names. Both at Harvard and at Princeton it dropped into third place, and it never recovered. It continued, however, as an important name during another half-century, gradually falling off. By decades from 1800 on, Samuel's position at Harvard was 3, 3, 5, 5, 10, 8. In 1800 Princeton put Samuel in seventh place, and in the 1810–19 decade Samuel failed to make the top ten.

The decline during the first half of the nineteenth century became a collapse in the second half. Only occasionally was

Samuel able to make a low place in the top ten. By this time the Old Testament names were beginning to seem archaic. The self-consciousness about Jewish names was also a factor in the decline of Samuel.

Since 1900 Samuel has remained viable, as indeed it will probably so remain for many years more. It is, however, a name with little present vitality. Its forms Sam and Sammy have been well established. It seems to have lacked any feminine, not having particularly appealed to the ladies.

Its numbers considered, the name has been that of comparatively few famous men. We may mention Adams, Houston, Morse, and Gompers. The fictional hero Uncle Sam is, however, an interesting national figure.

Sandy, *see* ALEXANDER.

Sarah ♀ As the account in Genesis explains, "And God said unto Abraham, 'As for Sarai thy wife, thou shalt not call her name Sarai, but Sarah shall her name be.' " We have here the direct evidence of what can be assumed from many other names of Genesis. Sarai has been translated as if Hebrew, with the unlikely result, for a name, of "contrition."

The most likely conclusion, here as with numerous other names of Genesis, would be that Sarai was the original non-Hebrew name in the patriarchal story and that it was, by a kind of folk-etymology, shifted to Sarah. This latter form, occurring in the Bible only twice, seems to be a genuine Hebrew word, though doubtless borrowed from some near-by language. Sarah can be translated as "princess," and thus is a complimentary term.

Sarah came into English popularity only with the Reformation. By the seventeenth century it was well established, standing often as high as third, exceeded only by Mary and Elizabeth, and occasionally by Anna. This prosperity continued in all the English colonies through the eighteenth century and on into the nineteenth. Sarah fell off considerably toward the end of that century, and came to be regarded as old-fashioned—often, indeed, giving place to its own variant, Sallie. It still, however, remains in use.

As is usual in name-history, the causes remain uncertain.

Why does Sarah so far exceed Rebecca and Rachel, the other patriarch's wives? One reason is certainly the literal meaning, "princess." But Sarah is not a very important character in the biblical text, and is not even a very lovable character, vindictively persecuting Hagar and Ishmael. Probably the most potent of the reasons for the popularity of the name lay in God's promise to Abraham with respect to Sarah on the occasion of the name-changing, in Genesis 17:16, "I will bless her, and give thee a son also of her . . . and she shall be a mother of nations."

The variant Sara was originally the Greek adaptation, since Greek lacks the letter *h*. It has never attained much popularity. On the other hand, SALLIE (or Sally) has tended to become a name in its own right. Sadie was chiefly a nineteenth-century variant, based upon the *r-d* shift.

Saul ♂ Probably Hebrew, "asked-for." This unusual origin may be justified by the reality that the tribes of Israel had "asked for" a king (I Samuel 8).

Saul was never much used in America. If David was to be a hero (as the frequent use of his name attests), Saul must be considered the opposition, accorded no more popularity than was accorded to other "evil" characters. Moreover, Saul was the original name of St. Paul, and the name-changing suggests that Saul was a particularly unsuitable name.

For reasons undetermined, Saul has enjoyed some popularity in the twentieth century.

Scipio ♂ Its use as a name for black men arose in the period of slavery. It springs from the great Roman family—in particular, from two of its members who bore the honorary name Africanus in recognition of their military exploits in that continent.

Though not as common as other Roman names (Cato, Pompey, Caesar), Scipio was in current use in the eighteenth and earlier nineteenth centuries, and was commonly shortened to Zip. Variant spellings are numerous, e.g. Sipio. Under cover of some of these, the name probably still is current.

Scott ♂ From the family name, originally indicating a person of Scottish origin. It has become commonly used as a given name in the twentieth century, thus being another example (as is

ROSS) of a Scottish family name becoming a commonly used personal name in the United States.

Selina ♀ Of uncertain origin, but most likely from a French form Celine, with an unusual alteration of spelling. Celine may be from a Latin form Coelina, "heavenly." The name is commonly related to the Greek *selene,* "moon." It is a rare name in English.

Selma ♀ It is derived from the so-called Ossianic poems. It is the name of a palace and, according to the text, means "beautiful appearance." Possibly it is a coinage by the author, James Macpherson, and it may have Irish connections.

It has been very rare, but is of some special interest as apparently suggesting other names in *-elma,* e.g. Delma, Thelma, Velma. (*See* THELMA.)

Seraphina ♀ A latinized form, from Hebrew *seraph,* a symbolic or imaginary creature. In Hebrew the word may be associated with a word for "burn," and thus with some kind of fire spirit. Just why it should have become the basis of a name for women is uncertain, but it was borne by an early saint (of uncertain date) and thus passed on, chiefly in the Romance languages. In the United States it has been so rare as scarcely to be considered viable.

Seth ♂ In spite of the many non-Hebrew names in the early chapters of Genesis, this one must be, somewhat tentatively, accepted as Hebrew, because of its aptness of meaning—"compensation, substitute," that is, another son to Adam and Eve after the catastrophe of Cain and Abel.

Seth was a moderately popular name in early New England, doubtless being sometimes given in recognition that the child was a compensation for an earlier son who had died. Also, the name was short, simple, and easy to pronounce.

Seth died out in the mid-nineteenth century, along with other biblical names.

Sharon ♀ In the Old Testament the name is that of a place. As "rose of Sharon" it appears in The Song of Solomon (2:1) as the symbol of the beloved. Since Rose was a well-established name in English, eighteenth-century usage could easily adopt the longer form, and so the name appeared as Rose-of-Sharon, probably a nineteenth-century development. (*See* ROSE.) It was shortened in pronunciation, with the spelling Rosasharn. The appearance of a character so named in Steinbeck's *Grapes of Wrath* (1939) must have disseminated the knowledge of this form.

A shorter form produced Sharon, which has established itself in later twentieth-century usage, sometimes making the top ten. (Cf. EBENEZER). The occasional Shirin is apparently a variant of Sharon.

Shearjashub ♂ Hebrew. The name occurs only once in the Bible (Isaiah 7:3) as that of a symbolic "son" of Isaiah. It is translated, in a marginal note to the King James Version, as "he-that-is-before-the-king-of-Assyria-shall-take-away-the-riches, etc." This translation obviously adds to the mysterious quality of the name.

Such mysterious and picturesque names attract occasional parents who are looking for some unusual name for their child. Shearjashub is thus found, though very rarely, in actual American usage during the period of biblical names. Cf. MA-HERSHALALHASHBAZ.

Sheila ♀ Irish, representing an adaptation of CELIA. In the twentieth century it has become a fairly popular name.

Sherman ♂ The surname is of occupational origin, i.e. shearman, a sheep-shearer. The given name doubtless owes much to the popularity of General W. T. Sherman among his Civil War veterans. The name has remained viable in the twentieth century.

Sherry ♀ The family name exists, but is rare. Probably the given name represents merely another spelling of Cherie or Cheri. It is rare, and modern in its occurrence. (*See* CHERE.)

Shirley ♂ ♀ As a place-name (meaning "shire-glade"), Shirley may be traced from Domesday Book (11th century). It became a family name, and in the nineteenth century and early twentieth century it appeared occasionally as a man's name in the United States.

As a woman's name (in England) it seems to date from Charlotte Brönte's novel *Shirley* (1849). The heroine of that novel was so called (fictionally speaking), being an only child, in order that her name could be associated with the estate, since the name would otherwise have been lost on her marriage. The novelist notes it as a "masculine cognomen."

Since Charlotte Brönte's novels were widely read both in England and in the United States, the idea that Shirley could be a woman's name became well established, especially in the South, where the use of family names as names for women was already current. By 1920 the men who were named Shirley were becoming highly conscious of their feminine identification, and almost no male babies were being so named.

With the almost unprecedented popularity of the child-actress Shirley Temple in the 1930's the name reached its high point, and was even more strongly fixed as being a woman's name. In Smith's list (1942) it stands at 25. Then the inevitable reaction set in. By 1950 the name was still fairly common for women, but after 1950 Shirley lost most of its vogue.

Sibyl, Sybil ♀ Though nonbiblical, the name Sibyl was accepted in the Christian tradition as that of a woman apparently possessing semidivine powers of prophecy. The name became a common one for women in England during the Middle Ages. The Puritans made little use of it, however, and it has been of rare occurrence in America.

Sidney, Sydney ♂ ♀ It is a family name taken over as a given name. It appeared first in the Harvard lists indicating a child born *c.* 1790, and there is a possibility that the English political figure Thomas Townshend (Viscount Sydney) was being honored for his favorable attitude toward the colonies during the Revolution.

The continuing use of Sidney, however, suggests the possibility that it is a feudal name (*see* HOWARD), since the Sidneys were a prominent English family, and Sir Philip Sidney (1554–86) was a Romantic hero. Certainly in later years the name assumed such connotations, and Mark Twain could use Sid Sawyer for the unpleasant younger brother of the typically American older brother named Tom. In spite of Mark Twain, Sidney continued in use. In fact, it shows a marked increase from 1870 to 1890, thus including the year of publication of *Huckleberry Finn*. The heroic figure of Sydney Carton in Dickens's *Tale of Two Cities* (1859) probably stimulated the use of the name.

With the passage of time the aristocratic aura of the name faded out, but Sidney remained viable. In the Smith list (1941) it is 86.

The use of Sidney as a woman's name is unusual enough to suggest a special origin, which Withycombe credits to the Irish name Sidony, derived from the Roman Catholic "Feast of the Sindon," i.e. "winding-sheet." On the other hand, other family names have produced feminines, e.g. Beverly and Shirley.

The variation between *i* and *y* is a matter of no importance, since early printers used the two letters interchangeably.

Silas ♂ Latin, an abbreviation of Silvanus, the name of the tree-god. It was an established name in the New Testament period. As the companion of Paul on his journey (Acts 15–18) Silas was a well-known biblical character, but his name was not much used in America.

For reasons which remain uncertain, Silas (usually in its shortened form, Si) came to have bucolic suggestions in the late nineteenth century (cf. REUBEN). This circumstance aided in the obsolescence of Silas.

Silvia, Sylvia ♀ Latin, "of-the-woods, silvan."

Rhaea Silvia was a figure in Roman mythology, and Silvia came into renewed use as a given name in Italy at the time of the Renaissance. Its use by Shakespeare in *Two Gentlemen of Verona* is probably one cause of its preservation in English.

Simeon ♂ Withycombe gives it as Hebrew, "hearkening" (or, possibly, "hyena"). Neither of these can be reasonably assumed for the name of a tribe. The likelihood is that, being a tribal name, Simeon is very old and, like many other names of Genesis, it may not even be Hebrew.

Like the names of the other tribes of Israel, Simeon was used during the period of biblical names, appearing chiefly in the eighteenth century. It was never a popular name. (*See* SIMON.)

Simon ♂ The name is a Greek development of SIMEON. Simon was a popular name; it was borne by eight persons in the New

Testament. The most notable of these was Simon Barjona, whose name was changed to PETER.

Simon appears steadily in the Harvard lists from 1660 to 1850, but faded out in the general decline of biblical names.

The popularity of the South American liberator Simón Bolívar led to some nineteenth-century usage. On the other hand, as the name of the villainous Simon Legree in *Uncle Tom's Cabin* (1859), the name must have fallen in esteem. It may be considered obsolete by 1875.

Solomon ♂ The name obviously contains the Hebrew word for "peace" (*shalom*). The suggestion is that Solomon had originally borne some other name and that Solomon itself was a name which was ascribed to him when the unwarlike nature of his reign had become known, and notable.

Though lacking the charisma of his father, David, the wise King Solomon is an important biblical character. The American colonists used his name regularly until it began to fade out with the decline of the biblical names after 1800.

Sonia ♀ Russian, a diminutive of SOPHIA. Probably transmitted at the literary level by the reading of Russian works in translation, Sonia survives in American use in the mid-twentieth century, but it has remained a rare name.

Sophia, Sophie ♀ Greek, "wisdom." Although several saints bear the name, the chief line of development is through the Byzantine Empire, especially through the great church Hagia Sophia, which was built by Justinian in the sixth century. The name became a popular one for women throughout the area of the Greek Church, which included the Slavic countries. From them the name spread eastward into Germany.

It failed to reach England until the seventeenth century, and had little vogue there until after the marriage (in 1761) of George III to a German princess bearing that name. Thus it hardly appears in colonial America, but developed (largely as Sophie) in the last years of the eighteenth century and extended through most of the nineteenth century as a popular name. It was becoming old-fashioned in the later part of that century, and has not figured much in the twentieth.

Stanley ♂ A repeated place-name ("stone-glade"), in England, it became a common family name, and, as such, became a given name in the nineteenth century. The Stanleys were an eminent English family, known to Romantic poetry by such a line as Scott's in *Marmion:*

Charge, Chester, charge! On, Stanley, on!

The adoption of the name in the United States is therefore to be tied in with the aristocratic namings of the nineteenth century. The name begins to appear about 1850, is commonest about 1890, and is still viable. Withycombe suggests a connection with the African explorer Stanley, who was a highly popular figure in the late nineteenth century, but in the United States, at least, the name was well launched before the emergence of that Stanley, who was born in 1841. Quite possibly Stanley was used as a given name in the United States earlier than it was in England.

Starr ♀ ♂ Though from a family name, which was derived from the word "star," the name is probably from some secondary meaning of the word, or by its use in an inn-sign—"At the Star." In modern usage this family name has been more commonly applied to women, probably considered as having a vague complimentary suggestion.

Stella ♀ Latin, "star." The name apparently was first used as a fictional one by Sir Philip Sidney in his sonnet sequence *Astrophel to Stella* (1591). In the United States it has had an occasional appearance from the mid-nineteenth century on, probably arising from its literary usage.

Stephanie ♀ This is a borrowing from the French, which has maintained the Greek *ph* in the name. It was negligible most of the time, but became popular in the mid-twentieth century. (*See* STEPHEN.)

Stephen ♂ Greek; literally, "crown." At the time of Christ it was a common name. Being the name of the first martyr, Stephen became established in Christian tradition as St. Stephen. A number of lesser saints also thus took their names. Stephen was in common English usage at the time of the colonization. As a biblical character, Stephen escaped the Puritan prejudice against nonbliblical saints.

The name provides an unusual example of constancy, since it always remained in use, but over the course of three hundred years never became highly popular. At last, in the mid-twentieth century, it attained some vogue, even appearing as sixth in one list.

The *ph* spelling preserves the Greek tradition, and is the common one for the given name. The *v* spelling represents the tradition of the Middle Ages, and is now more commonly used for the family name.

Stewart ♂ From the family name, which is from the Anglo-Saxon *stiweard*—in modern English, "steward." The exact meaning in early times is somewhat uncertain, but the office of steward in the king's household became highly important, and was adopted by the hereditary stewards of Scotland as a surname and then was passed on to the clan. It is thus chiefly a name of Scottish origin.

In spite of the uninspiring short form Stew, the name is fairly common as a given name, possibly profiting from the popularity of Scottish names in general.

Susanna[h], Susan ♀ Hebrew, "lily," the name of the chief character (even to be called the heroine) of the famous tale Susanna and the Elders. This story, to be found in the biblical Apocrypha, was highly popular in the Christian tradition of the Middle Ages, and has maintained itself to some degree in modern times by being anthologized as the first detective story.

The name was already established in England before the colonization, and early American listings include it as a common name, spelled Susanna or Susannah. Susan appeared rarely at first, but became the predominating form in the eighteenth century.

Generally standing in the second ten, the name occasionally reached the top ten, and would stand higher except that Susanna and Susan are generally listed as separate names.

By the later nineteenth century the name had declined sharply and was "old-fashioned" to most people. It revived (and even set new marks for itself) in the twentieth century, as such names are likely to do. In two lists of the 1950's Susan stands in second and third place. In fact, if Suzanne should be included, the combined count would even edge the name up appreciably.

Indeed, much of the popularity that is credited to Susan must be shared with the derived forms. Susan itself is an obvious contraction of the original Susanna. The ordinary development has resulted in Sue, and Suzie or Susy. Even the phonetically unusual Sukey was highly popular in the eighteenth and early nineteenth centuries, and has enjoyed a modern revival. In addition, the French form Suzanne has come into favor in the twentieth century.

Sybil, *see* SIBYL.

Sydney, *see* SIDNEY.

Sylvia, *see* SILVIA.

T

Tabitha ♀ Aramaic, "deer, antelope," probably conceived as a symbol of grace and beauty. It was the name of a woman who was, as the story is told in Acts 9, restored to life by St. Peter. Probably for closer identification she is mentioned as "a certain disciple named Tabitha, which by interpretation [into Greek] is called Dorcas."

Though partaking to some extent of the general popularity of the biblical names, Tabitha never itself became really popular. Its greater use may have been prevented by the string of meanings which attached themselves to the short form, Tabby. At various times it has meant a house-cat, a spinster, a gossip.

Tamar ♀ Hebrew, "palm-tree." Loughead gives it in her list, but I have not found it, and it must have been excessively rare, even during the flourishing of biblical names. The word clearly means "palm-tree" in Hebrew, but there may be some secondary meaning, in the sense of incest, since both the biblical women of the name were thus involved. These "unpleasant" associations of the name have cut its use down to the vanishing point. (Tamara, in rare use during the twentieth century, is probably a different name, of Slavic or Baltic origin.)

Tamsen, Tamson, Tamsin ♀ A Scottish development from "Tom's-son" is possible, but it is more likely from "Thomasin" with -*in* as the diminutive-feminine, and an *o-a* shift, which again is Scottish. In the United States it was viable in the nineteenth century, but has made little showing since that time.

Temperance ♀ The word does not appear in the Old Testament. In the New Testament the translators used it to express four different Greek words, but even so it occurs only six times.

The meaning it had, in the Puritan era, had no special connection with abstinence from alcoholic liquors, but merely suggested self-control and moderation. Like the virtue which it inculcated, it was moderately used as a name in the seventeenth century, but it disappeared later, and has not been revived.

Terence ♂ From Latin *Terentius,* the name of a tribe, meaning unknown. The name seems to have come into use in Ireland, where it was employed, on the basis of similarity of sound, to replace one or two of the native Celtic names (cf. MALACHI).

In the United States the name generally maintained its Irish associations through the nineteenth century, and to some extent it has done so to the present on the basis of tradition. Terence, in the late twentieth century, was still in active usage.

Perhaps unfortunately, the diminutive Terry has moved into being chiefly a feminine. We can only expect some confusion and ambiguity—the most likely result being the survival of Terry as a woman's name and the decline of Terence.

Thaddeus ♂ The language and meaning are uncertain, but possibly Aramaic, "praise." In Matthew 10:3 it is the name of an Apostle, given as "Lebbaeus, whose surname was Thaddæus."

In New England the name was viable (but not much used) through the eighteenth century and until about the middle of the nineteenth century.

Thaddeus was commoner in the countries of the Eastern Church than of the Western, and Jane Porter's popular novel *Thaddeus of Warsaw* (1803) may have helped the name maintain itself in English-speaking countries.

Thankful ♀ Probably to suggest the phrase "be-thankful." In Plymouth Colony of the seventeenth century Thankful generally stood about third in frequency among the abstracts. Even so, it is not a really popular name. Thankful disappeared after 1700.

Thelma ♀ It is apparently a coinage by the novelist Marie Corelli, appearing as the name of the chief character in the novel *Thelma, a Norwegian Princess* (1898). It seems however, to have no linguistic connection with Norwegian. (*See* SELMA.)

My lists have not yielded Thelma as a personal name before the publication of the novel, but after that time it occurs often enough to be considered viable.

Theodore ♂ Greek, "God's-gift," one of the number of names which thank God for the birth of a child, e.g. (in Greek) Dorothea, Dorothy; (in Hebrew) Nathan, Elnathan, Nathaniel. Theodora and (less commonly) Theodosia are the feminines for Theodore.

In spite of a number of saints bearing the name, it was scarcely used in England during the Middle Ages, and was considered a name of the Eastern Church and of the countries under that domination. For example, it was commonly used in Russia.

It began to appear in England during the seventeenth century, probably because of increased contacts with eastern and central Europe. At the end of that century Theodore was appearing in American usage.

Once established, it continued steadily—though it was never common—through the eighteenth century. It was more used in the nineteenth, with a modest "boom" around 1850. Theodore Roosevelt, the highly popular President (born 1858), helped to continue the interest in the name, and it has remained viable. He also helped to fix Ted and Teddy as the by-forms.

Theodore may thus be seen as a name with a somewhat unusual history in that, after a late introduction, it settled down as a stable name, with little variation.

Theophilus ♂ Greek, "God-loving," or "loved-by-God." The name is that of the "most excellent Theophilus" to whom Luke addressed both his Gospel and Acts. It was occasionally used in early New England, but seems to have gone quite out of favor with the decline of the biblical names.

T[h]eresa ♀ The name is of uncertain origin, but it has strong Spanish associations. It became more widely known because of St. Teresa of Ávila (1515–82). It was somewhat popular in England after 1700 because of the alliance with Austria, whose queen was Maria Theresa. In the colonies it was always rare, but it has survived as viable into the late twentieth century, and even with some increase, perhaps because of a certain popularity of Spanish names, such as Linda.

Theron ♂ Greek[?]. It was the name of a well-known ruler in ancient Sicily, but there seems to be little likelihood of American boys having been named for him. Neither does the literal meaning (from *ther,* "a wild beast") offer any good reason for such naming. The name is rare—it seems to have been most used in 1880–1900.

Thomas ♂ The name of an Apostle. It is Aramaic, the common language of Palestine in the time of Christ. Meaning "twin," it may be a kind of nickname which became fixed as an independent name.

After the Norman Conquest, as Christian names replaced the ancient Anglo-Saxon dithemics, Thomas became current. The murder of Thomas à Becket in 1170 transformed him into a saint and national hero, and his name prospered accordingly. In fact, it came to stand typically in third place, exceeded only by John and William. Thomas thus became much more characteristic of English than it is of French, Spanish, or other European languages, producing such prototypes as Tom Jones, Tom Sawyer, Tommy Atkins, Uncle Tom, and the piper's son.

Being a New Testament saint's name, it survived the Reformation with little damage. It was common among the early immigrants to America, being the second most numerous name in Raleigh's colony. During the seventeenth century it frequently nosed out William and stood in second place. In the eighteenth century it fell off, perhaps because of the growing popularity of Old Testament names. Though we remember Jefferson and Paine, it was not a very common name in the Continental regiments. In the nineteenth century it recovered its older popularity. In the twentieth century Thomas generally fails to make the first ten but remains still current. The name has also been fortunate in having highly popular bynames—Tom and Tommy.

The *th*-spelling (not used in the bynames) is a normal transliteration from a Greek *theta*. The anomalous *t*- pronunciation represents usage among the Norman conquerors, who did not use the *th*- sound.

Feminizations, such as Thomasina, have never become popular, though in the twentieth century Tommy has become a common nickname for girls bearing such family names as Thomas or Thompson.

Timothy ♂ Greek; clearly with the ideas "honor, respect," and "God." The actual meaning may be "honor-to-God!" or "we-honor-God!" or even "may-God-be-honored!"

Timothy was the companion of Paul in the Book of Acts, and two biblical epistles are addressed to him. Though recognized as a saint, Timothy only came to be used as an English name in the post-Reformation period. Among the early immigrants to Massachusetts it appeared as a regularly used name, though not common, and it continued in use through the seventeenth and eighteenth centuries.

After a small flurry of popularity around 1800 it fell off, and in the later nineteenth century it was scarcely viable. It has, however, recovered and has had some continuing use down to the mid-twentieth century.

Titus ♂ Latin, of uncertain meaning. Though the name was borne by a companion of St. Paul and is that of a book of the New Testament, it was never much used in the United States, probably being associated with the Roman emperor rather than with Paul's friend. Its usage, such as it was, seems to have centered around the middle of the nineteenth century.

Tobias ♂ The Greek form of the Hebrew name Tobiah, "God-is-good." Tobias is a principal character in the Apocryphal Book of Tobit—notable, if for nothing else, in that he has a dog.

The names of characters in the Apocrypha were not much used in the colonies (*see* JUDITH, SUSANNA), but Tobias was viable down into the early nineteenth century. It was regularly shortened to Toby, and in that form still turns up occasionally.

[A note on the dog. Reluctantly, the compiler of this book has not been able to expand his activities into cynonymy, the vast and rich field of the names of dogs. He is, however, prepared to stand ground against a proposition, widely advocated, that Toby's dog was named Moreover. Such fallacy arises by a willful misinterpretation of the line "Moreover the dog went with him"!]

Toni ♀ Derived from Antonia, it developed some popularity in the mid-twentieth century. The masculine is regularly Tony. (*See* ANTONY.)

Tremble ♀ Probably to express some such idea as "tremble-before-God," though there is no such exact wording in the Bible. (Cf. FEAR.) It was a very rare name, even in the period of biblical names.

Tristram ♂ Though the name may originally have been Celtic, meaning "tumult," the French writers of romances self-consciously connected it with their own *triste,* "sad," because of the sorrows involved in the famous love affair of Tristram and Iseult.

The name occurs in the United States (e.g. for a Harvard student *c.* 1750), but it is so rare as hardly even to be called viable.

Troilus ♂ Greek[?]. The first part of the name is presumably from the name of the city, Troy; the rest is uncertain. Unimportant in the *Iliad,* Troilus become a great figure of romance in the Middle Ages, along with his love Cressida. Spelled Troyles, the name appears as that of a slave in the eighteenth century, in accordance with the custom of endowing blacks with classical names.

Troy ♂ It is from the family name rather than from any influence of the Homeric poems. It seems to be a viable given name in the twentieth century. The family name is from the city of Troyes in France.

U

Ulysses ♂ It is the Latin form of the name of the Homeric hero, Odysseus, of uncertain language and meaning. The name is very rare in the United States, and occurs in the decades following the Civil War. It is obviously a tribute to General (and President) Ulysses S. Grant.

Una ♀ Of uncertain origin. One possibility is that it is an adaptation of a Celtic Irish name which was borrowed by the English. Such a borrowing seems unlikely; it is, at least, undemonstrated. Una occurs in Spenser's *Faerie Queene*, where it is obviously the feminine of Latin *unus*, "one," and is used symbolically in the sense of "unity, consistency," in opposition to the treacherous Duessa (from *duo*, "two"). It has been a rare name in the United States, but has been viable since the later nineteenth century.

Uriah ♂ "God-is-light." The story, as recorded in II Samuel, presents Uriah as a high-minded and conscientious soldier and David as a sensual, treacherous, and vicious king. Yet—perhaps it is merely the way of the world—the charismatic and successful David has had many thousands bear his name. And did you ever hear of anyone being called Uriah? Yet in these United States there were a few—occasional ones whose parents, apparently, thought for themselves.

As if, however, really to clinch the matter, Dickens selected

Uriah as the name of his most repulsive character, in his ever-popular *David Copperfield.* (And note there again the name David!) Who, after the advent of Heep, would touch the name Uriah?

Urian, Urien ♂ It is probably of Welsh origin, meaning unknown. It occurs rarely in America—in most instances, presumably, in a Welsh context.

Uriel ♂ Hebrew, "God-is-light." Except for the different divine name, this is the same as Uriah. As the name of two unimportant biblical characters, Uriel scarcely merited survival in colonial New England. Its literal meaning and perhaps its connection with Uriah may be responsible for its occasional use.

Urien, *see* URIAN.

Ursula ♀ Latin, diminutive of *ursa,* "she-bear." The namings, however, are from St. Ursula, widely known in medieval times from her association with the story of the 11,000 virgins. The name, though it may be called viable, has always been rare in the United States, whose inhabitants were apparently not enamored of such wholesale virginity.

Uzziah ♂ Hebrew, "God-is-strong." It is the name of five biblical characters, including a king of Judah. Its occurrence in America is questionable, but its apparent Greek form is to be found. *See* OZIAS.

V

Valeria, Valerie ♀ Feminines of Valerius, the Roman tribal name. As the name of two saints, one of them of French extraction, Valerie is current in French. Partly from French influence, the name has remained viable in the United States.

Varina ♀ Of uncertain origin, possibly from the Russian name Varvara (Barbara) by way of a diminutive Varinka.

Velma ♀ After the success of THELMA the ending -*elma* seems to have been created by analogy. Another such coinage in the twentieth century was Delma.

Venus ♀ The name, from the ancient Roman goddess, occurs as a slave name, but is very rare. As a rule, classical names for female slaves are hard to find, whereas they were fairly common among male slaves. Besides Venus, we have Diana, Dido, and Phoebe. The overwhelming majority of slave women, however, bore biblical names from a very early period.

Vera ♀ Latin, "true," but more directly from Russian, "faith." It probably became known because some novelists used it in the late nineteenth century. It has not had more than occasional use in the United States.

Veronica ♀ Latin, from the form *vera iconica,* "having-to-do-with-the-true-image," the reference being to the representation of the face of Christ on the handkerchief of the woman who thus came to be St. Veronica. The name has recently come somewhat into use in America.

Victor ♂ Latin, "victor, conqueror." It has not left much imprint on American naming, having been both late and rare. It still, however, remains viable.

Victoria ♀ Latin, "victory." Queen Victoria, herself named after her German mother, brought the name into English usage. She reigned long and successfully, and was personally popular. Her name, however, though appearing on cities, states, and natural features all over the world, was not more than moderately popular as a personal name among the British, and much less so, understandably, in the United States. It remains viable, however, even in the counterculture.

Vincent ♂ Latin, from *vincens,* "conquering." As the name of several notable saints, Vincent has had some use, especially among Catholics. It remains viable in the mid-twentieth century.

Viola, Violet ♀ It is a flower-name (*see* LILY), but as a flower it has been usually known by its diminutive, Violet. Viola is probably known more commonly from its use for a character in Shakespeare's *Twelfth Night.* It has been a rare name.

Virginia ♀ Latin. In the United States the name is inescapably tied up with the place-name Virginia, which was bestowed in 1584 by Queen Elizabeth I. The meaning is clearly "virgin-land." Since Elizabeth was frequently celebrated as the Virgin Queen, the naming was really a naming for herself. The name was also known as that of one of the heroines of the Roman Republic.

In 1587 the first English child to be born in America was christened Virginia. She was, however, lost along with the rest of the Raleigh colony, and no direct tradition of naming resulted from Virginia Dare.

Actually, if used at all in the colonial period, Virginia must have been very rare. It began to appear in the nineteenth century, and enjoyed a sudden burst of popularity about 1900. It still remains a fairly common name.

Vivian, Vivien ♀ Theoretically, Vivian should be a man's name; Vivien, a woman's name. Vivian is from the name of several saints. Vivien may be a misreading of the Celtic form Ninian, and it appears in Tennyson's *Idylls of the King* as a woman's name. Actually, the record available fails to show any American man named Vivian (or Vivien), and we may question whether any such exist. (Cf. EVELYN.)

W

Wallace ♂ From the Scottish surname—in particular, from William Wallace, the medieval hero of the Scottish War of Independence. In the United States it has been primarily a surname, but has also become popular as a given name, having lost any close association with a Scottish tradition.

Walter ♂ Germanic, *vald*, "rule," *-harja*, "folk, people." The name came to England with the Normans, by whom it was much favored. It was still in circulation at the time of the Reformation, but had become somewhat rare.

In the colonies the name was not favored, and approached extinction. Around 1800 it became more popular, possibly because Romanticism favored medieval names. This growth continued through the century until the name became a common one—in the decade of 1900–1909 breaking into the top ten at Harvard, though only at tenth place. In the later twentieth century it has lost most of this popularity, but remains viable.

The older abbreviation was Wat. In the United States, where the influence of spelling has usually been strong, the abbreviation has regularly been Walt, as in the notable example of Walt Whitman.

Wanda ♀ Germanic, probably to be connected with *vand*, "stem, branch." It may have been a nineteenth-century adoption from German usage. In any case, it has remained rare.

Warren ♂ From the family name, which indicates a person associated with a rabbit warren. The popularity of the name rests upon the hero-status of General Joseph Warren, killed in the Battle of Bunker Hill.

Washington ♂ From the family name, which is derived from a place in England. It was a fairly popular name in the Revolutionary period and the early nineteenth century, e.g. Washington Irving, the writer, and Washington Allston, the poet-painter.

It declined in popularity, partly because newer heroes competed with Washington, but also because it was of awkward length. Its common abbreviation was Wash, and that was certainly unheroic. The name has scarcely been viable in the twentieth century.

Wayne ♂ The surname arose from some association with a wain (wagon)—sometimes, probably, a shortening of Wainwright, a wagonbuilder. The common use as a given name is doubtless chiefly after General Anthony Wayne, a hero of both the Revolution and the Indian wars. In the twentieth century the name still shows much vitality.

Wealthy, Welthy ♀ This name is best considered an abstract. It occurs rarely as late as the nineteenth century. The word is biblical, and the name might be a reference to Psalms 66:12, "thou broughtest us out into a wealthy place." The meaning was probably "healthy," rather than the modern meaning.

Wendy ♀ It seems to have had no existence before its use by J. M. Barrie for a character in *Peter Pan* (1904). Presumably he coined the name. Its resemblance to Wanda is close, but may be merely accidental. The remarkable feature about the name is its growth in usage from that recent origin. In the later twentieth century it has become a popular name in the United States. It has even acquired a variant spelling, Wendi.

Wilfred, Wilfrid ♂ Anglo-Saxon; from *will*, "will," and *frith*, "peace." The name went out of use after the Norman Conquest. It was revived in the nineteenth century in England as a part of the Romantic attempt to restore medieval usages, being connected with the so-called Tractarian movement. It has become fairly common in England, but scarcely exists in the

United States—if known at all, being considered an anglicism.

William ♂ Germanic, *vilja,* "will," and *helma,* "helmet." As with many Germanic names, the literal meaning is of little importance as compared with its ethnic and social history. The Normans brought the name to England in the eleventh century, and it became the favorite Norman name, producing a very great deal of repetition.

From being a name favored by the aristocratic Norman minority, William came to be generally used. During the reign of Elizabeth I it was the commonest man's name (see Withycombe, 3rd ed., p. xxviii), totaling 22.5 per cent of the whole, with John at 15.5 per cent and Thomas at 13.5 per cent. The situation thus shows a nonbiblical name which was preferred to even the most used New Testament names. It shows also that William had become essentially a traditional and secular name in England, not much influenced by religion.

William fell off in popularity somewhat in the seventeenth century, but was still a common name among immigrants to the American colonies, usually standing below John and about even with Thomas.

In the New England colonies William faced the full competition of the biblical names. For instance, in Plymouth Colony (1640–99) William stood in seventh place, all others of the first ten being biblical names, if Ebenezer can be so included. In Boston for the period 1630–69 William stood in ninth place, with only 2.3 per cent of the names.

In the Harvard lists, William has a spotty appearance in the seventeenth century, making the first ten about half the time but sometimes falling off to only a single representative. In the eighteenth century, however, William stood consistently in the first ten, with a continuous rise from fifth or seventh at the beginning and standing steadily at third place from 1740 to 1790.

After 1800—with the disappearance of the competition of the biblical names—William rose to second place and then, in 1820, took first place. From 1850 until 1910 it continued to hold first place in the Harvard lists. (Note that for actual calendar dates, we must subtract 20 from the Harvard lists.)

Other evidence, especially the Princeton lists, confirm the testimony of Harvard.

In the general disturbance in American culture of the mid-twentieth century the shift away from the traditional William became sharp. In Lawson's list (children born *c.* 1950) William barely makes tenth place. In a California school list for children born *c.* 1940, William failed to make the top ten, though its form Bill/Billy stood third, in a tie with Peter. In a similar school list of children born *c.* 1960 William was an undistinguished name far down in the list, and Bill a single.

By the middle of the twentieth century the thousand-year-long reign of William seems to come to an end. But it may not be so! The possibility remains that some new shift in cultural habit may lead to a revival of the name. So many famous men in the Anglo-American tradition have borne it that it must constantly be present in parents' minds when a name is sought. Any strong renewal of that tradition may call William into prominence again.

During most of its history, William has had the short form Will, with its diminutive Willie. This form, however, was not wholly successful in the United States, whose people seem to have considered Will as poetic and old-fashioned, with a suggestion of British usage. In modern usage Bill and Billy came greatly to exceed it—in fact, almost to destroy it.

The shift from *w* to *b* is not a common one, and demands a *v* as an intermediate step. The situation suggests a British rather than an American origin, and the *w-v-b* transition is characteristic of southern England—in fact, of London.

Although further research is needed to establish the history of Bill, we can venture the opinion that it originated—or, at least, came into general use—in England during the earlier eighteenth century. From England it probably reached the colonies by the ordinary process of migration. If we are correct that it was city-born, the suggestions of Bill could be sophisticated on the one hand, but on the other they could be supermale, with the implications of toughness and even of a crime. Such a figure is Bill Sykes of Dickens's *Oliver Twist* (1839), and Dickens chose his characters' names carefully. Bill, even yet, fails to show the humorous associations of Jack, Jimmy, and diminutives of other "big" names.

Wilson, Willis ♂ Being a very common surname, Wilson has also become one of the commoner names among those transferred from surnames to given names. A particular reason for this popularity is probably that the popular short form Bill is allowable with this name.

Willis, itself probably a form of Wilson, is also so used, doubtless for the same reasons. Wilbur is also of the same group.

Winifred ♀ Welsh. The literal meaning is uncertain, but *win* is probably the same as the commoner *gwen*, that is, "white." The popularity of the name goes back to St. Winifred. It was generally used in a Welsh context, and occurs in one of the early Jamestown lists. Though never common, it has remained in use continuously.

Wrestling, *see* NAPHTALI.

X Y Z

Xanthippe ♀ Greek, "light-colored horse." The name occurs rarely in colonial times. Its only source is apparently the wife of Socrates, a woman very unfavorably presented. A naming for her may be one of the occasional namings from sheer ignorance rather than from love. It is sometimes spelled Zanthippy. It has several other variants, e.g. Zantippy, Xantippe.

Ximena ♀ Uncertain. The usage indicates an origin in northern Spain, and it may possibly be Basque. In the United States it has been a very rare name, probably of Romantic origin, since Ximena is chiefly known as the wife of the Cid.

Yolanda ♀ Probably a coinage, under Romantic influence, though Withycombe (using the spelling Yolande) derives it from the Old French form Violante, itself from Viola. In the later twentieth century it has shown some activity.

York ♂ As a family name, York is derived from the northern city and county of England, and has thence passed to being a given name.

Curiously, York appears as one of the commonest names for slaves. It may have arisen from some similar sounding African name, but no good possibility can be cited.

The Duke of York (later King James II) was an important political symbol during the late seventeenth century, but one has difficulty in thus trying to account for the situation.

Yvonne ♀ Celtic (according to Withycombe), but of unknown meaning. The modern form is a diminutive-feminine of Ivo or

Ivon, commonly used as men's names among the Anglo-Normans. There seems to be no continuous tradition of the name, and its modern use may be from a literary borrowing, or even a coinage. Its usage is chiefly of the twentieth century.

Zabdiel ♂ Hebrew, "God-endows." On the basis of two mentions in genealogies, Zabdiel made an occasional appearance during the period of biblical names, perhaps because of its meaning, which is close to that of Nathaniel and its related names.

Zadoc ♂ Hebrew, "righteous." It is the name of nine biblical characters, including a prominent priest in the reign of David. Though short and of excellent meaning, Zadoc remained rare, occurring only in the period of biblical names.

Zalmon, *see* SALMON.

Zebina ♂ Probably Hebrew, but of uncertain meaning, occurring only once in the Bible, in a list (Ezra 10:43). It may have been a name chosen by lot, and it is rare even in the period of biblical names.

Zebulin ♂ Probably not a Hebrew name, meaning unknown. Familiar as one of the tribes of Israel, it was used occasionally in the period of biblical names. Zebulon (so spelled) Pike (born 1779), for whom Pike's Peak is named, seems to be its outstanding example.

Zechariah, Zachariah, Zacharias, Zachary ♂ Hebrew, "renowned-is-God." It is the title of one of the books of the Bible as well as being a highly popular name in the Old Testament, borne by 26 people there mentioned. Zacharias is the Greek form, appearing in the New Testament. From it the English form Zachary has developed. President Zachary Taylor is one of the few notable Americans to have borne this name.

Zedekiah ♂ Hebrew, "God-is-strength." It is a name of some prominence in the Bible, being that of the puppet-king whom Nebuchadnezzar set up in Jerusalem, at the same time changing the name from Mattaniah, "gift-of-God." The significance of the change is uncertain. Zedekiah appeared occasionally during the period of biblical names. Matanniah has not appeared in the available lists.

Zelda ♀ Probably a coined name, *c.* 1900, it has become known in the mid-twentieth century as the given name of the wife of the writer Scott Fitzgerald.

Zenas ♂ Greek[?]. It may be connected with Zeus, the pagan god, or with Zenobia, but must be considered uncertain. "Zenas the lawyer" (Titus 3:13) is once mentioned in the Bible. It might have been a name especially of lawyers, but members of that profession are not commonly so dedicated at the time of their naming. Like New Testament names in general, Zenas showed little popularity in the period of biblical names, but some staying power. It was still occasionally appearing down to 1900.

Zenobia ♀ A Graeco-Latin form of some Semitic name. The meaning is unknown. It was the name of the famous queen of Palmyra in the third century A.D. Its use by Hawthorne in *The Blythedale Romance* may almost be said to have made an American name of it, but it has always been rare.

Zephaniah ♂ Hebrew, "God-is-darkness," perhaps with the meaning "God-is-hidden." The name of a book of the Bible and its author, Zephaniah was well enough known to appear occasionally during the period of biblical names.

Zillah ♀ Like so many of the early names in Genesis, Zillah may be from some other language than Hebrew, and of unknown meaning. Meanings such as "shade, protection" are quite unsupported. Yonge and Withycombe give the name as a favorite among the gipsies, with whom it may have been of nonbiblical origin. Direct borrowing from the gipsies is unlikely, but a Romantic novel may have served as intermediary. In any case, Zillah has been a very rare name in the United States.

Zoheth ♂ Hebrew, "strong." On the basis of a single mention (I Chronicles 4:20) the name was occasionally used. It was perhaps one of those chosen by lot.

Zuriel ♂ Hebrew, "God-is-a-rock." Occasionally appearing in America during the period of biblical names, probably because of its attractive meaning and possibly because it is the next to last (alphabetically speaking) name in the Bible, being outplaced only by Zurishaddai, of the same meaning but more cumbersome than Zuriel. In the Bible itself Zuriel appears only once, being merely listed in Numbers 3:35 as the chief of a house.

NOTES

1. Shifting *r*. As a rule, names can be considered a part of the living language. When the sounds of a language shift, so also do the sounds of the names. Thus we know that Chaucer pronounced names such as Hubert and Agnes somewhat differently from the way we now render them, but that situation is of little importance in the history of names, since the rest of the language has also shifted similarly.

One sound of Middle English, however, has changed so strongly in names as to show in the modern spelling and pronunciation. This is the shift away from *r*. This sound was a difficult one—for children, especially. Ordinary words maintained the pronunciation well enough to keep the spelling, but in many names *r* shifted to *l*. Thus we have Mary becoming Molly, Sarah passing into Sally and Sadie; Dorothy going over to Doll or Dolly; Harry and Harold showing up as Hal.

All these new forms began as variants, but came to be important names in their own right, so that their influence upon our naming habits has been considerable. The names affected have been chiefly those of women, for whom a softer sound has apparently been more desired.

Some very common names for men show the avoidance of *r*, though not the liking for *l*. Robert thus goes to Bob. In the Middle English period, however, it often shifted to Nobb or

Hob. Richard also lost *r* but rejected *l,* becoming Dick or Hick or Hudd. (The last two forms are preserved in family names.) Similarly, Roger became Hodge.

2. Intrusive *n.* Anyone who is interested in names may have wondered about Ned as a form for Edward. Actually there have been other similar shifts. Thus we have Noll for Oliver, Nabby for Abigail, Nell (and hence Nellie) for Ellen or Eleanor, Nan for Ann.

This custom thrived chiefly in the seventeenth century—the famous Nell Gwynne, for instance, was actually Eleanor. On the other hand, it is rare or possibly nonexistent in names which were uncommon in the seventeenth century, such as Arthur and Anthony.

Some scholars explain this intrusive *n* as the result of baby-talk, because the custom had developed of addressing children as "mine." Thus "Mine Ed" became "My Ned." Then the *n* shifted across to the name, and people could say Ned even though they used other words than "mine." But this explanation is not certain.

As with the *r*-names, the *n*-names developed into some very popular ones. Nellie was a high-ranking woman's name in most of the nineteenth century.

3. The forms of names. The great majority of names in English exist in three forms. In addition to the regular or established form (e.g. Thomas, Susan) there is a short form (Tom, Sue) and a form (Tommy, Susie) which may be somewhat uncertainly denoted as a feminine or diminutive, or better perhaps by the awkward term feminine-diminutive.

These forms are sometimes called nicknames, but that term is better confined to a name that has no phonetic relationship to the basic one, but is of different origin, most commonly a descriptive term, such as Red or Lefty. In many instances the association is fanciful or punning, as when a man named Rhodes or Miller is called Dusty. Nicknames flourish among small groups of people, and their colorful quality has largely lapsed from American life with the growth of cities. They seem chiefly to flourish now in sports and politics.

To return to the variants, the short form usually consists of the accented syllable of the name, as already illustrated with Thomas and Susan. In long names, such as Alexander and Elizabeth, there may be some options. Thus Alexander shortens to Aleck or Alex (rarely to Al), and Elizabeth may be Eliza or Liz or Beth. The short form is the one generally used in informal speech.

Monosyllabic names, such as George, generally fail to have a short form. In other names the change may involve the shortening of a vowel, as when James yields Jim.

The short form is less commonly used for feminines, e.g. Mary and Sarah. Their *l*-forms, however, yield Moll and Sal. A few short forms have developed irregularly. (For example, see JOHN, HENRY, FRANCIS, BARBARA.)

The feminine-diminutive is so described because it is less commonly used for men than for women and children. It is formed regularly by the suffix -*y* or -*ie* used with the short form, as with Jimmy, Margie. It may, however, occur even when a short form is lacking, as with Georgie.

4. The influence of diminutives. In the Middle English period and down through Shakespeare's time, the diminutive suffixes -*kin* and -*in* (or -*on*) were in common use. In modern usage -*in* is no longer active, though it survives as a misunderstood fossil in ROBIN. In addition, some feminine forms were borrowed from the French with the feminine ending -*ine*.

The diminutive -*kin* (commonly masculine) is incorporated into some very important names, such as JACK, FRANK, and HANK.

5. The linguistic problem. In the difficult area of etymology every effort has been made to ensure accuracy, but still to be brief and to keep away from the intricacies of linguistic scholarship, in which the user of this book will generally be untrained and comparatively uninterested. The language of

origin, as given, is that from which the name was immediately received into English, though in many instances the word itself may be traced back clear to Indo-European. In such names as Hope and Grace no etymology is even suggested, since these names spring directly from their meaning in the common English language.

6. Names from Ebla. Announced in 1976 was a major archeological site at Ebla in Syria. A "library" of 15,000 inscribed tablets in a North Semitic language was an important feature of the discovery. These tablets date from around the year 2000 B.C. Their language is only distantly related to Hebrew. In the inscriptions on these tablets many names of persons are included, some of them showing clear relationship to the names in Genesis, e.g. Abramu (Abram), Esaum (Esau), Dau-'u-dum (David), Sa-'u-lum (Saul), Mikalu (Michael), Isralu (Israel).

There seems to be little doubt that we have here the origin (or an early stage) of these Old Testament names. The investigation, however, is still in progress, and years will elapse before the decipherment of the tablets is made generally available. In the meantime the readers of the entries in this book have already been warned that the early biblical names were actually not Hebrew. The situation is somewhat awkward, but the decision has necessarily been not to make the attempt to refer these names to Eblaic, since they have not, as yet, been thoroughly studied.

7. By common custom in the United States certain names apply to men and certain others to women. There is, however, no hard and fast procedure, and the symbols ♂ (male) and ♀ (female), which are here used, must be taken only as applicable to the general practice, not to an absolute rule.

ACKNOWLEDGMENTS
AND SOURCES

For their assistance, generously contributed, I wish to thank James D. Hart, Jo Raleigh, and Theodosia Stewart. I wish also to thank E. D. Lawson, Wilbur Zelinsky, and Elsdon C. Smith.

The over-all basis of this book has been my own countings of the individual names, which cover a wide field.

They begin with the collation of the birth lists of five parishes of London for the decade 1540–49; though these are not American, they present some useful background. Proceeding in time and in geographical scope, I have compiled the lists of early colonists and of their progeny—at Roanoke, Jamestown, Massachusetts, and Plymouth.

By decades, either by total count or by sampling, I have tabulated the whole course of naming at Harvard and Princeton. Comparable lists for women are not available, but I have collected the list of Mount Holyoke College (1837–1924), and also have some useful samplings of Vassar College.

Another important source has been the muster rolls of four regiments of the Continental Army. For later periods, the analysis of school lists has been highly serviceable.

The chief useful works are:

American Name Society, *Names*, vols. 1–26.
Bardsley, Charles W., *Curiosities of Puritan Nomenclature*. London, 1880.
Dunkling, Leslie, *First Names First*. New York, 1977.

Dunkling, Leslie, *The Guinness Book of Names.* London, 1974.

Loughead, Flora Haines, *Dictionary of Given Names.* Glendale, Calif., 1933, 1974.

Partridge, Eric, *Name this Child.* New York, 1942.

Puckett, Newbell Miles, and Murry Heller, *Black Names in America, Origins and Usage.* Boston, 1975.

Pyles, Thomas, "Bible Belt Onomastics, or some Curiosities of Anti-Pedobaptist Nomenclature," *Names,* 1959, pp. 84–100.

Reaney, P. H., *A Dictionary of British Surnames,* London, 1958, 1961.

Saints, The Book of (comp. by the Benedictine Monks of St. Augustine's Abbey), 3d ed. New York, 1934.

Smith, Elsdon C., *New Dictionary of American Family Names.* New York, 1956.

——, *Personal Names, A Biliography.* New York, 1952.

——, *The Story of Our Names.* New York, 1950.

Stewart, George R., *American Ways of Life.* New York, 1954.

——, "Men's Names in Plymouth and Massachusetts in the Seventeenth Century," *University of California Publications in Enlish.* Berkeley and Los Angeles, 1948.

Withycombe, E. G., *The Oxford Dictionary of English Christian Names.* New York and London, 1945, 1977.

Yonge, Charlotte, *History of Christian Names,* 2 vols. London, 1863.

Young, Robert, *Analytical Concordance for the Bible.* New York, 1880.